'A beautifully researched, evocative adventure of the high seas. In Mary Ann, unexpectedly called to lead, Tilar Mazzeo has found a true hero of the sea and brought her into vivid focus.'
**Wyl Menmuir, author of *The Draw of the Sea***

'Captivating and immersive . . . Propelled by evocative writing and painstaking research, you feel transported . . . A remarkable story that deserves this definitive narrative.'
**Matthew Pearl, author of *Save Our Souls***

'Forged upon the anvil of Cape Horn, this is a story that embraces all the time-tested bromides of men at sea: leadership, nautical knowhow, unyielding resolve and, above all, raw courage. But it is not about weathered old shellbacks, it's about a nineteen-year-old "slip of a girl" who takes command of a clipper ship when her husband, the captain, collapses from tuberculosis during a storm off the continental tip of South America . . . I was spellbound to the last page. It captures everything that draws us to the sea.'
**Mensun Bound, author of *The Ship Beneath the Ice***

'Tilar J. Mazzeo has written a riveting story about a woman we might otherwise never know and brilliantly sets it within a larger history about the upward mobility and wealth that the seas offered – and just as quickly took away. A fantastic read!'
**Paulina Bren, author of *She-Wolves***

'Through meticulous research and vivid descriptions, Mazzeo reveals how Mary Ann Patten's unwavering perseverance and brilliant navigation prevailed against the most formidable obstacles.'
**Lydia Reeder, author of *The Cure for Women***

'Mary Ann Patten's remarkable feat of seamanship has been rescued and brought to vivid life.'
**Caroline Alexander, author of *The Bounty***

**Also by Tilar J. Mazzeo**

*Sisters in Resistance*

*Eliza Hamilton*

*Irena's Children*

*The Widow Clicquot*

*The Hotel on Place Vendôme*

*The Secret of Chanel No. 5*

# TO THE
# EDGE
## OF THE
# WORLD

A Perilous Storm, a Mutinous Crew
and the Woman Who Defied Them All

TILAR J. MAZZEO

Elliott&Thompson

First published in the United States in 2025 as *The Sea Captain's Wife* by St. Martin's Press, an imprint of St. Martin's Publishing Group

First published in the UK in 2026 by
Elliott and Thompson
2 John Street
London WC1N 2ES
www.eandtbooks.com

Represented by:
Authorised Rep Compliance Ltd
Ground Floor, 71 Lower Baggot Street
Dublin, D02 P593
Ireland
www.arccompliance.com

ISBN (hardback): 978-1-78396-917-3
ISBN (trade paperback): 978-1-78396-871-8

Copyright © Tilar J. Mazzeo 2025

The Author has asserted her rights under the Copyright, Designs and Patents Act, 1988, to be identified as Author of this Work.

All rights reserved. No part of this publication may be reproduced, stored in or introduced into a retrieval system, or transmitted, in any form, or by any means (electronic, mechanical, photocopying, recording or otherwise) without the prior written permission of the publisher. Any person who does any unauthorised act in relation to this publication may be liable to criminal prosecution and civil claims for damages.

Jacket images: Alamy; Shutterstock; Portrait of Mary Ann Patten: National Portrait Gallery, Smithsonian Institution

Map illustrations by Rhys Davies

Designed by Donna Sinisgalli Noetzel

9 8 7 6 5 4 3 2 1

A catalogue record for this book is available from the British Library.

Printed by CPI Group (UK) Ltd, Croydon, CR0 4YY

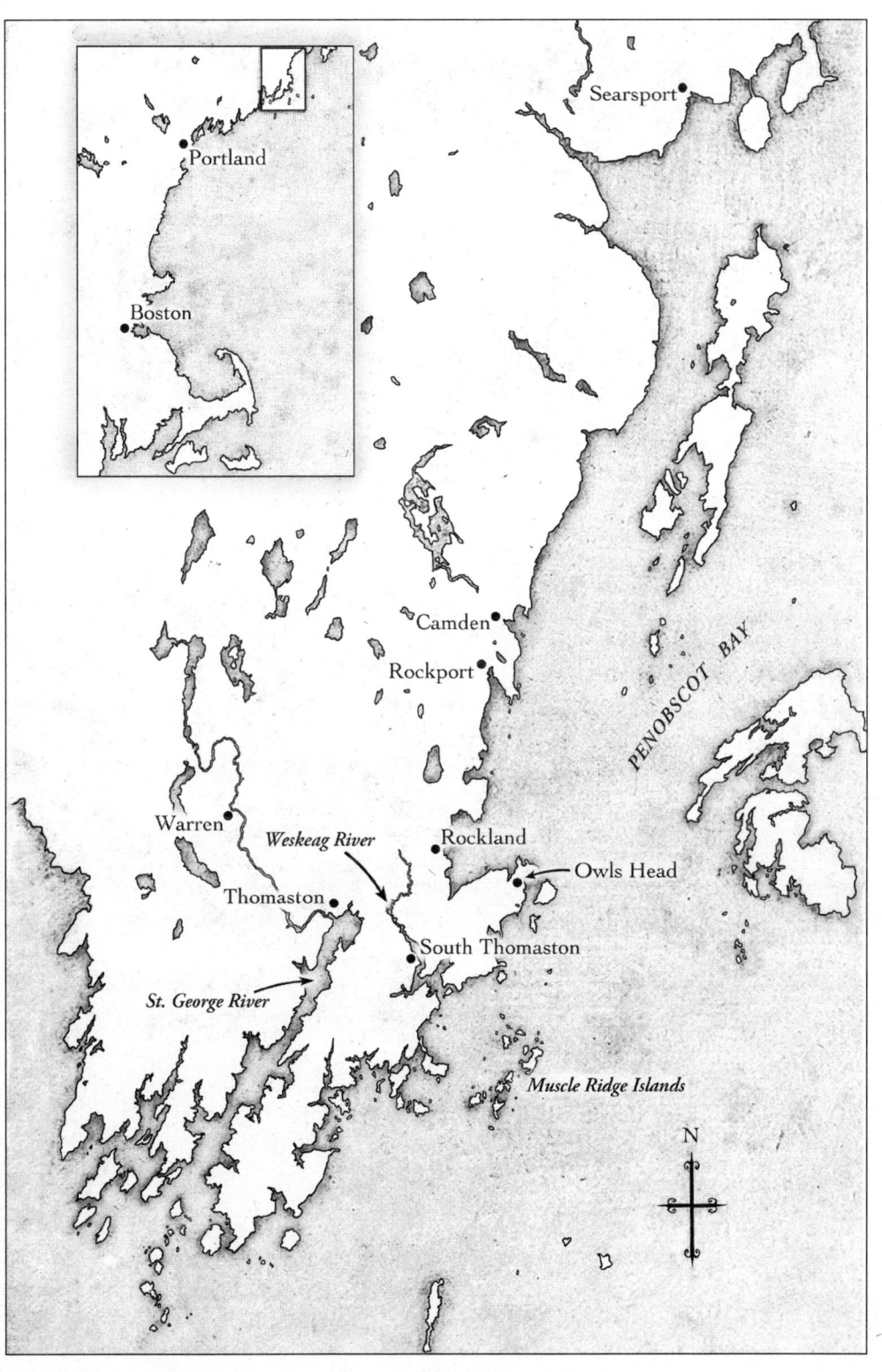

# CONTENTS

| | | |
|---|---|---|
| | *Epigraph* | xi |
| | **Prologue** | 1 |
| 1: | Penobscot Bay | 5 |
| 2: | Boston | 20 |
| 3: | Business in Great Waters | 33 |
| 4: | The Road to Liverpool | 51 |
| 5: | Pathfinder of the Seas | 69 |
| 6: | The First Circumnavigation | 82 |
| 7: | Westward Ho! | 101 |
| 8: | All the Tea in China | 117 |
| 9: | Cape Horn | 136 |
| 10: | The Tempest | 146 |
| 11: | The Land of Mist and Snow | 157 |
| 12: | The Long Way Round | 174 |
| 13: | The Iron Embrace of the Isthmus | 187 |
| 14: | A Mighty Pretty Woman and a Heroine | 201 |
| 15: | The Sea Captain's Widow | 222 |
| | Epilogue: *Are There Seas in Heaven, Joshua?* | 239 |
| | *Acknowledgments* | 245 |
| | *Notes* | 247 |

All I could see from where I stood

Was three long mountains and a wood;

I turned and looked another way,

And saw three islands in a bay.

So with my eyes I traced the line

Of the horizon, thin and fine,

Straight around till I was come

Back to where I'd started from.

—"Renascence," Edna St. Vincent Millay

# TO THE
# EDGE
## OF THE
# WORLD

# Prologue

This story begins in another place, another time, in a world of which only fragments remain.

Close your eyes and imagine, first, a cold and angry emptiness. The emptiness roars around you. You are on a sea, hurtling where the wind and water take you. You fall and you rise in darkness. The falling is fast and unforgiving and twists your gut as you count the seconds downward. The rising is worse. The sea towers forty feet above you, and you know only the terror that comes before falling.

Into this emptiness, build yourself a ship. A mighty, ghostly clipper. She is long and lean. Two hundred feet or more from bow to stern, painted coffin black to ride this darkness. You stand on her deck, held aloft with each angry swell by a million board feet of pitch pine laid out in planking, which moans and bends with the force of the ocean: her flesh and muscle. A forest of timber ribs is her backbone. Above this hull, three barren masts rise, a hundred feet above the sea. In fair winds, these ancient, empty trees are strung with 3,500 yards or more of crackling stiff canvas to carry you with unimagined speed around the globe and home again if you are lucky. This night, her yardarms are howling, empty crucifixes. This ship is *Neptune's Car*—the mythic chariot of a jealous god of storm and sea. Her name: a tribute to appease a fickle master.

Let the globe of our world spin slowly. Set this chariot upon a point, a latitude, a longitude. Turn west to the New World. Follow the line south from New York City and south some more, past Brazil, to the very last reaches, a place called Tierra del Fuego, the land of fire. Put your finger somewhere in that furious passage, between the end of the Earth and the frozen land of ice, Antarctica. Here is our tempest.

Trace your finger around the tip of the continent, westward again, past the fearsome headland of Cape Horn and then past Robinson Crusoe Island. Let your finger take you, following a point somewhere in the great Southern Ocean, back northward, up the coast of two continents, along the edge of the Pacific, until you reach San Francisco: your destination, the city of gold dust.

We are on a dangerous journey. A journey in which wealthy ship-owners pit young men against each other with the promise of riches, urging them on to reckless dangers, in the name of another man's lucre. The year is 1856. The season is early September: just before spring in the southern hemisphere, too early for this voyage. Somewhere in the darkness, three other ships, our competitors, careen the waves with us. Not all of us will survive this journey.

At the helm of our ship is a man, the captain, Joshua. He is twenty-nine, but his face is already weather-beaten and tired. The headaches blind him. He castigates himself now. He had misgivings before he saw this ship out of New York's harbor. He has been ill. He feels his force draining. Sometimes there is a cough; sometimes a fever. He has stood on this deck, sleepless, vigilant, for eight days and nights fighting the blast and the water. At the ropes and in the rigging far above the twisting sea are his crew. Men and boys, barefoot on icy decks too slick for shoe leather. They, too, are frightened, tired. One among them, shackled in chains below these decks, is angry, vengeful.

There is a woman, too, the sole female inhabitant of this bark. She is small and plump, and her black, plaited hair cannot be contained in this tempest. She is the sea captain's wife and just nineteen: Mary Ann. Her wide skirts and oilskin cloak, her only defense against a polar wind, disguise for the moment the warm, gentle swell in her belly.

She wants desperately for them to win this race. The prize means, for her and Joshua, freedom. With this purse, with the sale of this cargo, destined to fuel a gold rush making more men rich in distant California, there will be enough. Enough to imagine a different future for them and their baby. Enough to buy a share of a ship and chart one's own course. Enough, they said to each other when they dreamed, to build a little farm on their land in Maine, where the Weskeag River meets the sea and the salt marshes stretch beyond for many acres.

But, first, they must survive.

For eight days and nights Joshua has stood on the quarterdeck and fought the sea. In the gray half-light of the ninth morning, there is no fight left in him. He slips to the deck and lets the darkness take him. There is a cry from somewhere among the crew: "Captain!" In the shadows below the deck, the angry, vengeful officer waits, indignation swelling, also expectant. His eyes narrow. Mary Ann understands. There will be no safe harbor in San Francisco, no freedom, no farm running down to the banks of the Weskeag River unless she fights for them.

This is the moment her story begins.

# 1

# Penobscot Bay

ᘒ

This was that Earth of which we have heard, made out of Chaos and Old Night. Here was no man's garden, but the unhandselled globe.

—Thoreau, *The Maine Woods*

But before the story of the sea, there was the story of the land.

As difficult as it may be, at the distance of nearly two centuries, to imagine a tempest at sea on a clipper ship at the bottom of the world, it is almost as difficult now to remember a time when the coast of Maine was at the center of a deeply connected and prosperous international culture. The global trade and quiet affluence that flowed along its shores stretched in a current of wealth that ran from New York and Boston northward, down east, as we say, all the way to Nova Scotia. All along the seacoast there were ports. Behind the ports, there were farms, and, in the fields of the farms, there were winding stone walls. Today, drive along the roads of Maine and look into the woods. The old stone walls now meander through forest that was once, not so long ago, open pasture.

It was the sea that made this area rich and populous, the sea that connected it to the world beyond, to places like San Francisco and London, Liverpool and Buenos Aires. It was the sea captains, those soldiers of fortune, who carried around the world and brought home those riches, profits on commodities like China tea or plantation-grown bales of cotton, traded along the way for lumber and ore, fur pelts, nitrogen-rich guano, silk and porcelain, and sometimes opium and enslaved or indentured people.

Sea captains were born as well as made. Nowhere birthed as many of them as Maine's Penobscot Bay, the great inlet of the Atlantic Ocean that runs, according to local knowledge, some forty miles long and not quite twenty miles wide, from about where the Saint George River runs into the sea between Cushing and Port Clyde in the south, to where the Penobscot River cuts inland north of Searsport.

The small coastal village of Searsport, Maine, on the northern end of Penobscot Bay, at the time of this story, boasted out of a population of 2,500 citizens, three hundred sea captains—10 percent of all the sea captains in America. In the period from 1800 to 1857, a full half of all the large sailing vessels produced in the United States were built at shipyards in Maine, many of them at the entrance to Penobscot Bay in Rockland.

Two hundred years ago, whether you lived in Charleston or Boston or San Francisco or even Hong Kong or Panama City, you would have known those names and the names of coastal ports like Belfast or Wiscasset, and you would not have needed the map you are even now turning toward to find them.

The sea tempered her captains, to be sure, but in the deep, sheltered harbors along Penobscot Bay, especially in coastal towns with fine natural harbors like Thomaston or Rockland or Searsport, knowledge had been passed from fathers to sons or uncles to nephews in a chain often unbroken for generations, just as patient, steely fortitude was the inheritance sea captains' wives passed to their daughters. Sea captains, when they came home with the fortunes made at sea, built grand homes with rooftop "widow's walks," where those wives and daughters could keep watch for ships on the horizon and for the storms that destroyed them.

When those captains sailed, it was not because the sea, but because the land, called to them.

The economic and cultural history of America in the nineteenth century is, above all, a story of a national period of expansion that gave rise to wave upon wave of land speculation. Prospectors flooded into California to stake their claim during the gold rush. Merchants with private militias speculated in land purchases everywhere from the isthmus of Panama to the midwestern prairies, laying down railroad track, building railway hotels, and seeking to control and capitalize on international transportation corridors. When intensive cotton farming ravaged the soil of the plantations of the Mississippi Delta, the price of untouched western farmland skyrocketed, precipitating the forced expropriation (and the lucrative resale) of Indigenous land, and, ultimately, with the question of whether those western states would employ free or slave labor, the Civil War. In coastal Maine, the great land grab was the battle to determine who owned and would profit from what was then simply known as the Knox and Waldo Patent.

That land speculation made some men rich almost beyond imagination, and it was not the land itself that created wealth but the global trade routes that could be made to pass through it. The tighter the bottleneck, the greater the fortune. The greatest mercantile fortunes were made first in the China tea trade, where the so-called Canton system restricted business to a handful of brokers until

1842. Later, there were riches for the taking in California. Those who came home millionaires from the gold rush, though, were rarely the forty-niners, who, though they could make the equivalent of $30,000 a day, were also enticed to spend it. The ones who cashed in were the merchants selling French champagne, Kentucky bourbon, and pickaxes in advance of the arrival of competitors and the shipowners who ferried that California gold back to the bankers in New York City—and took a percentage of its value in commission.

If shipowners and merchant brokers took the lion's share of the wealth from this global marketplace, a sea captain also took a portion. Sea captains were paid not only on salary but on commission. An established sea captain with a quarter share took 25 percent of the profits. A young sea captain beginning his career might earn 5 or 10 percent of the charges paid for the cargo that he risked his life and the lives of his crew to deliver. A rich and enterprising sea captain who owned his own ship and transported his own cargo took everything. Those riches earned at sea made possible the ownership of land that also passed from generation to generation at a moment in American history when land values were rising (and occasionally falling) dramatically.

That chain of generational transmission was often far more broken, especially in the Knox and Waldo Patent. It was, in fact, one long story of possession and dispossession. Along the harbors of Penobscot Bay, captains—especially sea captains who were able to purchase their own vessels and, by doing so, control their own fortunes—built great mansions that ran down to the banks of the mighty rivers. On those rivers, they built mills and farms and quarries, producing more of the goods their ships carried in a stunning vertical integration.

And the story of the land on the banks of the Weskeag River in Penobscot Bay that Joshua and Mary Ann dreamed of coming home to? That story began before either of them were born. By the time

Joshua Adams Patten's mother first cradled him in her arms, it was a story that already stretched back generations.

**Joshua's part of** that story began with his father and his grandfather.

His father was Abel Warren "Uriah" Patten, and Abel Patten was born in 1787 to the Revolutionary War sergeant Nathaniel Patten Jr. and his wife, Mehitabel, known as "Hettie." At the time of Abel's birth, the family lived in a small and remote village not too far from Raby, New Hampshire.

Nathaniel had fought in the American Revolution against the British as a young man in his early twenties, in a close-knit company of men commanded by Captain Adams Bailey. When the American Revolution ended in 1783, he returned to New Hampshire as a farmer, and the family developed a close friendship with their neighbors, the Peabody family.

In the next dozen years, Nathaniel and Hettie Patten had six sons and one daughter, among whom Abel Patten—born on January 13, 1787, the year in which the United States' Constitution also came into the world—was the second. Sometime around 1800, the family moved to Maine, to the town of Penobscot, at the far northern end of the Penobscot Bay, where the Patten family was granted a large tract of farmland. Here, they mostly remained for the next several generations. They also remained in touch with the Peabodys and the Baileys.

In time, Nathaniel's second son, Abel, grew to be a difficult and unpopular man, prone to disputes over land with his neighbors. Our Abel styled himself "Abel Patten, Esq.," a public servant and would-be gentleman whose zeal for real estate, land speculation, and legal instruments of title displayed itself alongside a particularly litigious and quarrelsome natural inclination. Like three of his other brothers, Abel was trained for the sea as a young man and rose to the rank of mariner.

As far as we know, he never attained the rank of master mariner or sea captain, and, unlike his brothers, he seems to have quit the sea and taken up work in an office by his late twenties.

Perhaps he quit the sea because he was in love. Abel did not marry until 1817, when he was thirty years old, and his bride was a twenty-year-old young woman from the other end of the great Penobscot Bay named Mary Sarah Peabody. She was a distant cousin of the Peabody family who had been his father's friends and neighbors in nearby New Hampshire.

**Mary Sarah Peabody** is a bit of an enigma. Part of the mystery surrounding her girlhood is the simple fact that the lives of young women in rural Maine were not part of the great narrative sweep of history. Few teenaged diaries make it into the archives for posterity. Somewhere, in an old family Bible, Mary's birth and marriage and death would have been recorded, but even the public records are scanty. Things are made even more troublesome by the fact that she was sometimes known as Mary Sarah and sometimes as Sarah Mary.

What we do know is that Mary Peabody was born sometime around 1797, and she came from an old and wealthy Maine family. By the time she married Abel Patten, the Peabodys of Maine had already been established in the villages at the mouth of the Saint George River for three generations, and they had a very particular family connection to a little group of islands in Penobscot Bay where her father, Solomon Peabody, had spent his childhood. These islands, known then as the Muscle Ridge Plantation and known today simply as the Muscle Ridge Islands, lie, like stones scattered by a careless hand across the sea, in a haphazard archipelago of more than a dozen shoals and uprisings, each ringed white with forbidding granite shores.

Mary was born on this rocky and mostly uninhabited outpost,

beyond the mouth of the Weskeag River, where it turns inland to South Thomaston. She was the second of at least a dozen children born to Solomon and his wife, Lydia. The couple would bear five daughters before their first son, Joshua, and his sister, Sarah, were born in 1805, also in the Muscle Ridge Islands.

Mary and her siblings, though, did not live on the Muscle Ridge Plantation for long: At a low ebb in their family fortunes, the Peabody family were soon forced to sell many of these island holdings and move inland. How the Peabody family came to own and then to lose possession of the Muscle Ridge Islands is a story lost to local history. All that remains to tell that tale are a series of incomplete deeds in the Knox County Library in Rockland, going back to a time before the American Revolution, showing that the Peabody family bought and sold and bought again these lands.

So many times were these deeds exchanged that the islands—surrounded by a treacherous reef and of limited economic value in an era of sail, even after the installation of a lighthouse in 1804 to warn unwary mariners—can only have had for the family some deeper, more resonant meaning. For Mary Patten, it was a legacy she wanted to pass someday, somehow, back to her children.

**The families who** lived in these small coastal villages in the 1820s knew each other's business, then as now, and many of their near neighbors were relations of one sort or another. The lives of the Peabody and Patten families were jumbled up the with lives of their Bailey and Hathorne neighbors especially.

The geography of the coast of Maine is a series of long, rocky fingers that stretch to the sea, with narrow bays between them. By the 1820s the young Patten family lived in the village of Saint George, on the finger running down today to Tenant's Harbor. It was here that in the winter of 1823 their first son, Enoch, was born, and, by the time of his birth, the couple had managed to buy back from their fellow townsman William Keef the portion of Mary's island patrimony known as Long Island, for which they paid $200.

The fastest way anywhere was, as always along the coast of Maine, by water, and on the finger across from the Patten family, on the peninsula that runs down to modern-day Cushing, lived Lemuel Bailey, and by all indications this Bailey family was connected to Captain Adams Bailey, the Revolutionary War commander of Abel's father. Lemuel Bailey, in time, married Mary's younger sister Sarah. It was the second generation in which the Patten, Peabody, and Bailey families were knotted together. By the 1820s, Lemuel and Sarah had a son named Lemuel Jr.

Just a bit to the south of the Baileys, on the point of land that lay between the Saint George River and Maple Juice Cove, was the Hathorne property, and they were also part of this tight knot of local families. Captain Adams Bailey in 1815 married Ellen Hathorne, a Massachusetts cousin of the local seafaring Hathorne family. In time, one of Mary and Sarah's distant cousins, Sophia Peabody, would marry an aspiring young writer from the Hathorne clan. That young man, Nathaniel, would add a "w" to the Hawthorne family name when he became famous as the author of literary classics (and nineteenth-century bestsellers) such as *The Scarlet Letter* and—importantly for our history here—*The House of the Seven Gables*, a novel published in 1851 about land speculation on the Weskeag River.

**And that is** about all that is known of the day-to-day lives of Abel and Mary Patten and their families in the 1820s and even into the 1830s. The couple were affluent but not rich, and the domestic lives of comfortably middle-class families were not then, and are not now, generally any better preserved than the lives of young women. We, too, are unlikely to have our diaries and love letters preserved in museums or libraries, though that does not mean that our lives and our loves did not happen. What remains is only the incomplete scaffolding of public records.

Enoch was born in 1822, when his mother was in her midtwenties. Another son, Uriah, was born in 1824, two years later. Joshua Adams Patten, the third son of Abel and Sarah, arrived on April 20, 1827. He was named after his maternal uncle, Joshua. His middle name, Adams—with the distinctive and atypical "s" spelling—strongly suggests that his second namesake was Captain Adams Bailey.

By the 1830s, young Joshua's parents were living in a house owned by his mother's Peabody relations in nearby Rockland, and in that next decade other siblings followed. There was another brother, Samuel, born in 1830; a sister, Sarah, in 1832; another brother, George, in 1833; and another sister, Charlotte, in 1836. There may have been other children as well, stillbirths or siblings who died in infancy. Twenty-five was quite late for a young, married woman to bear her first child in the early nineteenth century; the average New England woman in 1830 bore six children and would bury two of them before they reached their fifth birthday. So fearsome and seemingly otherworldly was the epidemic of tuberculosis that rural New Englanders, fearing death was stalking them, were swept up in a vampire panic that began in 1782 and lasted another century.

Mary and Abel Patten did bury at least one of their children in the 1830s. There is an old headstone in a graveyard in Rockland, where Patten and Bailey children share a plot, that records that in September 1835 the family interred their eldest son, Enoch, at the age of twelve, for reasons that are unrecorded.

The only other public record is the record of the land. In 1832, still apparently determined to repossess Mary's lost patrimony, the Patten family once more put their resources into reclaiming the islands that lay beyond the mouth of the Weskeag River. They acquired that year from Elijah Hall the title to much of the ancestral archipelago. For Abel it was land speculation. For Mary it was a homecoming.

**Only in 1839**, the year that Mary Patten, now in her early forties, gave birth to her eighth and last child, John, does the record of their lives grow more granular.

Abel Patten seems to have left off shipping sometime in his twenties for other pursuits, but his sons were sent away young to learn to be mariners. Their eldest surviving son, Uriah, was fifteen in 1839, and he was already away at sea that year. He is likely to have shipped out for the first time a year earlier, at fourteen, cleaving to the tradition of his mother's family: His grandfather and several uncles were sea captains.

Joshua was twelve that year, and he, too, would go to sea soon, assigned to the forecastle to work his way up through the ranks of ship's boy to seaman. Little John, only six that year, when his time came would also become a sea captain. The best indication of the Patten's middle-class status is the fact that all of the Patten boys went to sea assigned to the forecastle and not the quarterdeck; they went, in other words, as teenaged common laborers and not as pampered young officers.

Their mother would not live to see any of this. She would only live to see her children's dispossession.

**The late 1830s** and early 1840s were years of economic turmoil and devastation for many American families, and the Pattens were not spared. The collapse of speculative bubbles in land and in southern cotton prices sent the United States spiraling into a financial panic in 1837. The fallout was an economic depression that would last, off and on, until the mid-1840s and was only completely reversed with the discovery of gold in California at the end of the decade.

Banks failed; the value of real estate (and, grotesquely, the resale value of the enslaved people who worked large plantations) plummeted; the Bank of England, controlling the global reserve currency in sterling, increased interest rates quickly, sending the American bond and credit markets haywire.

In 1840, Mary's father, Solomon Peabody, died, and Mary inherited another portion of the family land in the Muscle Ridge Islands. By 1842, Abel, like a lot of other people five years into a serious economic depression, was broke and needed to cash out assets. The assets he decided to liquidate were his wife's inheritance.

The decision to put the Peabody family lands up for sale was the occasion for a curious and undignified spat in local press, which played out in the paid advertisement section of *The Lime Rock Gazette*, the Rockland newspaper. It would later spawn a lawsuit about claims to adverse possession that dragged on for decades.

Abel's advertisement was published on February 1, 1842:

> Granite quarries for sale. The subscriber has nine Islands for Sale, situated at the mouth of George's River, known as Peabody's Island, containing 95 acres, Pleasant Island, 75; Western, 52, and others of smaller size,—seven of them containing good Granite Quarries, handsomely laid in sheets.— Said Islands have good harbors, bold water, and are well situated for wharfs. N. B. All persons are hereby cautioned against taking any property whatever from said islands, without the consent of the subscriber.

Now, the Muscle Ridge Islands are not at the mouth of the Saint George River; they are at the mouth of the Weskeag. One might suppose that these were other lands that had come into the family's possession were it not for two facts, the first of which is that Pleasant Island certainly is one of the Muscle Ridge Islands.

The second fact is more interesting: the counter-advertisement, published three days later, by three irate local residents of Thomaston, Israel Gregory, Joseph Hewett, and C. Brockman. These gentlemen diagnosed what—and who—they saw as the problem frankly:

> Islands for Sale. The Subscribers offer for sale a number of Islands situated at the entrance of Penobscot Bay, about 8 miles from Owls Head, (being the same advertised by Abel W. Patten, who has about the same claim to them as he has knowledge of their location) on which are houses, barns, wells, fish-houses, wharves and other convenience for prosecuting the fisheries. The buildings are all in good order. The whole will be sold at a bargain.

What are we to make of this strange quarrel in the classified section? The "bargain" sale of the islands and the competition to liquidate property is not, in itself, surprising, given national economic conditions. Nor is the broader disagreement about the chain of title particularly unusual. These islands are so numerous and the titles and deeds in this part of Penobscot Bay at this moment in its history so tangled, the conflict was almost inevitable.

What is surprising is how Abel could have got his geography so backward. No resident of Thomaston, Maine, would possibly confuse the Saint George and Weskeag, any more than a lifelong resident of Manhattan would confuse the East River with the Hudson. For a mariner, the mistake is mind-boggling. Abel cannot have ever seen his wife's patrimony; if he had, he simply would not have made the error.

Money was undoubtedly tight. Sacrifices were necessary. But

an emotional rift between Abel and his family was growing. Mary's children, especially after their mother's death and their father's remarriage, would come to feel about this archipelago very differently. Joshua would set his heart on returning to the river that ran out to the sea toward those islands.

It is why, from a clipper ship in a tempest at the end of the world, in the land between ice and fire, he dreamed of going home there.

**Joshua and Mary Ann's** voyage and that dark night in that tempest are still a decade or more ahead of us.

For the moment, in 1842, his father-in-law recently buried and the law, as he knows full well, giving right to a man and a husband, Abel has advertised for sale the lands of his wife's family, lands that the Peabodys have been struggling for a generation or more to reclaim and that he, Abel, cannot locate on a map.

Mary at least would not have to suffer long with the knowledge. By the end of 1843, she was almost certainly already ill with whatever infirmity it was that would kill her the following year. She died that winter, in the nadir that in Maine is February, not yet fifty.

Joshua was sixteen and at sea when his mother was buried. He stood, according to his seaman's card in 1844, five feet three inches tall, with gray eyes and fair hair. His older brother, Uriah, stood four inches taller and, at eighteen, would soon be promoted to sea captain. Joshua was probably already sailing with one of the clippers that were ferrying immigrant passengers from Liverpool to Boston. That winter, the potato blight was already spreading across Ireland, carried there on an American clipper as part of the passenger provisions. By 1845, the Great Famine had started, and, to meet the demand, clippers crammed ever more passengers into steerage.

The brothers are unlikely to have learned of their mother's death immediately, though they may well have been present for her burial.

The family would have to wait until the spring, when the ground thawed, to dig her grave. She would remain, until then, in one of the crypts that were ubiquitous in New England graveyards, in a pragmatic acceptance of the realities of a northern winter.

By spring, Joshua's brother Uriah certainly knew of his mother's death. He must have been home from sea and in nearby Lincolnville sometime in March or April 1844, because it was in one of those two months that Joanna "Ann" Batchelder, the daughter of an elderly Thomaston fisherman named Hezekiah, became pregnant.

When Uriah and Ann were married on October 12, 1844, the bride was at least seven months pregnant, perhaps more. One hopes that the delay was due to the time it took to get a message to Uriah at sea that summer, though the quick deterioration of their marriage suggests there may have been some ungentlemanly foot-dragging.

When Mary died, Abel's first thought was a quick remarriage. He needed a mother for the younger Patten children and a woman to keep the house for them. He married his wife's recently widowed younger sister, Sarah, then just forty. A widower marrying his wife's sister would not have raised, in the 1840s, a single eyebrow. Indeed, it would have been seen as a sensible and responsible solution to the complex problem of children and stepchildren and inheritances.

Joshua's new stepmother—and his aunt—also had deep ties to the Muscle Ridge Islands. Like her sister, she'd been born on the Muscle Ridge Plantation as had been Joshua's cousin—and new stepbrother—Lemuel Jr., already a sea captain.

**Abel was still** determined to offload the Peabody family lands. Sarah, with the residue of her widow's estate, was determined to buy them. Abel and Sarah's remaining siblings sold to her first Pleasant Island and then Long Island, Peabody Island, and Bush Island, for the sum of a hundred dollars, half what they had sold for fifty years earlier.

It was, in effect, a transfer of their mother's inheritance from Joshua and his siblings to their new stepsibling and cousin. Joshua and Uriah might have felt it as an injustice had it not been for their aunt's generosity toward all the Patten children in the years that followed. Sarah stepped into the role of matriarch. When Uriah received his appointment as sea captain, his first purchase was to buy back a large portion of the Muscle Ridge Islands, with Sarah's blessing.

In 1850, when Joshua turned twenty-two and was himself elevated to first mate, his first purchase was a piece of land in South Thomaston, on the western bank of the Weskeag, at the mouth of the river that leads to the sea and to the Muscle Ridge Islands just beyond them, also with the support of his aunt. He bought it from Elijah Hall, the man who a generation earlier had sold those islands back to his mother for the sum of eighty dollars, and the Patten boys thought of that land as their living connection to their mother.

# 2

# Boston

> We must come down from our heights, and leave our straight paths, for the byways and low places of life, if we would learn truths by strong contrasts; and in hovels, in forecastles, and among our own outcasts in foreign lands.
>
> —Richard Henry Dana Jr., *Two Years Before the Mast*

When Joshua came home from sea in those first years after his mother's death, he stayed with Sarah and his siblings in Rockland.

But, by 1850, the Patten family had fractured. Only Joshua's sixteen-year-old sister, Charlotte, and young John, his mother's last child, now eleven, were still living at home with his stepmother. The marriage of Sarah and Abel had never been a love match. Abel had needed a mother for his children. Sarah had wanted to keep the Peabody legacy intact and had done her duty. Love was more than anyone reasonably had a right to expect of her. And no one did.

Joshua's sister Sarah had married a young corporal in the Ninth Infantry. Younger brothers Samuel and George were sailing. They had been sent to sea young, like Joshua and Uriah, no later than fourteen or fifteen.

Joshua's cousin and stepbrother, Lemuel Jr., a mariner and thirty-one that year, had moved to nearby Brunswick, where he was living with two of his Patten cousins, Nathaniel and Mark. All three young men were mariners, happily married with wives and toddlers.

Joshua's brother Uriah, now a sea captain, was a father, but Uriah and Ann's marriage, never happy, was floundering. Uriah and Ann lived at first in Lincolnville, near Ann's family, and then a bit down the coast in Camden, also sharing a home with a fellow mariner, a bachelor named Nathaniel Sylvester. According to 1850 census records, the two young men owned between them that year property worth more than a thousand dollars—some $35,000 in modern values—not enough to make either of them rich but a respectable beginning. Ann was left to manage housekeeping for both men. She was lonely. And she was too sick to manage the burden. In fact, Ann's first pregnancy had been a disaster.

Before long, Uriah would commit Ann against her will to the notorious Maine Insane Hospital in Augusta, where she would spend the better part of her thirties and die in her early forties.

One struggles to see Uriah Patten's decision to incarcerate his young wife through the prism of another place and time. One tries to remember that medical science was different in the 1840s and 1850s. But the fact is that poor Ann was involuntarily committed as a "lunatic" for the seizures and abdominal pain that began immediately following the birth of her child (who does not seem to have survived) and for what was almost certainly untreated (and unrecognized) postpartum eclampsia. It was a tragedy packaged as a nightmare.

On the third night of her imprisonment in the insane hospital,

Ann attempted to throw herself out the window in a desperate bid to escape, cutting, the asylum doctor noted, her "arm & throat quite badly." She remained for most of a decade an inmate of the asylum, despite the doctor conceding in her medical record that she "Appears very lady like, & in fact shows no insane symptoms."

Ann was very ill and was, undoubtedly, sometimes at wits' end, even as early as 1850. The medical record later documents that she was irritable with her husband, had been known to smash some housewares in exasperation, and, once or twice in a decade, may have gone so far as to use "profane and vulgar" language. A grieving, ailing woman at her wits' end in the middle of the nineteenth century was one step away from a diagnosis of literal madness, especially if a marriage suffered after long periods of absence and grew intolerable.

The records of the Maine Insane Hospital show that Ann was not the only defiant sea captain's wife confined in that gray stone fortress. Captain's wives are alarmingly overrepresented. AMHI—the Augusta Mental Health Institute, as it was later renamed—was, until as late as 2004, part of a larger national system of quasi-penal institutions that included the local "poor farm." It still stands forbiddingly over the Kennebec River, the oldest surviving "lunatic asylum" anywhere in America.

**Joshua, on his** trips home from Boston, took in all of this. Lemuel, Nathaniel, Mark, and their blooming children. Uriah and Ann and madness. His aunt and his father, and their distant marriage.

Wherever Abel Patten was by 1850, it was elsewhere. He was not at home with his wife or his children in Rockland. He was not obviously ill; Abel would live for nearly another decade yet, into his midseventies, and would return to Maine before passing. He may have been living out of state, involved in some land deal or another to repair his fortunes; 1850 was boom time again in America, and he may have been working land speculation deals in New Hampshire or Massachusetts. Perhaps in financial extremis he had returned to sea, though at nearly sixty-five by 1850, it would take a bold captain to bring onboard a mate like Abel Patten.

Joshua's focus in these early years of the 1850s, anyhow, was on something bigger. National political tensions were running high that decade in America, with Northerners and Southerners resorting to fistfights and loaded revolvers on the floor of Congress over the question of the westward expansion of slavery. The economy had not only rebounded but was roaring. Gold had been discovered in California, and Joshua's stepbrother, Lemuel, now promoted to captain, was already talking of heading west, around Cape Horn, to make his fortune. Nathaniel and Mark and their wives were prepared to take the gamble on the West with him. Lemuel's wife, Mary, was determined to stay in Maine, with family. She didn't yet see what the others saw was coming. The world and that economy was turning away from New England.

Telegraphs were a breathtaking technology, sending messages at rapid speeds, though there was not, as yet, an undersea transatlantic cable. That would take until 1858 to send its first message, between President James Buchanan and Britain's Queen Victoria, with the queen congratulating the president on "the successful completion of this great international work" in a telegram that took sixteen hours to travel across the Atlantic—not the ten days a message took to travel by vessel. Within a month of this marvel, the system would collapse, and it would take nearly a decade to be restored. But everyone now knew it was possible, and when it came, it would be the end of an era.

Until the late 1860s and that moment came, the world belonged to the age of sail. More importantly, it belonged to the clippers and to the men who raced them—because every voyage was a race against the clock, the stakes of which were fame and fortune. For an aspiring sea captain, the new "extreme" clipper ship designs, capable of carrying cargo at unimaginable speeds of up to twenty knots, were the pinnacle of risk and reward. That was the kind of ship that Joshua longed to captain.

And when he, too, had made his fortune—when he owned his own ship or when he had set aside a nest egg big enough to retire on—he would build a house on his land on the banks of the Weskeag River, above where, when the tide turned, the rapids reversed their direction. He would look out toward Penobscot Bay and his mother's islands.

He had bought that land in 1850. In 1851, he met the girl he was going to marry. And he was determined that the marriage he was going to have would be modeled on those of his stepbrother Lemuel and his cousin Nathaniel and not on the marriage of Uriah and Ann—or on either of the marriages of his father.

**That girl was** Mary Ann. Born Mary Ann Brown, she grew up a world away from the relative affluence of the landowning Patten, Bailey, Hathorne, and Peabody families and their long and intimate small-town coastal village connections.

Mary Ann was born in Chelsea, Massachusetts, a working-class seaport just across the river from Boston proper, a teeming urban center, on April 6, 1837, the child of two recent English immigrants to the United States, George Brown and his wife, Elizabeth Margaret (Spavin). Her parents had married a decade earlier, in 1827, in Yorkshire, and emigrated to America in the early 1830s. A son, George, had been born around 1829 in Britain.

Mary Ann's parents left Britain during the reign of King William IV—the "sailor king"—a third son who had been raised to a career in the Navy. Never expected to be in the line of succession, he had been permitted to carry on a long-standing, passionate love affair with an actress by whom he had ten children but whom he would never be allowed to marry. Despite it all, he ascended to the monarchy in his late sixties after the deaths of both his older brothers. When he, too, died, "officially" childless in 1837, the young woman who came to the throne inaugurated the long Victorian era.

The Brown family left Britain as the slave trade—but not the profits from slavery—was being outlawed in Britain and in her remaining colonies from Canada to the Caribbean in 1833, but just as the following year the rights of the poor were being circumscribed dramatically. The Poor Act of 1834, passed around the time Mary Ann's parents were emigrating, established compulsory workhouses for the destitute and their children. These are the workhouses described by novelist Charles Dickens in *Oliver Twist* and (think: Ebenezer Scrooge) *A Christmas Carol*.

When the story of that terrible voyage at the bottom of the world became famous later, some journalists rushed to claim that Mary Ann Brown was from a "well-to-do" family and had been raised with every luxury. Those same journalists claimed that Mary Ann had blond hair and blue eyes (a quick glance at her photograph shows definitively otherwise), and we can dismiss this as romantic wishful thinking.

Mary Ann Brown did not grow up middle class. She did not even grow up respectably working class. She grew up in a poor immigrant family in North Boston. The confusion seems to stem from a misunderstanding of how it was that a girl from her background came, rather exceptionally, to have been educated.

Her father, George Brown, was a seaman, among the lower ranks of sailors. The fact that George Brown would never rise above that condition, in an era in which there was such a shortage of sailors, competent or incompetent, that captains were known to resort to "shanghaiing"—kidnapping crew—suggests that he was, at best, unlucky and, at worst, shall we just say, unsteady. Sailing as a seaman was dangerous and low-paid work, performed under severe discipline, in deeply unpleasant conditions, and in the company of men who not infrequently boasted criminal records and murderous tempers. A literate man with even a modicum of talent could rise to the rank of mate after just a few voyages, such was the shortage of maritime labor.

George Brown did not, apparently, have even a modicum of talent. He was also likely to have been illiterate and, as a consequence, unable to master the mathematics and recordkeeping required for navigation and for promotion. That may have been part of the reason the family prioritized literacy for the Brown children—daughters included. Because, while George Brown may have been beleaguered and poor and even, perhaps, "unsteady," he wanted something else for his children. That was why, after all, they had come to Boston and left behind family.

Seamen were known for rough living aboard ship and even rougher living in port, and they were notorious drinkers, gamblers, brawlers, and womanizers. Whether George Brown Sr. was unsteady in these ways, no one knows, but Mary Ann grew up in the North End of Boston, then a neighborhood on the downswing and quickly becoming a bawdy maritime red-light district.

In the 1830s, Boston was still a small city, with a population of only 150,000. In 1837, the year that Mary Ann was born, the Brown family moved to a tenement at 7 Unity Court, four blocks back from the wharfs and in the shadow of the Old North Church, from where Paul Revere set out on his famous ride in 1775. The narrow lane at Unity Court and its four-story brick-and-granite mews houses still stand today, though number seven no longer exists and the old, small tenements have long since been converted into expensive town houses.

From 1835 to 1836, a Harvard undergraduate from across the

Charles River named Richard Dana set out to sea from Boston to "double" Cape Horn, as the transit around that notorious South American headland was known in the era of the clippers. In 1840, Dana's account of that voyage, *Two Years Before the Mast*, made him a national celebrity. Dana describes the North End of Boston, and especially the notorious area around Ann Street (now North Street), not five minutes by foot from the Unity Court tenements, in the years around when Mary Ann was born, as a district of rough saloons, cheap boardinghouses, and open prostitution.

Crews coming in from sea were unruly. A sailor's last chore upon arriving in port was furling the sails and making the vessel "shipshape." From the decks, as they wrapped up their work, the crews sang boisterous and occasionally bawdy sea shanties, with choruses that echoed back and forth across the docks, from vessel to vessel. Only when the sails were stored was their voyage finished and did the shanties go silent, and, when they were paid, it was often for a year of back wages. Money like that could burn a hole in a sailor's pocket. Brightly rouged buxom lasses were paid to make sure of it.

To those who made their living by relieving these seamen of a large portion of their wages, the shanties might as well have been the Old North Church bell tolling the faithful to worship. "[T]he landlords, runners, and sharks in Ann Street," Dana wrote of Boston's North End, thus "learned that there was a rich prize for them down in the bay." Within minutes of receiving their pay packets, the crews were surrounded by hustlers and madams, plied with alcohol that they sometimes had not tasted for a year or more aboard dry ships, and introduced to boardinghouses that generally did not trouble themselves to disguise that they did double duty as brothels. More than half of Boston's brothels and an astonishing number of bars were jammed into this small quarter.

When their pockets were emptied, "crimpers" hired to round up crew for shorthanded captains would deliver intoxicated customers—

"some seamen, but many not"—who were "hoisted, literally dead to the world, aboard the clippers." They would awake only to discover they had drunkenly signed the "articles"—a shipping contract—and were unwitting crew on a multiyear voyage from which there was no quitting. Many of them had never been off dry land.

The area near the wharves of North Boston was as insalubrious as it was intemperate. Venereal diseases were the least of it: Smallpox, yellow fever, scarlet fever, cholera, typhoid, and, especially, tuberculosis were common diseases in the damp, confined spaces of long sea voyages and in the crowed red-light districts of ports of call. Often entire crews were felled by illness.

Experience soon taught any seaman to tell the difference. Ship fever (typhus) and typhoid brought sweats and delirium, smallpox raised angry pustules, dysentery destroyed the bowels, with a "putrid" throat (diphtheria) the tongue turned black. The best treatment for the "Black Tongue," the doctors said, was silver nitrate, mercury, or, if all else failed, "as much brandy as the patient can digest"; for catarrhal fever—influenza—a few drops of arsenic. Scarlet fever, the leading cause of death for children, raised a brilliant rash that caused misery at any age.

But the most fearsome of all was the "white plague," with the bright eyes and flushed cheeks and bloody coughing. Sufferers wasted away to frail skeletons "consumed" by tuberculosis—or "consumption." For reasons no doctor understood, the ravages of the disease were worst in young people and in the small, close-knit towns of New England. "What a dreadful scourge is consumption. It seizes upon the loveliest of earth's flowers and blights and withers them away," wrote one distraught husband in the 1840s.

The suffering caused by the disease in the nineteenth century is almost unimaginable. By the beginning of that century, tuberculosis had already killed nearly 15 percent of all the people who had ever lived in the United States and Europe. By the end of that century,

80 percent of the population would be infected with a bacillus that had an 80 percent rate of mortality.

**The North End** of Boston at mid-nineteenth century was (and largely remains) a warren of narrow alleys and cobble streets, dominated by its proximity to the water. When the Brown family lived there, the main arterial was already known as Hanover Street, and at the end of Hanover Street was the Winnisimmet Ferry depot, which since 1631 had shuttled workmen, passengers, horses, and cargo from the North End to nearby Chelsea.

If you had stood at the end of Hanover Street in the 1830s or 1840s, facing the waterfront, and looked to your left, there was Gray's Wharf and Comey's Yard and all the main maritime operations along Commercial Street. Over your left shoulder were Henchman's Lane, the burial grounds, and ultimately Foster Street and Unity Street, where the Old North Church was located and where Mary Ann and her family lived in the 1830s and 1840s.

Had you looked to your right in those decades, you would have seen Wood Wharf, Battery Wharf, and come to the railway station. Just over your right shoulder here was Salutation Street, where Mary Ann and her family lived by the 1850s.

Looking farther along the waterfront to your right, you'd have spotted Union Wharf, Sargent Wharf, Scarlet Wharf, Lewis Wharf, and the East Boston ferry. Tucked back from the port here was Ann Street and the heart of the red-light district.

The distance from the water today is deceptive. In the nineteenth century, Foster Street ended at the docks. Today, after those wharfs were backfilled and concreted, the entire baseball fields and tennis courts at Langone Park and the acres of parking lots at the Coast Guard installations separate you from the water. Mary Ann grew up in far closer proximity to the Atlantic and to the ships that came and went from Boston Harbor than any resident today of the North End can readily imagine.

No public record has been found to suggest that the family owned a property at any of these addresses. Typical of immigrants in the North End in the 1840s, the Brown family lived in rented tenement accommodations, with a number of families crammed into "makeshift plats and polluted alleys," generally moving every few years.

Seamen like George Brown were away from home for months or even years at a time, leaving wives and mothers at the head of many North End households. Only 5 percent of seamen in the mid-nineteenth century spent even a quarter of the year at home. Mary Ann's mother, Elizabeth Brown, was a devout woman, and she aspired to respectability precisely because of her family's economic struggles as new immigrants. One of the first things she did on arriving in Boston in 1833 was to join the congregation at the Old North Church.

Mrs. Brown's pew assignment, though, was shared and transient, just like the family's accommodations. Elizabeth Brown rented a seat (and in some years, two seats) in a shared pew, alongside a number of other solitary women whose husbands were also often seamen. In 1833, she shared pew ten with Mrs. Yates, Miss Smith, and Mrs. Peterson. A few years later, her fellow worshippers in pew thirteen included two other married—but solitary—ladies.

Renting a seat in a pew was a substantial investment in a family's community standing for a working immigrant household. Elizabeth Brown paid between five and ten dollars a year (about a week's wages for a shipwright) to reserve a seat in the church on Sundays and, more importantly, for the right to enroll her children in the Sunday School, the first in the nation, where the children—boys and girls—of local lamplighters, mast-makers, grocers, laborers, seamstresses, and seamen could be educated.

The Sunday School at the Old North Church was a groundbreaking social project and, when it opened in 1815, it was the first such school in the nation. Sunday schools had started as a movement in Britain in the 1780s, with the goal of teaching working-class children the "Three Rs" of reading, writing, and arithmetic, along with liberal doses of catechism, memorization, and lessons on cleanliness and gratitude. Some part of the charitable mission of the wealthy patrons was to tidy up their servants and tradesmen and to instill in them Christian values like duty and obedience; they were also a stepladder for working families, however. Sunday schools provided a rare opportunity for a free public education and made possible some class mobility.

Neither Mary Ann's name nor the names of her older brother George or their next two brothers Tobias "John" (born in 1838) and Edward (born in 1839) appear on the attendance lists at the "academy" on Salem Street. The names of all their younger siblings do, however, especially during the period in which the family was living on Salutation Street in the later part of the 1840s, by the time Mary Ann was about ten.

The younger Brown children continued to attend the academy into the 1850s. Her siblings William (born in 1842), Isabella Elizabeth (born in 1844), and Thomas (born in 1846) all attended the "Infant School" at various points as elementary school–aged children, where the curriculum focused on reading and religious instruction.

Isabella would go on to marry the bellringer's son. By the age of thirteen or fourteen, the boys would be sent to sea or apprenticed on the docks. In 1850, brother George Brown Jr., now twenty-one, was living at home but employed on the docks as a ship's caulker. Edward and William would both follow him into that profession. The Brown boys, unsurprisingly, all grew up to work in and around the shipyards of Boston. But they would not grow up to be sea captains.

Why did the Brown children born in the latter part of the 1830s not attend Sunday School when the siblings born in the 1840s consistently did? Money. With George Brown Sr. at sea and a half dozen children to feed, Elizabeth was compelled to take on some form of paid labor. Doing laundry at home was a common sideline for married women with small children, though there were other forms of domestic service. The 1830s and early 1840s were a lean period for the Brown family, and the older children worked beside their mother. By the late 1840s, when George Jr. was able to help support the family and the nationwide depression turned to boom times, the family's outlook improved. When it did, the younger children were enrolled in the Sunday School academy.

The older children, however, were literate. Mary Ann could read and write by the time she was a preteen, and subscription records in the parish archives from the late 1840s show that a John Brown, probably Mary Ann's second brother, had a library account allowing the family to check books out of the Sunday School collection. The schools encouraged families to take home books and encouraged older siblings and even parents learning alongside the younger students. Reading, writing, mathematics: This was an education typical for sea captains' daughters, for middle-class girls like the Hathorne girls in Salem; for a girl of Mary Ann's immigrant and working-class background, it was extremely lucky.

We know that Mary Ann learned to read and do sums and that she had a quick intelligence because, had she not, a few years later in a storm at the bottom of the world, her story and the story of all those aboard *Neptune's Car* would have ended in a different kind of disaster.

# 3

# Business in Great Waters

></>

They that go down to the sea in ships, that do business in great waters; they see the works of the Lord, and his wonders in the deep.

—Psalm 107:23–24 (KJV)

Joshua Patten was twenty-three the year he became a master mariner.

Mariner was a rank, and sailors had their own hierarchy of qualifications. A young lad starting out was a ship's boy. This was how Joshua and all the Patten boys started. His first job was to run errands.

An "ordinary seaman"—the next rung on the ladder—was a sailor who didn't yet "know the ropes": the complex system of rigging required to set the sails. His brother Uriah was a seaman before the age of sixteen, as was typical. Joshua is also likely to have made seaman early.

An "able seaman" not only knew the ropes but was a good helmsman, qualified to take a turn at the wheel and pilot a vessel to instruction when on watch, but a seaman did not have the skills of navigation. One rose to the rank of "AB" after two years as a seaman, and this is where the career of Mary Ann's father faltered.

Those who could navigate were "mariners" and might serve aboard a ship as a "mate." "Master mariners" were those mariners qualified to command a vessel; they were, in other words, sea captains. Attaining the rank of a master mariner required six years at sea, at least two as an officer and one as a first mate, and attaining the age of twenty-one.

When Joshua was first put to sea in the 1840s, Penobscot Bay was one of the great hubs of the American merchant sailing fleet. In 1845, seventeen oceangoing vessels were built in the Thomaston area and local mariners could be found "in almost every commercial mart, near or remote." The *Lime Rock Gazette* reported the arrival and departure in Rockland each week of "barks, schooners, and packets from around the Atlantic."

Joshua's first few years at sea were spent crossing the Atlantic on the passenger clippers between Boston and Liverpool, though he may have spent some time when first starting out on the passenger-ferry schooner run between Boston and Rockland. Generally, a mariner would serve as a mate aboard a vessel before being appointed to its command, and sea captains were constantly moving up to larger and more prestigious vessels, because those were the most lucrative runs for a master.

Being a sea captain required a certain steady forbearance in the 1850s. As one nineteenth-century sea captain explained, looking back on the era of sail in his youth,

The packet captain, no matter what his age might be, was usually spoken of as 'the old man' . . . and [it] required an unusual combination of qualities. . . . Above all things it was necessary that the captains should be thorough seamen and navigators; also that they should be men of robust health and great physical endurance, as their duties often kept them on deck for days and nights together in storm, cold, and fog. Then there were frequently desperate characters among the crew and steerage passengers, who required to be handled with moral courage and physical force, while the cabin passengers were usually gentlemen and gentlewomen of good breeding, accustomed to courtesy and politeness, which they expected to find in the captains with whom they sailed. These requirements evolved a remarkable type of men, hearty, bluff, and jovial, without coarseness, who would never be mistaken for anything but gentlemen.

Young Joshua Patten had the right temperament.

In 1851, the year of his promotion, Joshua had been at sea for eight, perhaps nine years already. His first command, either that year or early in the year following, was as the master of an American-registered three-masted merchant bark called the *St. Andrew*, which "plied between New York and South[ern] American ports." The *St. Andrew* sailed in those years, according to ship records, among Baltimore, Savannah, Jamaica, and Charleston for New York merchant houses, and Joshua soon knew all those ports as familiar places.

It was a good and respectable job. A coastal captain working short runs along the Eastern Seaboard could easily earn several thousand dollars a year, perhaps double if he were good and the distances were long, enough to look forward to a comfortable future. In modern terms, it was the equivalent of a salary in the low six figures. Joshua's career, in other words, was unfolding along a promising but well-trodden path for a young mariner from a good background.

Once a man became a sea captain, however, his career hit a fork in the road. One turning led to a modestly affluent lifestyle, a moderate level of risk, and a good work-life balance, to use the modern parlance. The other turning led to adventure on the high seas, fame, fortune, and mortal danger.

Those who remained coastal captains lived comfortable, middle-class lives; they also were home frequently enough to see their wives and watch their children grow tall and sturdy. Then there were those who became celebrated sea captains: the men who circumnavigated the world, took great risks, faced down the elements, gambled on nature for a living, and sometimes came home extremely wealthy men, able to retire before their number was up and the sea took them.

Joshua already knew which one of those careers he wanted. The trouble was he hadn't counted on falling in love.

**They met in** 1852, and, at barely fifteen, Mary Ann was not yet looking for courtship either.

Mary Ann Brown was light and small. Those who knew her later described her as fey and ethereal and extraordinarily pretty. In the one daguerreotype of her that has survived, she has big brown eyes, plump cheeks, and jet-black hair that she wore parted down the middle.

There is no record of how or where she and Joshua met, though it had to have been somewhere along the waterfront of Boston.

Her brothers worked as caulkers. Their job was to make tight and waterproof the hulls and decks of wooden vessels, scraping away the old stuffing, filling the gaps afresh with hemp "oakum" and hot pitch, preparing the body of the ship for the copper sheathing that protected her underbelly from barnacles and the wood-boring mollusks known simply as shipworm.

Mary Ann was spared being sent out to labor in the workshops and factories, where agitating for a ten-hour workday for children was considered a progressive reformist passion, but she was old enough to be expected to bake, cook, clean, sew, and iron beside her mother. Among her daily tasks would have been taking lunches down to the docks for her brothers. Perhaps it was here among the milling seamen and shipyard workers that she first met Joshua.

More likely, their eyes met in Old North Church one Sunday morning. The Old North Church had been at the center of the social and religious life of the Brown family already for two decades. Joshua became a parishioner in 1852, during the period of his first command of the *St. Andrew*. The arrival of a new sea captain in the congregation would have been a cause for some excitement. A sea captain was a gentleman and a man of substance, even if he were not yet five-and-twenty.

Courtship in mid-nineteenth century New England had its own traditions, and Mary Ann and Joshua's affection would have deepened at Christmastime church dances under the bright lanterns at the Old North Church, with the girls dressed in layers of lace and frills, hoping not to be left wallflowers. From church gatherings and shy conversation at the end of service, Joshua would have progressed, with Mrs. Brown's permission, to sitting for an hour in the family's little front parlor.

There, little gifts were passed between them. In summer, a young chap falling in love might bring a bouquet and speak through the language of flowers; in winter, more common was a love token, a coin onto which a young lady might find her engraved initials. There would, of course, too, have been Joshua's floridly formal love letters. Writing love letters was an essential element of any budding romance in the 1850s, even if the couple lived only a stone's throw apart and saw each other daily. No young lady could be properly assured of a young man's sensibilities and affection without a passionate declaration to review with her sisters.

Mrs. Brown looked on benignly. There was no reason to dislike Joshua, although Mary Ann was, in truth, too young to be courting. Still, only a cold heart could have thwarted such a happy story unfolding, and Mrs. Brown apparently was not coldhearted.

By January, the young people had, with the blessing of Mary Ann's mother, the kind of understanding that allowed them a bit more freedom. Joshua could have proposed an excursion. Winter sleighing out to Chestnut Hill, wrapped up together under thickly scented fur blankets, was on the mind of every young paramour in Boston. The sleighs were immense: eight horses deep, carrying forty or more young people (and their shivering chaperones). A local composer one evening in Simpson's Tavern in 1850 came up with a song, which began "Jingle bells" and ended with the today-forgotten verse, "Now the ground is white / Go it while you're young, / Take the girls tonight / and sing this sleighing song," rendering that old tradition timeless.

Or there were a dozen other ways a young couple falling in love in Boston in the 1850s might contrive to be together, laughing. They might stroll down to Boston Common to watch the boys "coasting," or sledding. They might touch hands for a moment as they whirled across a frozen pond on a cold, sunny afternoon. Ice skating in 1850s America was a passion.

And by the time Valentine's Day came along—because ornate and elaborate Valentine's Day cards were essential—Mary Ann and Joshua had declared not only their affection but their intentions: They wanted to get married.

Mary Ann's mother did not attempt to dissuade them. She simply said that they would have to wait until her father was home from sea in the springtime. When George Brown returned, the ceremony was hastily arranged. Joshua would have returned to his ship, too, within a week or two of their wedding.

Mary Ann and Joshua were married on April 1, 1853, by the rector of the Old North Church, William Smithett, with Mary Ann's father signing the record book to give his permission. Joshua was just shy of his twentieth-sixth birthday. Mary Ann was not yet sixteen.

When her father came home, everyone could see the obvious. George Brown had almost certainly already contracted tuberculosis. George knew it, too, the day he gave away his fifteen-year-old daughter in marriage.

**From their marriage** in the spring of 1853 until the beginning of 1855, the details of Mary Ann and Joshua's life together are scanty but tantalizing. All the indications are that they were laying the foundations for a return to Joshua's hometown in Maine.

In 1852, in anticipation of their marriage, Joshua had traveled before Christmas to Rockland by steamboat to put in place the necessary arrangements. Until he had saved enough money to build a sea captain's home on the Weskeag land, they would need a small house for Mary Ann and for children who were surely soon to come.

Joshua turned to his stepmother, Sarah. She owned a little house on the south side of Rockland, just northeast of what is today the intersection of South Main Street and Thomaston Street, and, to help Joshua start his family, Sarah offered to sell it to him along with a small plot of land. Joshua paid $264 for the home, which he owned mortgage free, and his new neighbors were other young sea captains, with wives and children.

Joshua also joined the local Masonic lodge in Rockland and received the white lambskin apron of an initiate, which would travel around the world with him in the captain's quarters. Joshua's brother and stepbrother both also joined the lodge at around this period as master mariners, and sea captains made up a large proportion of lodge membership in the 1850s. The substantial initiation fees were a prudent investment. The Masonic fellowship provided the most reliable form of travel "insurance" available to any sea captain—or to his widow or orphaned children—in the event of misadventure. As one historian astutely quips: "Any clear-thinking wife contemplating taking her family away from home might well decide that this [insurance] more than compensated for her husband's long evenings at the lodge." Any clear-thinking sea captain looking to marry and start a family might make the same calculus.

**There would be** no honeymoon or chance to travel up to Maine to decorate their new little home and to choose furniture and curtains or plan a garden. Joshua was scheduled to ship out of New York again at the end of April, and he would need to oversee the final preparations in person. By mid-April, he was on the steamer for Manhattan.

Mary Ann, they decided, would spend the spring of 1853 in Boston with her mother, and they would travel up to Maine together as soon as Joshua could persuade the ship's owners to let him have a few weeks on the schedule. Joshua was fond of his stepmother and aunt and was sure that Sarah would welcome Mary Ann, but their first introduction would need to be by letter.

The *St. Andrew* was headed that spring from New York to Liverpool. The *Sun* newspaper of London published, as an item of marine intelligence on May 30, 1853, that Captain Patten's ship "had been sighted recently off the coast of Liverpool on a northwest heading," about a month after departure—an uneventful and decidedly average passage.

At sea Joshua would not hear the terrible news from Rockland even when he arrived in Liverpool. Word would not make its way across the Atlantic for weeks, and Joshua would only learn when he landed back in New York and received Mary Ann's waiting letters that most of his hometown no longer existed.

At three o'clock on the morning of May 23, in the downtown merchant offices of Samuel Pillsbury, there had been a fire. No one knew afterward quite how it started. By the time the fire was spotted in the early hours of the morning, the entire building was engulfed in flames and sparks were jumping from one wooden building to the next down Main Street.

When the Commercial Hotel began burning, guests rushed into the street in their bedclothes. When the firefighters attempted to turn on the hydrants to fight the blaze, nothing happened. The pumps had been turned off down at the pond by repairmen working on the system, and there was no water. Someone set off on a run down to the pumps, someone else rushed to call for the water engines, but the fire was faster. The blaze jumped the street, setting alight one of the great wharves, bringing it crashing into the water, and soon more than a million board feet of timber in the lumber yard was fueling the conflagration. Terrified horses in the livery stables were released and tore through a burning Main Street.

By the time the fire was brought under control, nearly the entire commercial center of Rockland—more than fifty homes and businesses—lay in smoldering ruin. The Commercial Hotel was gone, along with four grocery stores, the local apothecary, the house of Captain Varrell, and the house of the local doctor. Destroyed was the Masonic lodge and all its papers.

Mary Ann's brothers heard the news on the docks when Captain Lambert arrived in Boston a few days later on the Rockland packet. The letters that flew between Mary Ann and her mother-in-law, Sarah, did not survive, so we can only guess at their contents, but it would have taken more than a week for Mary Ann to receive confirmation that their little home on South Main Street, along with the Patten family residence, were still standing. When Joshua arrived back in Boston that summer, he and Mary Ann traveled north to witness the reconstruction.

**They seem to** have stayed in Maine most of the summer and into the autumn. Joshua was at loose ends, waiting for a new commission. He had relinquished command of the *St. Andrew*. The *Cornelia Lawrence*, an emigrant passenger ship destined for the route between New York and Liverpool, was awaiting launch, and Joshua had been promised command of her, instead, when she was ready. He had expected her to launch that summer.

The *Cornelia Lawrence* was not one of the great "extreme" clippers that could make a man rich, but she was a transatlantic packet for the old Black Star Line, and it was an important promotion. Crossing the Atlantic Ocean was nothing new for Joshua. As mariner and later captain on the emigrant packets, he had made the voyage more than a dozen times already.

It was a hard decision for a young couple in love. What kind of command should Joshua look for? It was really just another way of asking what kind of life and marriage they wanted to build together. It was hard to be married to a sea captain.

Joshua could easily have found work, like Captain Lambert, on the run from Rockland to Boston, plying the coastal waters. Captain Lambert could be home sometimes to see his family.

The transatlantic packet service and the *Cornelia Lawrence*, on the other hand, would mean more time away. But the New York to Liverpool route wasn't impossible. These were short crossings, three or four weeks in each direction, on a regular schedule, and captains on the packets were home more than most mariners. Mary Ann understood the reality. She was a seaman's daughter, and she had married a sea captain. Still, the young couple struggled with the idea of so many months a year away from each other.

The trouble was the launch of the *Cornelia Lawrence* kept getting postponed. At first, they welcomed this belated honeymoon. The summer of 1853 was exceptionally hot and dry, gardens were parched, and everyone in the town was seeking the sea breezes. Just a mile or so down the road from their little house, the waters of Rockland Harbor and the great Penobscot Bay ran into a shallow cove with great mudflats. At low tide, the sand was covered with the bubbles of buried clams, where the rakers hunched over their harvests. To the left and toward the open sea was the peninsula known today as Owls Head. Straight down the road another two or three miles, through rolling farmland, one came to the mouth of the Weskeag River, which "broadens into several large coves before emptying into the Muscle Ridge Channel."

The Indigenous people called this place Wessaweskeag—"wizard's point," the place of magic. Town planners renamed it South Thomaston in 1848. Locals today know it simply as the Gig, and you will get strange looks if you call it anything else. In 1853, the small village at the head of the river boasted a gristmill, a sawmill, a post office, new lime kilns, a shipyard, and more than a dozen houses. Mary Ann and Joshua may have traveled there in August or September to see the destruction wrought by gales that damaged a number of vessels in the harbor. It had been a strange summer, and in August when the town turned out to watch a comet streak across the night sky some people said that it was a warning of a hard winter. It was this small, fledgling village where Joshua dreamed of them settling and raising their children.

But he would need, first, to earn enough money as a sea captain to support a family. And the autumn of 1853 was frustrating. At Christmas, he was still without a ship. A howling nor'easter dropped feet of snow over the holiday, confining even the most intrepid Mainers to their homes, and as Joshua and Mary Ann grimly welcomed the new year on January 1, 1854, more snow started falling.

The snow continued for a week, stopping even the mail and the telegram service.

The snow just kept falling and somewhere south of them the *Cornelia Lawrence* was still sitting in the shipyard. Watching their savings diminish, Joshua was growing impatient and a little worried.

Then, in the spring of 1854, a new opportunity popped up unexpectedly. Captain Patten was offered the temporary command of the *Flying Scud*, a 220-foot-long extreme clipper that had launched in Damariscotta, Maine, on November 2, 1853. There was a gap in the ship's schedule. The next fall, she was destined to be put in the service of an emigrant packet line from New York to Australia.

Damariscotta is not twenty-five miles from Rockland, and this was the *Flying Scud*'s maiden voyage. Joshua would finally have his chance to earn the kind of hard-sailing reputation that by summer would launch him into the fast-paced and dangerous world of international extreme clipper deliveries as an up-and-comer.

It was thanks to a dramatic impromptu race against the celebrated master Captain Samuel Samuels that had the sea captains and ship's owners talking.

**Clipper ships, especially** the so-called extreme clippers like the *Flying Scud*, were marvels of engineering, but, like performance race cars, they were built for power and speed, not safety. The 1850s were the golden age of these astonishing sailing vessels, and the captains who sailed them hardest and fastest were international celebrities. A clipper could travel at previously unimaginable speeds and cut days or even weeks off the long sea voyages that integrated trade in a global economy. They were, if you will, the "just-in-time" portion of the nineteenth-century supply chain, the expedited couriers of the 1850s. When it had to be there and fast, it had to be clipper.

Speed cost, but it also paid. Speed paid off for the shipowners and the cargo owners, who charged a premium for the clipper service, and it paid for the captains, who were rewarded for delivering results. A sea captain who could transport goods and passengers from New York to San Francisco in under one hundred days could generally count on a salary of $3,000 plus a bonus of several thousand dollars more, for a total compensation, in modern terms, of over $200,000. A captain ferrying passengers could generally double that amount with the receipts for passage. It was a fine wage, easily twice what Joshua could earn as a coastal captain on the run between Rockland and Boston.

But the salary was not how clipper captains became fabulously wealthy. The real money came from fast international cargo transport.

The extreme clippers were large ships, anywhere from 150 to nearly 300 feet long; 200 feet from bow to stern was common. They were three-, four-, sometimes five-masted ships, rigged tall and square, with gleaming black hulls and bright, copper bottoms, and carrying ten thousand square feet or more of canvas sail, controlled by a complex system of lines. "Learning the ropes" to qualify as an able seaman was no metaphor. The *Flying Scud* flew seventeen sails. Ambitious young captains used every inch of those sails to press for speed, reducing the canvas only when the wind's power was too great to manage. Sometimes, captains didn't reef their sails even then, with occasionally fatal consequences. For these were also narrow boats, with sharp lines, designed to cut swiftly through the water, generally overpowered and often under-ballasted.

The evolution of the clipper was largely due to American and then, later, British innovation and to the intense mercantile competition between the empire and her former colony. From the early use of the nimble Baltimore-built clippers that ran the British blockades during the War of 1812 and the opium clippers that smuggled narcotics in and out of China, to the innovation of the "extreme" clippers after 1845 that Joshua was sailing and that raced to bring the spring tea harvests to New York and London markets, it was always about speed and lucrative cargo.

But the height of the clipper ship era began in 1848, the same year that South Thomaston became a town, with the discovery of gold in far-off California. The wealth of one fueled the prosperity of the other.

The transcontinental railroad did not yet exist. Neither did the canal in Panama. Slow and sturdy frigates were not fit for purpose when there was a frantic race to move mining equipment and eager young men to the other side of a continent in a hurry. There were fortunes to be made; prospectors rushed to get their claim in early. When gold was discovered next in Australia in 1851, the push to build clippers only accelerated.

The public was fascinated by the stories of extreme maritime adventure aboard the clippers, and passengers' journals of these voyages to California or Australia were often collected and published in volumes of thrilling sea stories. One such nineteenth-century volume recounted for an eager reading public a storm at sea aboard the clipper the *Sagamore*. "Tacking a large square-rigged vessel is considerable of a job at any time, but at night, and in a hurricane, it is an arduous task," one unfortunate passenger reported:

> The stiffened braces, wet with icy salt water, got tangled up, and occasionally a man would make a mistake amid the maze of ropes . . . Several times [the ship] went over so far that captain and mates hardly dared to breathe for fear she was on her side and would never right . . . At each roll, the bulwarks went far under, allowing a flood to come roaring and tumbling aboard; washing about the main deck, tangling up ropes, and knocking men off their feet.

A ship's boy was not a seaman until he had survived at least three or four offshore voyages. Survival was not assured: A full 75 percent of the ship's logs from this period record the death at sea of at least one crew member.

Speed did not pay for the crew in these circumstances. Crews and captains had competing objectives. Sailing conservatively in foul weather, even if the ship lost speed by it, was safer for a sailor. Men were lost at sea all the time by falling from a mast or being knocked off their feet and off the decks, and few could swim well enough to tread water for long. There was no easy way to turn a ship around, no way to save them in time. Besides: Crew were paid by the month. Captains, on the other hand, had every incentive, especially in the clipper trade, to push their crew to the limit.

Merchant sailing ships were not floating democracies. At sea, a captain's power was nearly unfettered. He was the master. He alone chose where they would sail, under what sail power, and at what risk to the ship and the crew. A seaman's contract was binding; there was no quitting in some distant port to find another vessel. A man who breached his shipping articles was a deserter and subject to arrest or forced return to a disgruntled captain. The captain had the authority to discipline any crew member who disobeyed his orders; a sailor wanted, if he could, to choose his captain carefully because there were "bully captains" who flogged sailors on sea voyages for minor infractions.

**Life onboard was** strictly divided along the lines of this hierarchy. The seamen—and on a clipper ship they might number thirty, forty, or even fifty or more, from as young as fourteen or fifteen to someone like the forty-year-old seaman George Brown in 1850—lived and passed their free time "before the mast," literally in the area of the ship known as the forecastle or "fo'scle." Here, a captain did not enter.

Generally located between the first and the second mast of a three-masted clipper, the forecastle was a raised utilitarian bunkhouse, built on deck, forward of the main hatch, with a galley at one end, the ship's carpenter's room at the other end, a long mess table down the center, and tightly stacked bunks on all sides of the mess table. A seaman who wished to relieve himself faced a trudge to the bow or the bucket, and relieving oneself on a pitching vessel at night required some agility. Even today, more than one unlucky sailor has pitched overboard taking a nighttime pee, and grog generally does not help matters. Privacy was not a seaman's lot, and neither was regular bathing.

The quarters occupied by the captain, his senior officers, any genteel paying passengers, and the agent of the ship's owners were located at the rear of the ship. Life at sea was never easy, but the conditions here were very different. A sea captain and his officers were not working-class mariners. The captain was a gentleman, waited upon by a steward, and his authority rested as much on maintaining a strict class separation from his crew as from meting out physical discipline. The men who commanded the fastest clippers had an international celebrity that today is almost unfathomable. They were the rock stars and elite athletes of the mid-nineteenth century. No member of the crew was permitted even to address the captain unbidden.

At the aft of the ship, the captain's quarters were also a raised bunkhouse stepped up above deck, but the proportions were entirely different. Where the roof of the forecastle was often used for lifeboat storage, the captain's quarters could be two stories high, with banks of leaded glass windows providing floods of natural light, spaces that often looked, more than anything, like the interior of a small and particularly beautiful chapel. On the top of the captain's quarters was the "poop deck," where the captain scanned the horizon and took navigational sightings. In the center of the main saloon was a large and spacious captain's table that opened onto the captain's office, where he kept the ship's library and the chartroom. To one side were the captain's personal suite of rooms, with a bedroom, private sitting room, and facilities, and ranged around the open dining room were staterooms for the first mate, the ship's agents, and any paying passengers. The 180-foot tea clipper *Foochow* had a half dozen additional staterooms and was probably typical.

The wine at captain's table was good, and the suite of staterooms at the aft of a clipper were luxurious. The storeroom and armory were both accessed through the captain's quarters, which also served as a kind of shipboard fortress in the event of mutiny or pirates. Polished wood gleamed in the saloon and master's stateroom (though the officers' cabins were small and spartan), and cozy fires burned in front of rich oriental carpets and other luxurious souvenirs of a captain's far-flung voyages. The *Witch of the Wave*, a clipper built in 1851 for the trade, was recorded as boasting "interiors of bird's eye maple . . . enameled cornices edged with gold [and] dark imitation marble pedestals." One sea captain's wife, Hannah Rebecca Burgess, writing in the same winter that Captain Patten commanded the *Flying Scud* to Liverpool, recorded in her journal that the staterooms aboard the clipper *Whirlwind* boasted a dining room "painted with Zinc paint of a cream color . . . beautifully ornamented with gilded work," a parlor "of Mahogany, rosewood, and satin wood," and a suite of staterooms for the captain and officers "carpeted with nice velvet tapestry."

Aboard a clipper were, notably, no women unless the captain's wife sailed with the ship or the captain took aboard paying female passengers. Joshua sailed the *Flying Scud* that winter solo. His time commanding emigrant packets had taught Joshua to dislike taking passengers, especially ladies. He much preferred to fill his staterooms with additional cargo.

The *Flying Scud* would sail from New York. Mary Ann remained in Boston during Joshua's absence. The parish register for the Old

North Church shows that on June 4, 1854, while waiting for Joshua's return, Mary Ann stood as sponsor at the christening of her first nephew, the son of her favorite and older brother, George, and his wife, Margaret.

The new parents marked their affection not only for Mary Ann but also for Joshua by naming the little boy Joshua Patten Brown.

# 4

# The Road to Liverpool

༃

> Each ship is an island, a floating colony of the tribe to which it belongs. Here are brought together the remotest limits of the earth; and in the collective spars and timbers of these ships, all the forests of the globe are represented, as in a grand parliament of masts. . . . A Liverpool dock is a grand caravansary inn.
>
> —Herman Melville, *Redburn: His First Voyage*

The *Flying Scud* was loading at Pier 11 on the East River, at the southern tip of Manhattan.

Joshua's last stop before the *Flying Scud* cast off the lines on March 23, 1854, was to the offices at 116 Wall Street, to receive his final instructions from the ship's owner, Canadian-born merchant Roderick William Cameron, whose two great passions were fast ships and racehorses.

Mr. Cameron, a burly man with an untamed lamb-chop beard and bushy eyebrows, was already rich enough to be enjoying the lavish life of a New York plutocrat, as his stretched waistcoat attested, and in 1853 and 1854 he was on a spending spree that included at least two new Maine-built clipper ships, the *Flying Scud*, for which he paid $100,000, and the Bath-built clipper *Windward*. Cameron did not have any nostalgic attachment to the region. Construction prices were 25 percent less expensive in Rockland than at the shipyards of Boston or Manhattan, and the northern men who built them were masters.

The *Flying Scud* and the *Windward* were the newest additions to a fleet of clippers at R. W. Cameron & Company, whose primary business interest was in ferrying immigrants with gold fever to Australia. From 1852 to 1854, he had at least seventeen different ships discharging emigrants in the antipodes, and steerage class aboard the Australian Pioneer Line, as he called the service, was notoriously crowded. As one historian has written of Cameron, "He seems from such evidence as survives today to have been intelligent, masterful, courteous, polished and cosmopolitan, but also aggressive, manipulative, self-centered, and indifferent to the humble and the unfortunate." After eighty days or more in steerage, in an overloaded vessel with rotting food provisions, few doubted the last bit.

Joshua's impression of his new employer is also not recorded, but the character of Mr. Cameron is unlikely to have concerned him greatly. This was not going to be long-term employment. He had given up on the *Cornelia Lawrence*. He was sick of the emigrant passenger run back and forth, New York to Liverpool. He was longing for a circumnavigation and the chance to make his own fortune. The decision to send the *Flying Scud* under Captain Patten on a quick Liverpool circuit was temporary, and Joshua knew it. What mattered to him was that it was one more rung up the ladder. The commission was meant to fill in a gap in the shipping magnate's schedule, and, though equipped to serve as a passenger ship, this trip was cargo. British ports like Liverpool specialized in the skill of "coppering" the bottom of clippers to increase their speed and revenue, and many newly launched vessels made their first run to Liverpool for coppering, in preparation for voyage to warmer, equatorial waters. This may have been the primary purposes of her maiden voyage.

The *Flying Scud* departed New York on March 23, 1854, and Joshua set sail already knowing the astonishing news that had arrived from Liverpool about a new world record. On the wharves and in the merchant houses along South Street, everyone from the tattooed seamen with their bell-bottom trousers and leathered palms to the shipowners in their silk top hats and with their waiting carriages were talking about it.

It had all started right here, after all: During the second week of January, just two-odd months earlier, another Rockland-built extreme clipper ship, the *Red Jacket*, had cleared New York harbor under the command of the forty-five-year-old Massachusetts Captain Asa Elridge, who had docked in Liverpool on January 24, some 3,000 nautical miles and thirteen days, one hour, and twenty-five minutes later. With a crew of sixty-five men, Elridge, already renowned among his peers as a gallant and steely-nerved sea captain, shaved an unbelievable two and a half weeks off what was typically a thirty-day crossing. Anything under three weeks eastbound transatlantic was impressive. To cross in thirteen days was a marvel.

In fact, thirteen days eastbound transatlantic was seen as so unimaginably fast and the local British coverage was so breathless that Captain Elridge found his ship's log questioned in the international press, with the (unfounded) implication that he was cheating in what one historian has described as essentially one ceaseless twenty-year-long round-the-world regatta.

The story repeated that day across the docks of south Manhattan got even more exciting. Hearing of a record in the making, the *Yarmouth Register* reported that in Liverpool "people rushed in thousands to the docks; every point of vantage was black with spectators awaiting the arrival of this incredible racer." When no pilot boat would brave the heavy fog to tow the *Red Jacket* the last leg into port, in a feat that combined seamanship and showmanship, Captain Elridge not only docked the majestic clipper under sail but backed her in to her berth under sail to thunderous applause at the docks, so as not to lose the record. It's hard to fathom the level of skill and unthinkable nerve it takes to back a two-hundred-odd-foot wooden vessel under sail into a berth without a modern bow-thruster or engine. Suffice it to say that was a reason these sea captains were considered celebrities on the order of legendary athletes.

Joshua headed back to the *Flying Scud* from Mr. Cameron's office to oversee the final loading, mulling. Captain Elridge's feat was something to consider. Joshua wanted to break that kind of record for speed. An international race was on, a race against time and the sea, on which depended skill, discipline, and good fortune. Joshua wanted to be part of that excitement and glory.

**The new "extreme"** clippers combined with rapid advances in the understanding of sea currents made Captain Elridge's feat possible. But what made a clipper "extreme" and accounted for its (then) breathtaking speed?

It was all about sail power and resistance.

Designing a sailboat to move through water quickly requires a series of compromises, each more daring than the last, and it's all a matter of physics. Consider in your mind's eye your typical sailboat: mast and sail up in the air, hull resting in the water, and the keel at the bottom. The rounded portion of a sailing vessel below water, the hull, has volume. It takes up space in the water. The greater the volume of the space, the greater the cargo one can place in the hold, but also the greater the resistance, because, as a sailing ship moves, it must displace the water as it advances.

One way to increase the speed of that hull through water is to increase the amount of sail and, thereby, sail power. This is why extreme clippers had tall masts and more than a dozen sails spread out in every conceivable direction. Another way to increase speed is to make the hull slender and the lines at the front of the ship, where it pushes through the displaced water, sharp and angular, to reduce resistance, though that comes at a price of space for cargo. This is what distinguishes the "extreme" clipper from her slower, wider, "beamier" clipper cousins.

There is one other way to make a ship sail faster, too: to make the part of it that travels through the water, that hull, longer. How fast a vessel can move through the water before the forces of displacement become overwhelming and the vessel begins to lose speed despite an increase in sail power (known to mariners as "hull speed") is a direct function of the length of the vessel. Extreme clippers were long. The *Great Republic*, built in 1853 in Boston, the longest clipper ever constructed, was 400 feet from bowsprit to stern. She launched to a crowd of 50,000 cheering spectators. To understand how intense the celebrity surrounding these clippers was, consider that Boston in 1853 had a population of fewer than 150,000.

Extreme clippers were sexy, fast, and capable of making the shipowners and the captains very, very wealthy because their speed meant that they could charge a premium on freight rates and could specialize in only the most profitable cargo.

**The lines were** cast off, and they were underway. When the Atlantic Seaboard was behind them, Joshua turned his attention eastward. Whether by chance or design, he quickly fell into a transatlantic competition with the clipper *Dreadnought* as his "antagonist."

The *Dreadnought* and the *Flying Scud* each left Manhattan loaded with cargo and mail destined for the manufacturing heart of England and with a complement of paying passengers. On their return voyage, passengers would be almost all they carried, most of whom would be desperate Irish immigrants crammed into "steerage" as human cargo fleeing economic disaster. Their mutual destination was Liverpool, which, because it possessed the only deepwater harbor on the West Coast of Britain, was unrivaled in international importance.

At the helm of the *Dreadnought* was Captain Samuel Samuels, a thirty-one-year-old master mariner already legendary for his speed and skill as a clipper captain and known along the wharves for his particularly harsh treatment of his seamen.

Captain Samuels had come up "before the mast." He'd run away to sea at the age of eleven as a ship's boy. At twenty-one, he was commanding a clipper as captain. To the paying passengers who booked the first-class staterooms, he was a soft-spoken, gentlemanly character, and for five years already, his wife, Anne, and his numerous children had been with him on nearly every voyage. On deck and with his crew, though, the captain brooked no opposition, was accompanied by his attack dog, Wallace, and had put down his fair share of mutinies at gun- or knifepoint. Captain Samuels had a reputation for being free with the lash and with the trigger. Neither Joshua nor any other commander in the emigrant packet run, where the crews were of the lowest standard and referred to without any affection by their masters as "packet rats," would have faulted him, but it didn't play well in the newspapers.

Unfortunately but perhaps not unsurprisingly, Captain Samuels never mentioned the encounter with the *Flying Scud* in his autobiography, but a young sailor aboard the *Dreadnought* left a journal recording the competition between the two captains as it unfolded. Joshua was also sighted along the way by at least one other ship, whose captain observed how aggressively the *Flying Scud* was sailing.

The antagonists sighted each other first on April 10, 1854, seventeen days out of Sandy Hook, the last barrier island outside New York Harbor, somewhere more than halfway across the Atlantic.

Captains communicated with each other at sea largely by a complex system of coded flags. A flag was raised, signaling a message. The responding captain acknowledged standing ready to receive by raising the answering pennant. A single flag might suffice to send a simple message. Raising the "Y" flag coming into port meant "I am carrying the mail." A lifted "P" or "blue Peter" warned laggard seamen that this ship is leaving, get a move on. The "G" was a request for a pilot to come into harbor, and a "V" was an urgent request for assistance. "HO" in combination meant "heave-to or I will shoot you"; "QY" was "barometer is falling" (and storm incoming). Longer messages could be sent, of course, in calm weather, each letter spelling out sentences, which, recorded in the logbook, would be reported in the next port and published in the newspapers as maritime intelligence. This is what is meant when a ship was referred to as "sighted" by another captain.

Whether Captain Samuels or Captain Patten started the competition, no one remembers, though, from the journal of the young seaman aboard the *Dreadnought*, it sounds like the instigator was Joshua. Perhaps the two captains laid down the gauntlet with some protracted exchange of sentences. It's unlikely. One of them just needed to hoist the "A" flag: speed trial. First, Joshua put on sail and told his crew to bring them taut. Captain Samuels responded. "[W]e clapped on all the sail we could," the journal of Charles Swinscoe recorded.

For a while the ships flew along, neck and neck, and then, to the outrage of Captain Samuels, the *Flying Scud* pulled ahead and passed them. Now, the race was on in earnest. "[S]he was giving us a pretty hard rub," Swinscoe remembered, despite Captain Samuels demanding a "pretty press of Canvas."

Unable to keep the heading, the *Dreadnought* was forced to tack and change direction to keep course. Captain Samuels was determined to make the turn with a lot of canvas flying. Changing the direction of a massive clipper required the deceleration of the ship, and losing speed and momentum was inevitable. Captain Samuels, now swearing mightily, came about violently and "came near to losing a man overboard, he'd shipp'd for able seaman. . . . [and] a passenger came near to being swept off the house on Deck by the main sail" as it came flying past him.

The *Dreadnought* stalled in the turn. The *Flying Scud* and a jubilant Captain Patten sailed on, out of sight. Captain Samuels was having none of it. He pushed his men, determined to make up lost distance, and the next week, with the coast of Britain just coming into view in the distance, the *Dreadnought* again caught sight of the *Flying Scud*.

Or, at least "we presumed it to be the *Flying Scud*, a new Clipper built to show the *Dreadnought* the road to Liverpool," Swinscoe recorded. "We were all watching her, up goes her flying jibs, then her Top Gallant . . . We sent up our Ensign, which they returned, then up goes *Dreadnought*, then *Flying Scud*" as Captain Patten and Captain Samuels raced to the finish line. "Several bottles of wine [were] cracked" and Captain Samuels, to urge his men on, "liquored the crew on the strength of it."

Then, somehow, again, the *Dreadnought* lost sight of her opponent.

The *Flying Scud* came into port with a decidedly average crossing time of twenty-nine days, but word spread across the docklands that, on two separate days at sea, Captain Samuels had been outsailed by a new young captain few had ever heard of. A fellow named Captain Patten.

Suddenly, Joshua was a master worth watching—and worth hiring.

**The city of** Liverpool—from the Old English "liever pol" or "muddy pool"—grew up on the eastern banks of the Mersey River, in a great tidal port that was the only safe natural harbor on the wild West Coast of Britain.

From the sea, what one saw first on the approach to the harbor in 1854 were the distant hills and the blackened fingers of smoke that drifted across the horizon. The textile mills to the northeast of Liverpool were the engines of commerce that drove the largest share of this great coming and going.

Beyond the headland of the Wirral Peninsula lay a great stretch of sandy beach, and, as the *Flying Scud* turned to the south, the passengers who stood on her decks caught sight of the broad, open mouth of the Mersey River and, farther along, to the port side, the brick terraces of the city of Liverpool, rising above that parliament of masts.

As the river came into view and they approached the sandbars and swift tidal currents, Joshua did not attempt to emulate Captain Eldridge's feat of showmanship. The *Flying Scud* lifted the flag to signal for a pilot and patiently waited to be guided into Liverpool's teaming harbor.

The passengers now could make out the wharves, nearly two hundred acres of wooden planks and walkways, and, behind them, heading up the hillside, the warehouses and the warren of streets with hotels, the railway terminus, mercantile establishments, shipping brokerages, and boardinghouses.

In the distance, to the south, was the main commercial area, with its freshly built New Custom House and the wide thoroughfare of

Bold Street. There, up the hillside, one could just make out the green splotches that were the genteel enclaves of St George's Square and Falkner Square, where the best accommodations and services for the well-heeled were located.

American packet ships on the emigrant run with large numbers of passengers in steerage arrived and departed from the Waterloo Dock, at the northern edge of the city, beyond which lay little more than a sprawling slum, where, as one contemporary observer noted, "we find destitution of every degree, and crime and suffering of every kind."

But this was primarily a cargo run, and merchant ships carrying cargo were brought to the bustling Albert Dock, in the more salubrious commercial heart of Liverpool, surrounded by modern innovations made possible by the immense wealth washing through the city.

The docklands were a marvel of engineering and ingenuity. The Mersey River experiences, twice a day, huge tidal swings. On some tides, the water rose or fell thirty feet between high and low tides, and, in order to accommodate tall merchant ships with deep keels, a massive system of docks developed. The Albert Dock, opened less than a decade earlier, was ringed with airy, dry warehouses on all sides to allow merchant vessels to unload cargo of cotton, tobacco, and sugar from America and the Caribbean as efficiently as possible. Because the warehouses were bonded, import duties could be paid when the goods were sold, and, while that was a boon to merchants, it was also a relief for captains, who could unload their ships without waiting for the custom agent to inspect and catalog the cargo.

When the mooring lines were thrown on and the *Flying Scud* was safely secured on the docks, the crush of voices and raw scents and bodies assaulted Joshua's senses. Stevedores crowded the gangways, ready to unload the cargo, and the crew, eager to be off to the cheap boardinghouses and the red-light district, set to making the ship port-ready while belting out shanties. The popular tune in the 1850s was "The Liverpool Judies," which rang out from the docks as a bawdy warning to young seamen, with lyrics that went:

*But the best of intentions, they never goes far.*
*After thirty-two days at the door of a bar*
*I tossed off me liquor and what do you think?*
*That rotten old bastard had drugs in me drink.*

*The next I remember, I woke in the morn*
*On a three skys'l [skysails] yarder bound south round Cape Horn.*
*With an old suit of oilskins and two pairs of socks*
*And a bloomin' great head and a dose of the pox.*

*Now all you young sailors take a warnin' by me.*
*Keep an eye on yer drinks when the liquor is free.*
*And pay no attention to runner or whore*
*When your hat's on your head and your feet's on the shore.*

The crew, for obvious reasons, generally waited until the master and mate had left the ship to belt out the verse that went:

*Here's a health to the Captain wherever he may be,*
*A bucko on land and a bully at sea,*
*But as for the chief mate, the dirty ol' brute,*
*We hope when he dies, straight to hell he'll skyhoot.*

And Joshua left the *Flying Scud* not long after the lines were secured, so his crew was free to belt out the tune as boisterously as they wished while making the ship port-ready. The stevedores and dockmasters and crew would see to the unloading and stowage. The second mate would see to making the vessel and her crew safe for shore leave. Joshua's duty as master was to make his way to the Customs House with the vessel's papers, and he would need to coordinate with the ship's agents and the American consulate.

Captain Patten had no need that late April afternoon to hail one of the horse-drawn taxis that carried passengers from one end of the metropolis to the other. The Albert Dock was in the heart of the city, and all the offices he needed to visit were within a few minutes' walk in any direction. Enjoying the spring sunshine and eager to dispel the "sea legs" that, after weeks of ocean travel, leave even the most sober mariner a bit unsteady, he set off walking briskly to the New Customs House. At the bottom of Brunswick Street, he may have stopped in first at the office of the American consul. If he did not stop now, he would have dropped in later.

The American consul was handsomely paid, but this particular consul in 1854 did not enjoy his employment. He would have much preferred not to have been in Liverpool at all. The consul complained that he was short-staffed and was required as part of his post to meet with every class of American, and he didn't have a great deal warm to say about any of those fellow countrymen. "I have received and been civil to at least 10,000 visitors," the consul lamented, "brutal ships' masters, drunken sailors, vagrant Yankees." And, of course, he had to meet them all: His job was to sign the import and export papers for merchant ships coming from and heading to America.

Joshua may also have encountered the unhappy consul again later that evening in a more convivial setting. American captains passing through Liverpool in the 1850s stayed, as a matter of established custom, at a boardinghouse at 153–155 Duke Street, owned and operated by a sixty-year-old matron, Mary Blodget, and her invalid American husband, Samuel, a retired shipping merchant. Her front parlor was "the rallying-point of the better class of American captains who made voyages to Liverpool," and the "better class" included any master of an extreme clipper.

The consul himself had lived at the boardinghouse on Duke Street for a time when he first arrived in Liverpool in 1853, and he continued to be a regular guest at Mrs. Blodget's in the evenings, where, as his son later remembered, despite his general disdain for his fellow countrymen, he admired these sea captains as:

> men who day by day and month by month hold their lives in their hands, and are practised in finding a way out of danger and difficulty. They had a code of good manners and polite behavior . . . great shrewdness, and were capable of really fine diplomacy, for the school they attended demanded such proficiency. . . . Some of them would bring their wives with them for the voyage; uniformly rather pretty women, a trifle dressy, somewhat fragile in appearance, but really sound enough; naive, simple, good souls, loving their husbands. . . . My father sat there foot to foot with them, played euchre with them, listened to their yarns, laughed at their jokes, and felt, probably, the spirit of his own old sea-captain ancestors stirring within him.

Nothing could have been more inevitable than a meeting of the two men, one arriving in port and the other charged with documenting that arrival. What the consul and Captain Patten spoke of when they encountered one another is not recorded, but it must have included more than mere shipping business and paperwork.

Because the American consul at Liverpool when the *Flying Scud* registered with the shipping office, of course, was Nathaniel Hawthorne. The consul's wife was Sophia Peabody Hawthorne—one of Joshua's distant cousins and one of the Salem heirs to the Hathorne lands in the old Knox and Waldo Patent. Another of the consul's cousins was the wife of Joshua's namesake, Captain Adams Bailey.

**Consul Hawthorne and** Captain Patten also shared another keen interest that year. Both of them were ardent supporters of a new and revolutionary theory of oceanography and the man behind that theory.

That story begins, in a roundabout way, in the middle of the South Pacific, on a remote atoll not quite a thousand miles northeast of Tahiti, and not quite three thousand miles south of Hawaii.

Here, a seventeen-year-old lieutenant from a wealthy Virginian family is on furlough from the US Navy and sets off on a secret and dangerous trading mission to the island of Nuku Hiva, in the archipelago known as the Marquesas Islands, with some shipmates, to try to persuade the native inhabitants of the island to trade sandalwood, which will fetch fabulous prices back in the global market.

When the ship in which they have arrived leaves loaded with the precious cargo in early 1813, John Minor Maury, as the young lieutenant is called, and some other members of his crew remain behind to bargain for the next load, which they expect to send on shortly.

Unfortunately for Lieutenant John Maury, news of the War of 1812 and the naval blockades meant that their ship would not be able to return for some time, even as they were every day expecting its arrival. Even more unfortunately, the natives, understandably furious at the discovery in the interval that they had been tricked by an earlier trading ship into accepting worthless trinkets, dispatched by machete one of the crew members, persuading John and his fellow sailors to steer clear of the locals and fend for themselves on the tropical outpost, waiting for a supply ship that they were no longer sure was coming. Such were the perils of a secret trade mission.

When the war ended and the US Navy eventually did arrive to pick up the young men some nineteen months later, John dined out on the tale, which grew and grew in dimensions, like any good sea story.

One of the people who heard this story and was captivated by it was John's youngest brother, Matthew Maury, who was eight or perhaps nine when his brother returned from sea in 1814–1815 to regale his family with his adventures. His shore leave over, John left home again for shipping, fighting pirates off the coast of China and ultimately dying in 1824, not yet thirty, from yellow fever.

Matthew, admiring his older brother, wanted to go to sea. His father, Richard Maury, heartbroken at the death of one of his sons, fought him. What do to with young Matthew, however, was a conundrum. When he was twelve, Matthew, terrifying his poor father further, fell from a tree while climbing and broke his back, prompting Richard to send his youngest son away to a boarding school academy. There, Matthew Maury learned to love mathematics.

When he graduated, with his back recovered, Matthew begged his father to let him attend the academy at West Point. His father refused; he wanted Matthew to become a doctor. So, at nineteen, Matthew ran away to sea in the spring of 1825, persuading a member of the state House of Representatives to appoint him as a midshipman in the US Navy. He sailed that summer aboard the frigate *Brandywine* traveling as far as the Mediterranean. Aboard, the young midshipman showed a remarkable aptitude for spherical trigonometry and navigation.

The next winter, he was given a berth on a four-year circumnavigation of the globe that took the talented young Lieutenant Matthew Maury around Cape Horn, to ports up and down the West Coast of South America, and to the Marquesas, where he saw the island on which his brother had been marooned, as he had dreamed of doing since childhood. Studying the native language late into the night for the weeks they were anchored off Nuka Hiva, he asked the local chief to tell him the story of John's time on the island. Before he returned home, he saw China and Hawaii, the Philippines and Java, crossed the Indian Ocean and the Cape of Good Hope at the tip of Africa, following in the footsteps of history's great navigators and explorers.

He fell in love with the sea and with navigation.

Then, when he returned to New York in 1830, now twenty-five and soon to be appointed a sea captain, he also fell in love with his eighteen-year-old cousin, Ann Hull Herndon, to whom he was very shortly engaged to marry.

Matthew considered resigning his commission. As Mary Ann and Joshua knew, it was agonizing to think about leaving behind someone to whom you were devoted, for a period of years—or, perhaps, because the sea was dangerous, forever. But he couldn't bring himself to quit. The sea was part of Matthew. He and Ann promised to wed as soon as he returned from this next voyage.

He assumed command of the *Falmouth*, a naval sloop, in 1831, destined for Cape Horn and the Far East, and that voyage would last three years, until 1834. Matthew spent those years trying to learn everything he could about the currents and tides that would allow him to get home faster.

Every day at sea, thinking of Ann, he took soundings and made measurements. He drew charts and plotted currents. Mathematics were his love letters to Ann, and, when he finally returned to New York and was given leave, he immediately acquired a horse, headed straight back to Ann, and married her, on July 15, 1834.

He also immediately started work on a book about everything he had learned about the sea and navigation. When that book was published in 1836, under the title *A New Theoretical and Practical Treatise on Navigation*, the Navy made it required reading for every young cadet at the academy.

Matthew Maury would not leave Ann for another circumnavigation. The Navy, keen to retain a brilliant young officer, moved him first into mining and then into astronomy, hydrography, and surveying as alternative appointments. Then, in a rainstorm in the autumn of 1839, a stagecoach in which he was riding was overturned, Matthew was thrown from the seat next to the driver, and his leg was shattered. When he recovered, with a limp and unable to sail again, the Navy appointed him to a permanent desk job, as the head of the Depot of Charts and Instruments.

In the musty depot office, Lieutenant Maury found stacks of ships' logs, sent in by generations of sea captains at the request of the US government. As he organized their contents, he started to mull a theory, the expansion of his research at sea on his long circumnavigation back to Ann.

What an amazing thing it was, after all, that mathematics could predict, to the instant if one could read celestial geometry, when a planet transits our sun. "With emotions too deep for the organs of speech," as Matthew put it, "the heart swells out with unutterable anthems; we then see that there is harmony in the heavens."

What if there were also a harmony and an invisible order in the seas? What if one did not sail by wind alone? What if there were unseen rivers in the sea that one could follow? If one could chart the ocean currents, based on this trove of data, would it be possible to sail from point to point around the globe more quickly, to come home to those one loved more swiftly and surely, by mapping new courses along these invisible marine highways? What if the fastest route was not the one that traversed the fewest miles but the one that was swept along by those unseen rivers? What if one could track the winds, too, as they changed course along these routes with the seasons, to predict their strength and prevailing direction? Perhaps the past weather could predict the future. He was sure it must be possible.

When Maury's *Wind and Current Chart of the North Atlantic* was published in 1847, it shocked the world and divided mariners. Lieutenant Maury was suddenly the topic of urgent national and international conversation. Vast sums of money and international fame rested on the speed of a clipper voyage. Young sea captains in the transport trade and many fortune-hungry shipowners rushed to adopt Maury and test the limits of his bold theory. Older captains were skeptical. Some wrote disagreeable letters to the newspapers attempting to refute this newfangled theory.

Joshua Patten and Nathaniel Hawthorne were both already persuaded.

# 5

# Pathfinder of the Seas

There is a river in the ocean. In the severest droughts it never fails, and in the mightiest floods it never overflows. Its banks and its bottom are of cold water, while its current is of warm. The Gulf of Mexico is its fountain, and its mouth is in the Arctic.

—Matthew Maury, *The Physical Geography of the Sea*

It would be difficult to overstate the importance of Maury's theories about oceanography in a world dominated by—and linked by—sail.

As the *National Intelligencer* explained the significance of Maury's work in 1848:

> Lines of multiplied routes [on the charts] furrow the ocean; they represent the actual tracks of a number of ships, the logbooks of which have been carefully examined in order to collect thence the dates, the winds, the currents, the temperature

of the water, the magnetic variation established by observation. . . . This chart, so rich as it is with actual results, is but the ground-work of the undertaking. When completed, thousands of new results will be obtained, so as to afford, by simple inspection, a detailed knowledge of the ocean, and the facility of choosing, according to the season, the route the most favorable to cross it with rapidity.

In May 1848, the first ship, the bark the *W. H. De Courcey*, attempted a transit sailing by the Maury charts only, and the result was electrifying: The captain shaved nearly two weeks off the previous record passage. Two weeks less time at sea was revolutionary, especially in the clipper trade where time was money. "No vessel should go to sea without these charts," the newspapers heralded: "We understand they will be given to any navigator who will send the track of his vessel with a record of his winds and currents."

Joshua willingly sent the logbook of his crossing to Lieutenant Maury and received his copy of the pilot charts, including the charts for the transit of Cape Horn and traversing Drake's Passage.

In time, those charts would prove, in the midst of a tempest at the bottom of the world, to be the one thing that could offer Mary Ann, who also desperately wanted to get home, any chance of salvation.

**Joshua remained in** Liverpool for six weeks while cargo was unloaded, new cargo was taken aboard, and the *Flying Scud* was made ready for a return transatlantic crossing. In late May or early June, the *Flying Scud* was moved over to the Salthouse Dock, where export loading started. On the return voyage this time, Joshua would also play host as captain to eleven first-class passengers, whose names, unfortunately, do not appear to have survived in the records, and to an unrecorded number of immigrants in steerage. During the crossing,

Joshua would be expected to dine with these guests at the captain's table and accommodate them in their strolls on deck in the evening.

The westbound voyage back to New York in early June was always longer and more tiresome for a captain. The Gulf Stream flows across the Atlantic at speeds of up to ten knots from west to east. That means that, westbound, they flow in the wrong direction. As they left the Mersey River behind them and set the sails toward the open water of the Irish Sea, Joshua steered the traditional course, which, because of those currents, was not due west toward Newfoundland and Labrador, but a thousand miles south, toward the coast of Portugal, where he would tuck between the islands of Madeira and the Azores to pick up the westbound trade winds to carry them back toward the North American continent.

By the time the *Flying Scud* arrived back in Manhattan on June 30, 1854, Joshua had been away just over three months. By the standards of the day, it was a quick trip for a sea captain. As soon has the paperwork was complete, he hurried up the coast to Mary Ann and to look for a new position.

**Joshua needed a** new command, and, like Matthew and Ann Maury, Joshua and Mary Ann remained torn about how to navigate a future as a couple.

There were all sorts of arguments for leaving transatlantic crossings and the dream of a circumnavigation behind and settling for a job running passenger schooners up and down the coast from Rockland to Boston. Joshua's family had deep roots in midcoast Maine. He was a member of the Masonic lodge and on his way to becoming a respected town worthy. They owned their own home on South Main Street, as well as the riverfront tract of land on the Weskeag where they saw their future. His brother Uriah and any number of his cousins and uncles were shipping out as sea captains along the coast, his younger brothers were working their way up through the ranks as seamen, and his stepmother was related by marriage to one of the prominent local shipbuilders. For a young man with Joshua's qualifications and his connections, there were plenty of opportunities in Rockland.

What complicated everything for Joshua and Mary Ann was simply this: Joshua dreamed of becoming one of his generation's fastest clipper captains. There was the allure of celebrity. There was the allure of a fortune. Like Matthew Maury, he also loved the sea.

He had tasted it. To command a clipper ship like the *Flying Scud* in 1854 was to reach the pinnacles of the profession. Joshua was undeniably drawn to the thrill of clipper sailing. Of course he was: He was a young man in his midtwenties. There was wealth and prestige. There was the sheer exhilaration of speed and flying across the waters.

But the sea captains who became rich were those who raced around the world and took improbable chances. Those voyages, as Matthew and Ann Maury already knew, were counted in years, not months, and for a young couple in love with each other, it didn't promise much of a marriage. And Joshua and Mary Ann were deeply in love.

He would not leave her. Their plans, as well as we can reconstruct them from the deeds and records, suggest that in the autumn of 1854, they were preparing themselves for a house, a family, a farm on the river.

All that changed one afternoon. Joshua never said precisely where he was when everything changed, but all the signs point to a shipyard in Rockland.

**Rockland Harbor takes** the shape of a great half circle, open to the east toward the Atlantic, and the main shipbuilding activity in the

1850s was clustered toward the northern end of the bay, where the deep water of the anchorage began to give way to sandy beach. Great wooden wharfs and boardwalks hung above the shoreline and creaked with the tides, and from the piers that jutted out toward deeper water Joshua could catch the sharp scents of drying fish and resinous caulking. These were the scents and sounds that Joshua had known since childhood.

One of those wharfs belonged to Captain Horace Merriam, who, in his forties, had himself reached the pinnacle of the shipbuilding profession and was designing and building some of the era's most celebrated clippers from a dockyard on North Main Street.

Joshua dropping by the Merriam shipyard when he was in Rockland would not have been in any way unusual. The Patten family home and the shipyard were both on Main Street, though at opposite ends of the route that ran along the harbor, but there was also a family connection. Joshua's stepmother and aunt, Sarah, was the widow of Lemuel Bailey. Joshua himself was named Joshua Adams Patten after Captain Adams Bailey, his grandfather's old war commander. The young Mrs. Merriam had been born Mary Parker Bailey, though, and the old gravestones in the local Achorn Cemetery, where the Pattens, Baileys, and Merriams lay buried next to each other, bear silent witness to these connections.

More than the ties of blood and marriage that linked their families, though, were the ties of profession. Joshua was a sea captain with stories to tell. What drew him down to the docks were simply the clippers. Captain Merriam had launched in 1853 a beauty of a clipper called *Live Yankee*. In the summer of 1854, the crews were putting the finishing touches on a new clipper, *Euterpe*, set to launch by late autumn and commissioned for the California trade by another Maine sea captain named Lorenzo Nickerson, on behalf of a New York City firm.

Captain Nickerson was a member of the Nickerson part of the

firm of Foster & Nickerson, which owned a fleet of Rockland- and Thomaston-built clippers. The Nickerson partners included Lorenzo; his brothers, John and Joshua; their brother-in-law, Mulford Howes; and their nephew, Amos, and they were the seafaring side of the business. The Foster side of the firm was New York City grocery distributor Abel Foster and his silent partner, James Adrian Suydam, the twenty-eight-year-old heir apparent of a powerful old Dutch mercantile family. Together, they ran a fleet of clippers supplying the California trade as "commission merchants."

Commission merchants were the middlemen of international trade. The business wasn't glamorous. From their warehouses on South Street in Manhattan, they loaded onto ships groceries, pharmaceutical tonics, pickaxes, and alcoholic spirits, which retailers in San Francisco would sell for grossly inflated prices to a captive market. They owned or chartered the clippers, fronted the insurance on the cargo, paid the captains who delivered it, and unloaded the product at its destination. It was, in a nutshell, supply chains and logistics. It might not have been glamorous, but it was exceedingly lucrative, because they took a percentage of the value of the cargo at each stage in the process.

Ships in the 1850s—and, in fact, registered vessels still today—are divided into sixty-four shares. The six investors at Foster & Nickerson controlled 48 of the 64 shares, or 75 percent, of the *Euterpe*. The remaining "quarter share" of the ship's profits, traditionally, was offered to the captain, in addition to salary and bonuses. This was how a sea captain began to make real money.

A quarter share was a partnership that drew a clipper captain in as a direct stakeholder in a vessel's success and into the business side of the cargo delivery, and, especially in the early 1850s, a clipper could make staggering profits. Shipowners could earn back the entire cost of the vessel, $100,000 or more, in just one run if they were good businessmen. In 1854, that was an independent fortune. A "competence" of $100,000 in capital was the amount that a sea captain needed to retire as a very wealthy gentleman. A "competence" of half that amount was enough for any man to build himself a fine farm on the banks of the Weskeag River, live out his days in comfort, and grow old surrounded by his grandchildren.

Most clipper captains were able to earn that $100,000 fortune in under a decade at sea, and, considering that most men were made master mariners in their early twenties, that meant a lucky sea captain might be able to afford to retire by thirty.

Many captains, even after making their fortune, continued shipping. Retiring in one's early forties was far more common, because the money and the thrill were a constant temptation. But any wise sea captain always balanced in his mind a certain calculus: Each circumnavigation also meant the real risk of dying. Mariners still have a saying that these captains understood all too well: There are old captains, and there are bold captains, but there are no old, bold captains. And to sail a clipper around the world—and especially through the dangerous waters off Cape Horn—was something beyond boldness.

**Joshua might have** admired the shipwrights at work on the *Euterpe* at Horace Merriam's wharves, but she did not lack a commander. The captain of the *Euterpe*, when she launched, would be the forty-year-old Rockland Captain George Washington Brown, no relation to Mary Ann's family. Captain Brown owned a local grocery store, a ship's chandlery, a mansion estate on the farmland then on the outskirts of town, and a quarter share of the *Euterpe*, which he would command on her maiden voyage in December.

Foster & Nickerson, however, owned one other clipper—the

only one of their ships not to have been built in Rockland or Thomaston—a 216-foot "extreme" clipper called *Neptune's Car*. And *Neptune's Car* that autumn did not have a master.

*Neptune's Car* had launched in 1853, and she had just returned from a yearlong circumnavigation under the command of Captain David Forbes. Accounts of Captain Forbes depend to a very great extent on the perspective of the person giving the summary of his character. Those in his native Connecticut described him as a "generous, whole-hearted man, outspoken in his convictions, and with an open hand to the poor and suffering" who had made "a fortune in the China trade"; those who served under him as crew considered him a merciless tyrant.

Captain Forbes's 1853–1854 voyage to California, China, and then on to Calcutta aboard *Neptune's Car* had been an exceptionally brutal passage, by any measure. The crew mutinied, and, rather than return to port and risk the cargo—and, as the owner of a quarter share, his personal capital—an angry Captain Forbes set off into international waters, where there was no law but his own, frogmarched the unruly seamen to the brig at gunpoint on the high seas, chained them belowdecks in murderously hot conditions without food or water, and then, to make up for lost time, set course straight into an Atlantic hurricane. When *Neptune's Car* was towed limping into port—but with all her cargo intact—the crew brought charges of cruelty against their master. Captain Forbes decided that, at forty-two, it was past time for him to call it quits and focus on enjoying an opulent retirement.

Foster & Nickerson, as a result, needed a new captain for *Neptune's Car* on short notice, and Lorenzo Nickerson was looking to find one quickly. Here, ogling his ships and keen for adventure, was the young Maine sea captain Joshua Patten, who had already caught the clipper fever.

The proposition that Foster & Nickerson made to Joshua that autumn was simple and intoxicating: a clipper run around the bottom of the world, this time as far as San Francisco and then on to Hong Kong, around the tip of Africa, back to Britain and America.

Because he was young and hungry, the ship's owners lowballed him. Instead of a quarter share of the profits, the owners offered him a smaller percentage of the freight charges, a salary, and the right to take on private cargo. It would not earn him an immediate competence, perhaps, but it was still an opportunity to make a great deal of money if he were clever. The risks were equally extraordinary.

**It is worth** pausing to consider in some detail the economics that Joshua and Mary Ann were weighing, because their desire for that "competence" and the financial freedom it represented explains both why Mary Ann supported Joshua's command of *Neptune's Car* and also why she made the decisions that she did a year or two later.

Joshua's contract with Nickerson & Foster does not seem to have survived, but if the terms of the contract were standard for a young captain not being given a quarter share, and they likely were, the offer would have run something like this: Captain Patten would be given a salary in the amount of $3,000 to deliver the ship from port to port. That meant he would be paid $3,000 when the ship arrived in San Francisco. There would be other payments for the onward voyage from California to China, China to London, and London back to New York City. Over a period of two or perhaps three years, the salary might amount to something over $10,000.

He would receive passage money directly from any passengers he carried, if any, an amount generally equal to several hundred dollars per person per leg of a voyage, with the captain paying expenses for feeding them. Most captains carried a dozen passengers, and a captain might easily earn another $5,000 or more on a circumnavigation if he were willing to entertain first-class passengers in the staterooms.

He would be given primage, which was a percentage of the "total gross freight earned by the ship"; freight rates in 1854 varied by route and by type of cargo. Transporting a pound of cotton from New York to Liverpool cost twenty-five cents. Sending a ton of tea from Shanghai to London cost $65.67, including primage. *Neptune's Car* had a cargo capacity of 1,616 tons; loaded with China tea, that was a gross freight charge of more than $105,000 for just that leg of a journey. Rates from New York to San Francisco are more difficult to establish, but in 1851 the clipper *Staghound* was charging $1.40 per cubic foot of any cargo destined for California.

A captain's percentage of the primage could vary, but circa 1853 a typical commission was 5 percent per delivery, and a typical circumnavigation had at least two highly profitable legs, the leg from New York to San Francisco and the leg from China to London. A captain making a quarter share could conceivably earn $30,000 in profit per circumnavigation. A younger captain, on a lowball contract like Joshua, could still reasonably expect to earn an additional $5,000.

He was required to purchase but also permitted to sell on his own account the dunnage, essentially the boxes and the moving blankets of the clipper transport trade; if a captain were clever, that dunnage might be soft goods like carpets or rattan, picked up cheaply in the East, and sold for a nice profit in New York or London. How one managed dunnage was one of the things that distinguished a savvy sea captain from a less-talented businessman.

Most importantly, a captain was also entitled to a certain amount of space in the ship's hold as personal cargo. The British allocated to a captain 56.5 tons for personal cargo for a ship roughly the size of *Neptune's Car*, and the American merchant ships are likely to have been at least as generous. This space a captain could either lease directly, retaining 100 percent of that freight fee, or, if he were entrepreneurial, he could purchase for resale, using a credit account provided by the ship's owners, his own cargo. If a captain sailing on the leg from China to London simply filled his share of the hold with tea taken on freight, his profit would be more than $3,700 in charges.

But, if the captain filled his cargo space with tea, purchased on his own account, his profits—but also his risk—multiplied. In the London wholesale market, an average-quality tea sold for $20 to $25 a pound, somewhere around $50,000 a ton, and profit margins ran the gamut from 10 percent to 25 percent depending on the product and the season. Back of the envelope math: A very astute sea captain, with good judgment in tea and good contacts in the London market, might easily clear $25,000 in private cargo profit on the China to London run alone. That might not be true for a young captain on his first round-the-world voyage with no knowledge of tea or the market and no capital to risk on private cargo—though Foster & Nickerson had sweetened Joshua's deal by agreeing to loan him on account the capital for private cargo investment. But it might very well be true for a seasoned captain on his second or third circumnavigation.

Then, if a captain were sailing against competitors, there was the money he could earn from what was, essentially, betting. Above all, a clipper captain's responsibility was to get his cargo safely from one port to the other, in the fastest time possible, and without making any unscheduled stops where import and custom duties or port charges would eat up the profit margins on which both he and the ship's owners depended. Foster & Nickerson's prize money offer to Captain Patten was $2,000 for any voyage from New York to San Francisco in a hundred days or fewer. The ship's owners regarded these bragging rights as an investment in marketing and advertising. A clipper that could make voyages in under a hundred days could command premium freight charges.

Assuming Joshua did not earn any prize money, carried no

passengers, and leased out his cargo allocation, he could expect to earn at least $15,000 on a round-the-world voyage. If he were to learn quickly and gamble with his own capital, he might double or triple that on a second journey, and he would also be in a position soon to demand a quarter share as the fair compensation for an experienced master.

All around him, in Rockland, he could plainly see what this had meant for the other sea captains. Federal census records did not record incomes in the 1850s, but they very often did record the value of real estate.

The common real estate values for a young family with good, steady employment were $500 or $800. Mary Ann and Joshua started out with a home purchased for under $300, and that would have been a fine start for two young people in the 1850s. In the few cases where someone is listed in the census as owning a home over $2,500, those men are invariably sea captains or farmers with large holdings.

**This was Joshua** and Mary Ann's plan, then: Joshua would sail fast and hard. They would save their competence. And then, in a decade, perhaps less if they were lucky, Joshua would retire and perhaps buy a ship with his brother Uriah to set up a merchant business. They would live for now in their little house on Main Street until they had saved enough build their waterfront farm on the banks of the Weskeag River, and there, Joshua would look out toward the sea, into the Muscle Ridge Channel, back toward his mother's islands. It was a simple and lovely dream of two young people who wanted a life and a home together.

To close the deal with Captain Patten for the command of *Neptune's Car*, the partners at Foster & Nickerson also agreed to the one other concession that Joshua and Mary Ann decided they most wanted: permission for the captain's wife to sail with him on this voyage.

They had already decided that, whatever the risks—and those risks, whether they understood them or not yet, were staggering—they would not be separated again.

# 6

# The First Circumnavigation

> In the immutability of their surroundings the foreign shores, the foreign faces, the changing immensity of life . . . there is nothing mysterious to a seaman unless it be the sea itself, which is the mistress of his existence and as inscrutable as Destiny.
>
> —Joseph Conrad, *Heart of Darkness*

A captain's wife sailing aboard a clipper on a round-the-world voyage in the mid-1850s was unusual, but it was not exceptional. When *Neptune's Car* was piloted out of New York Harbor in January 1855, there were seamen who said that a woman onboard—derisively known as a "hen frigate"—was unlucky.

Captain's wives did sometimes sail with their husbands, even with children, especially on long circumnavigations. In 1854, during the season when Joshua took the *Flying Scud* from New York to Liverpool, Hannah Rebecca Burgess, the wife of a Massachusetts sea captain William Burgess, sailed around the world aboard the clipper *Whirlwind* and left a diary chronicling her circumnavigation. Between 1849 and 1851, Susannah Weynton circumnavigated the globe with her sea captain husband on a Hudson Bay supply ship destined for Vancouver Island, making her the first British woman to sail the Strait of Georgia. She also left a diary.

Captain Samuels's wife, Anne, sailed with him and their children from 1848 to 1856, and Captain Samuels's autobiography records that Captain Legge sailed with his daughter aboard and Captain Pine with a wife who was a fine navigator. Most famously, Eleanor Creesy, the wife of Captain Josiah Creesy Jr., was something of a sensation, having taken, with the support of an admiring husband, the celestial navigation readings aboard the record-setting clipper ship *Flying Cloud* in 1851, using Matthew Maury's new sailing directions.

And, in fact, the day that *Neptune's Car* was towed out of New York Harbor, it was the beginning of a gentleman's race to San Francisco, and Joshua's antagonist, Maine sea captain Samuel Bancroft Hussey, was sailing with his sixteen-year-old daughter as a companion.

The contest between Joshua and Captain Hussey had been agreed upon that autumn in Boston. Captain Hussey was the master of the Boston-built clipper the *Westward Ho!*, just returned from Calcutta, where he and his wife, Sybil, resided in palatial splendor, surrounded by carefully tended tropical gardens and a phalanx of servants. For men willing to live in the East, the riches were unimaginable.

Captain Hussey's fourteen-year-old son, Francis, had gone to sea that year to "learn the ropes," and Hussey was picking up their daughter, Melissa, at the end of her private education at the Charlestown Female Seminary, an expensive Christian boarding school across the Charles River from Boston proper. Melissa would travel with her father back to Calcutta, and a captain's daughter sailing around Cape Horn with her father was unusual enough that the newspapers remarked upon it.

**Joshua and Mary Ann** had been in Boston before Christmas, passing through to say goodbye to her family before traveling to New York City to prepare *Neptune's Car* for departure. It might be years before Mary Ann would see her parents again, and her father, George, with the telltale cough and fading life force, was ill with the tuberculosis that would kill him. Medical science in 1855 had no conception yet of the risk to which his disease exposed the entire Brown—and Patten—family.

The race started out as a friendly contest, with Joshua as the young up-and-comer against the very wealthy and very experienced Captain Hussey, an "old salt" in his midfifties. The arrangement was a wager to see which of them would make San Francisco first. Captain Hussey would depart from Boston after retrieving Melissa and would time the start of his race from the moment he passed the Boston Light, on the harbor's last barrier island. *Neptune's Car* would set sail from Manhattan, and, because one does not sail a clipper out of New York Harbor but must be towed through the Narrows and then piloted past the sandbars at Sandy Hook, her race would begin once Joshua had discharged the pilot.

Foster & Nickerson had no stake in the personal wager between Captain Patten and Captain Hussey, but the ship's owners had every reason to wish for *Neptune's Car* to make a journey worth boasting over. The fastest clippers commanded the highest rates for cargo, and they all made their money on the margins. Advertising cards for clippers never failed to mention when a ship had made a record-setting voyage. So the ship's owners offered Joshua the standard bonus, an additional incentive to push his crew to the limit: If he could make it to San Francisco in under a hundred days, they would pay him a cash prize of $2,000, on top of his salary and primage and private cargo. But Joshua's primary object was not the money; it was the thrill of the competition.

The *Westward Ho!* began her race at 4:45 P.M. on January 13, 1855. *Neptune's Car* cleared Sandy Hook one day and fifteen minutes later, at 5:30 P.M. on January 14, a day behind a third clipper, the *Elizabeth F. Willetts*, under the command of Captain Charles Sisson, also headed for Cape Horn and San Francisco. At Sandy Hook, Joshua recorded in the ship's log, he discharged the pilot, turned to the East, into the falling darkness, and "made all sail to best advantage."

**How to chart** one's course from here was, for any captain, the essential question. One does not turn a clipper toward a point on a chart and simply sail forward. Sailing by the wind means traveling where the winds are and where Lieutenant Maury's current charts would take you. Maury, collating hundreds of ships' logs to make a statistical analysis, recommended that captains heading for the tip of South America sail very considerably east, far into the North Atlantic, before turning south to catch the trade winds. Mariners who turned too soon risked suffering in the doldrums.

Atlantic sailors, of course, had known of the existence of the Gulf Stream, a river running near the surface of the ocean and driven by the prevailing winds as they ricocheted off landmasses, since time immemorial. The river began with the southeastern trades in the South Atlantic that picked up off the coast of West Africa and were deflected back toward South America, splintering off the coast of Brazil.

One portion of this westbound current flows northward, toward the Gulf of Mexico, along the southern coast of the United States, at the speed of eighty or ninety miles per day, until the promontory at Cape Hatteras throws it again back across the North Atlantic, east toward continental Europe; this is the Gulf Stream.

In the middle of this great ocean gyre in the Atlantic, like the calm in the eye of a hurricane, is the stillness of the electric blue water of the Sargasso Sea, spreading roughly east from Bermuda. Avoiding that great calm, where one could float for days without wind or fresh water, was every sea captain's object, and it was part of the problem that Matthew Maury was solving.

Leaving Sandy Hook behind them, the lanterns flickering gold against the dark-paneled walls and the pilot chart spread out on the great wooden table in the captain's quarters, Joshua took Maury's advice and charted a course far away from the Eastern Seaboard.

When they found the Gulf Stream off the coast and felt their pace quicken, heard the faster rushing that tells any experienced mariner that conditions are changing, the frigid weather of January in New York gave way to the balmier temperatures of Bermuda. They followed now a diagonal line through the North Atlantic, running southeasterly hundreds of miles off the coast of South America.

Aboard *Neptune's Car* in those, Mary Ann's first, days at sea Joshua and his crew fell into a rhythm that at first she did not recognize. At sea, their days were divided into four-hour watches, with duties and command rotating through a day's twenty-four hours.

Mary Ann quickly learned how strict the hierarchy was at sea and how small a role she had in it. Joshua issued all his commands though his first mate, and there was no fraternizing with his crew or his officers. Sea captains brooked no opposition, and to question the captain's decision was tantamount to insurrection. This habit of a lifetime may explain why Ann Patten would not be the only sea captain's wife to be confined to the asylum for domestic insubordination. To undermine that authority was to risk encouraging mutiny, and mutiny put everyone and the cargo and the profits of the owners and the captains in danger. Some captains were known to stand on deck with a loaded pistol when giving orders. Joshua was discreet, but he carried one.

As Richard Dana described the splendid power and isolation of the captain—and his wife, if he were to have with him such a singular companion:

> The captain . . . is lord paramount. He stands no watch, comes and goes when he pleases, is accountable to no one, and must be obeyed in everything, without a question even from his chief officer. He has the power to turn his officers off duty, and even to break them and make them do duty as sailors in the forecastle. . . . [He] has no companion but his own dignity, and few pleasures . . . beyond the consciousness of possessing supreme power, and, occasionally, the exercise of it.

Yankee clipper captains, especially, had a reputation for brutal discipline, and with good reason. Faced with a shortage of crew—because who would risk his life as a badly paid seaman if you could be a rich prospector in California with gold dust spilling out of your pockets?—clippers, as one sea captain put it, "were manned by an international proletariat of the sea, vagrants with an attitude." A portion of any crew were determined malingers and incompetent. Another portion were hardened criminals, escaping justice somewhere, generally under no name their mother would recognize, looking for an opportunity to mutiny and abscond with cargo. *Neptune's Car* was no exception.

If the captain confined his commands to the first mate and maintained a lofty countenance, life for Mary Ann was even more isolating. As captain's wife she was permitted to speak with only four classes of people: her husband, their steward, the first mate, and any passengers. Stewards, like cooks, were often "Free Blacks," and Mary Ann had grown up in proximity to the "negro" boardinghouse at 157 Ann Street. Everyone in the North End had known about a brawl involving a thousand men in 1843 when a white boatswain had been compelled by a Black seaman to step off a sidewalk. But the crew aboard clippers often came from around the world, and a seaman might as easily be from Sweden as from China.

The captain's wife was at a distance from all of them, not as a matter of race or nation, but simply by virtue of hierarchy and gender. Only if there were another "genteel" woman aboard as a passenger could Mary Ann hope to find a confidant and an equal, and, on this voyage, *Neptune's Car* carried no passengers.

For the first several days at sea, Mary Ann could not read or pass her time with needlework in the captain's quarters. The sweats and nausea of "mal de mer"—seasickness—crippled many new sailors. The very word "nausea" has the Greek word for the sea, "naus," buried within it. And the fastest way to make yourself queasy in a rolling ship is to remain belowdecks focused on what Mary Ann would have called "close work," activities like reading or darning.

The causes of seasickness were not well understood in the 1850s. Indeed, they are not entirely understood today, except that it is, essentially, a disorder of perception, in which our eye and our inner ear cannot resolve the dissonance created by a body being at once at rest and in motion. If the cause was not well understood, the effects were no mystery. As one physician put it in 1846: "If we were to judge of a disease from the painful sensations that it causes, rather than from the danger it involves, we should be forced to classify seasickness in the rank of the scourges of humanity."

The best prevention for seasickness is not any medicine, though in the ship's medical manual Mary Ann could read all sorts of suggestions, ranging from sniffing lavender oil to drinking powdered sulfur mixed with sugar and water. As every sailor knows, the best prevention—and nothing is foolproof—is to get oneself up on deck, in the fresh air, and to not take your eye off the horizon until the brain is habituated to the rolling. As the captain's wife, however, she could not wander the decks. To go "before the mast" especially would have been a shocking transgression. But the weather side of the quarterdeck, at the aft of the ship, a ceremonial location, was open to her. Here, Mary Ann looked out to sea for hours. When the sickness passed, in the gilded cage of the staterooms her solitary embroidery awaiting her, her first experience at sea must have been one of surprise followed by crushing loneliness and boredom.

And for how long, really, could she spend her life embroidering on a rolling deep-sea vessel? Their voyage would last at least a year. Two years was not uncommon. She was young, only seventeen when *Neptune's Car* left New York Harbor. She was looking already for something else to keep her hands and her mind occupied.

**The Gulf Stream** carried *Neptune's Car* along with winds that Joshua recorded in the ship's log as "calm and variable." But they could not ride the Gulf Stream forever; Africa was not their destination. Joshua would have to decide where to leave the Gulf Stream behind and to turn to find a southbound current. In between those currents could be some infuriating sailing.

One of the trickiest parts of the voyage from the racing perspective was knowing where to cross "the line" and enter the great quietness at the center of the gyre. One had to cross it. Make the wrong decisions, and a captain could easily find himself, as the poet Samuel Taylor Coleridge put it in his 1798 poem *The Rime of the Ancient Mariner*, "Day after day, day after day, / . . . stuck, nor breath nor motion; / As idle as a painted ship / Upon a painted ocean."

Within five degrees latitude on either side of the equator is a region that has plagued mariners since the first ship crossed the Atlantic, the Intertropical Convergence Zone, known to sailors simply as the "doldrums." Sailors had long known the quietness, and they had long known, too, the lethargy and malaise of mind and spirit that the term "doldrum" signified. The term as it applied to the windless regions of the equator, though, was another of the inspirations of Lieutenant Matthew Maury. At the equator, "the line" between the northern and southern hemispheres of the globe, the winds and currents switch, and in the space between, what Maury named the "equatorial doldrums," there is a great and maddening quiet.

Joshua and Mary Ann hit the equatorial doldrums on February 6, 1855, a little more than three weeks out of Manhattan. Whether Joshua could make it to San Francisco in a hundred days or less and whether he could beat Captain Hussey would depend a great deal on how swiftly he could leave the doldrums behind them.

Perhaps because of the great stillness in the Atlantic in the region of the equator, the celebrations when a ship crossed the line were— and are—raucous; they involve drink, disorderly behavior, and some elaborate costumes. It was a carnival at sea. For one day, the crew was in charge. King Neptune, with his trident and his court, swept in and demanded to interrogate each of the ship's "greenhorns" or "polliwogs," which included any creature, from seamen to shipboard livestock, who had not before crossed the equator. All sorts of unpleasant, rowdy things might await a "polliwog," from a shaved head to a pint of seawater down the gullet or, for a man who could not swim, a terrifying dunk in the ocean. For the paying passengers, the baptism was gentler: some gags about "seeing the line" and the captain good-naturedly fooling the ladies into searching the horizon with the spyglass for it. The order of the day was, in short, a great deal of tomfoolery, before the new initiates could all be declared "shellbacks" and "sons of Neptune."

*Neptune's Car* crossed the line at 9:30 in the morning at 32°50' W longitude, in the lightest of winds, some five hundred miles off the coast of Brazil, and Joshua played his role in the dramatics with good grace. He was already earning a reputation as an even-tempered and fair captain, willing to leave discipline to his officers. But some of the crew said that their young captain was too lax, too weak. It would end, they muttered, badly.

**For several long** days, they drifted just south of the line. Then, they found the first whisper of wind, and a great cheer went up. The crew scrambled to set the sails, to catch breeze, and a ripple in their wake told Mary Ann that they were moving. Soon, the doldrums were behind them; they were on their way south.

It was a short reprieve.

Conditions deteriorated south of the equator quickly. At first, they were buffeted by squalls and heavy swells from the east, and, in the captain's quarters, the rolling ocean made drinking hot tea in the morning a two-handed adventure. Even those who had not been seasick before could find themselves queasy in this weather. *Neptune's Car* was built for these waves, even if those aboard her were not, and her bow sliced through the water.

For two weeks, they plowed through large and rocky seas, making swift if turbulent progress. Then, on February 22, 150 miles off the coast of Buenos Aires, the temperature plummeted twenty degrees overnight to the low sixties, thick "Fogg" surrounded them, and Joshua watched with concern as the barometer started falling rapidly.

A falling barometer meant danger. Even today mariners rely on the barometer as an essential instrument. It measures changes in atmospheric pressure, which falls with an approaching low-pressure system or storm, and remains an excellent and sometimes at sea the only early warning that it is time to reef the sails and batten down the hatches. For a week they battled intense storm conditions and shifting winds strong enough to split some of the sails. The waves grew steep and ragged. Now there was no hot tea; Mary Ann and Joshua some nights settled for a cold dinner.

After two more weeks of heavy weather but good speed down the coast of Brazil, they entered the critical zone: the entrance to the Strait of Lemaire, the narrow chute south of the Falkland Islands, between the rocky end of Tierra del Fuego and the equally rocky shores of the Isla de los Estados. They would need to run the gauntlet, and then on the other side all hell would break loose.

The doldrums might be maddening. Stormy conditions might be rattling. But Drake's Passage, the untamed body of water that lies between the tip of South America and Antarctica, as one makes the turn westward at the end of the Strait of Lemaire into open water, can be murderous. This is the world's most dangerous sailing.

On March 6, late summer in the southern hemisphere, they slammed into a roaring gale on the approach to the strait. The heavy seas churned up dangerous, hull-busting driftwood. When they entered the strait, there would be swift currents and limited sea room. Mary Ann, in the captain's cabin, could be forgiven for looking in the ship's library for a well-thumbed copy of the Bible.

**None of this** was a surprise. This is what it was—and remains—to attempt to round Cape Horn and the reason mariners everywhere still respect this passage.

The reason Cape Horn and Drake's Passage, the body of water that separates the Horn from Antarctica, is so wild is based in simple geography and, once again, on the power of Matthew Maury's currents. Here at the bottom of the world there are no landmasses to stop the flow of water as it rips along in an eastbound current.

In the northern hemisphere, the Gulf Stream pushes water across the Atlantic at perhaps three nautical miles per hour, a current worth treating with respect as a sailor. Wind at sea is measured in nautical miles per hour or "knots." To convert a nautical mile to a statutory mile, 1.151 is the multiplier. The currents in Drake's Passage, at the bottom of the world, run at about four knots, but they are whipped up, over a thousand miles of fetch, by winds that average—and often exceed, because it is not always average—as much as sixty knots. The effect is a mass of water pushing you eastward at fifteen or twenty knots. That is a force worth being terrified of as a sailor. This mighty river of wind, sea, and wave is known as the Antarctic Circumpolar Current.

How to explain how sobering those numbers are? Unless you have been at sea and transited Cape Horn or unless you have been at the helm of a sailboat beating against a strong current, it is difficult to imagine the desolation of that passage.

At a bit over twenty knots of wind in open sea, the sea grows rough, and waves begin to have an amplitude of as much as five feet, and you will see whitecaps breaking.

Remember that the amplitude of a wave is measured at sea level, but that the true height of a wave, from peak to trough, is greater. Because you will fall as well as rise those five feet in each cycle, your experience of a wave when you are at sea and its actual height is double. When you reflect that a wave with five feet of amplitude is ten feet of motion, you will understand why most sailors of small boats make for shore over twenty knots and why this is when the Coast Guard begins issuing small-craft warnings.

At thirty knots, the amplitude of the waves climbs higher and higher, seven or eight feet tall—fifteen or sixteen feet from top to bottom—and "spindrift" appears, that spray of water at the top of a breaking wave carried by the wind. In Homer's *Odyssey*, spindrift was personified as a nymph who rescued drowning sailors, because in thirty knots of wind, drowning is a definite possibility. "Gale" force winds begin in the midthirties. These are the winds where a wise captain's wife gives up on walking the quarterdeck.

At forty knots, one no longer has a sense of waves but rather of the entire sea rolling. Waves from peak to trough now might be twenty feet tall, a fall through space of several stories. These are the waves that bring cold suppers.

At fifty knots, the crests of the waves hang as they roll, like those long breaker waves you see in surfing competitions on television or in that famous Japanese woodcut *The Hollow of the Deep-Sea Wave off Kanagawa* (1831). These swells might now be as great as thirty feet tall, peak to trough, but imagine that, instead of long, rolling waves, they come one after another, with little distance between them. The entire sea in fifty-knot winds looks white from the waves breaking everywhere around you. No one has an appetite in fifty knots. The instinct for fight or flight is hardwired in us. Aboard a ship in these seas, there is no fighting the water and no fleeing.

At sixty knots, you are in trouble. The wave height can be forty-five feet or more. The waves become so tall that from the bottom of a trough, the hull of even a tall ship like *Neptune's Car* would disappear from view in the valley. Anything over sixty-four knots is a hurricane, and the waves are described simply as "phenomenal." This is when, if you are a nineteenth-century sea captain's wife, you reach for that well-thumbed Bible.

In Drake's Passage, the winds average forty to sixty knots. Average.

And wave heights, too, are averages. In any set of waves, some are larger or smaller than others. Then there are the outliers. Sailors have told stories for millennia of the "three sisters," a sudden set of waves, coming out of nowhere, each bigger than the last, more than twice as tall as the other waves around them.

Many mysterious disappearances at sea are thought to be accounted for by them, including the loss in 1853 of the emigrant clipper *Annie Jane*, en route from Liverpool to Atlantic Canada, with 500 passengers. Struck by a towering rogue wave, when water crashed over the decks the wooden planks shattered, instantly crushing 200 passengers in steerage. Of the remaining 300 aboard, 198 went down with the ship when she sank to the bottom. Washed up on the shore were 102 survivors, clinging to some of the wreckage. They told the story of a wave of monstrous proportions.

Rogue waves are not the stuff of legend or sea stories. In fact, they are far more common than anyone has previously imagined, though their existence was not confirmed until as late as the 1990s. The largest wave ever recorded, off the coast of western Scotland, at 95 feet, was documented in the year 2000. Off the coast of Vancouver Island, British Columbia, a rogue wave measuring 58 feet, or four stories, tall, came crashing onto a beach out of nowhere in 2020, and anyone who lives on the Pacific Coast of North America knows (or should know) that you never turn your back to the sea for just this reason.

Just how common are rogue waves? Statistical analysis calculates that a ship at sea encounters more than 40,000 waves each week, or 55 million waves in a twenty-five-year lifespan. One in every 10,000 waves are thought to be "rogue," defined as at least double the size of the wave average in current conditions. That's four rogue waves a week for a ship like *Neptune's Car* on a circumnavigation. And rogue waves don't matter when the sea state is a few feet. The difference between four feet and eight feet can be startling, perhaps, but it doesn't place a ship in peril. When the waves around you are thirty feet, though, "double" starts very much to matter. And rogue waves are most likely to occur in heavy winds and swift sea currents; in other words, in places like Drake's Passage.

And, as bad as all this sounds, the truth is that water is stronger than wind. None of this accounts for what is truly terrifying about Drake's Passage in a storm, and that is the speed of those waves.

With all their sails aloft, in a stiff wind, Joshua and the crew aboard *Neptune's Car* might make as much as twenty knots for a short period—faster than the average speed of a modern container ship with its million gallons or more of bunker fuel in its belly. But some of the water that runs through Drake's Passage runs as much as twenty-five knots, and, if one is heading from east to west, making for San Francisco, all that water is running against you, pushing you inexorably backward. That is why the saying in Drake's Passage is simply this: "Make Westerly"; one way or the other, you have to do whatever needs to be done to make forward progress in that direction.

Because, behind you, if you are pushed backward, are the ice fields of the Southern Ocean and, ultimately, Antarctica.

What does it feel like to fight twenty knots of current at the helm? It takes a lot of muscle. While the wild West Coast of Vancouver Island bears the brunt of Pacific storms and the monstrous waves they can generate, the narrow fjords on the eastern side of the archipelago have some of the most treacherous narrows and tidal rapids in any coastal cruising ground. When hydrographer Captain George Henry Richard arrived to survey these waters in the late 1850s for the British government, accompanied by his wife, Mary, he described whirlpools and boiling waters in narrows where we know today that the current runs only a dozen knots at the maximum. Only a foolhardy sailor takes those rapids at anything other than slack tide, that moment of stasis when the currents are at their least, because even at half that current a vessel twists and turns in the water, and the helm fights your body. In Drake's Passage, there is no slack tide, though the current can be greater or lesser, just an inexorable mass of water pushing you eastward.

It might seem that making westerly against such an opposing current is as easy as some basic mathematics. If you can go forward twenty knots but are pushed back at a speed of fifteen knots, you are still making five knots of progress, surely? Except sailboats do not move forward in straight lines; they only move forward on the angle. To sail straight into the wind is known, in sailor's parlance, as "coming into irons," because like a shackled man, locked belowdecks by an angry captain, you are going nowhere except where the current takes you. And in Drake's Passage on a westbound transit, that is only backward toward danger.

Nor does a wise mariner sail at a ninety-degree angle in heavy wind, though the wind and sea will try to push a vessel in that direction. Wind does not always come from the direction we would wish it as mariners. A strong and steady hand on the helm is imperative. In storm-force winds, the "weather helm" will fight you.

If your vessel turns to the weather and you take a wave "abeam" or broadside, this is a tried-and-true method of rolling your vessel in heavy seas, either knocking her sideways, until the tip of the mast touches the water, or, worse, making a hellish 360-degree underwater turn.

The keels of sailing vessels are heavily weighted with ballast, usually iron, and when a sailboat flips over it will generally right itself. But the tipping and turning is dreadful. In a full roll, masts are generally torn off the decks, leaving the ship, if she survives, helpless. Anything not secured belowdecks is thrown airborne. Heavy objects—and clippers were vessels filled to brimming with cargo—slam into the sides of the ship, into other objects, and into people, and then break through the hull at velocity. Water pours in, and it all takes place in darkness and a freezing chaos. When a vessel sinks from a breach in the hull, she generally sinks in minutes. Sinks like a stone, down and down, to the bottom of the sea, which is an average of 11,150 feet below water in Drake's Passage. There is no time for lifeboats. Some commercial mariners still say that it is best not to know how to swim because that way, it is easier to drown quickly.

**Every mile in** Drake's Passage was hard earned, but the conditions Joshua confronted on the eastern side of South America on this, his first transit around Cape Horn as captain, were not in the least unusual. This was all considered an easy passage. It would be another fifty years and the turn of the twentieth century before even whalers would routinely attempt summer operations on the other side of

Drake's Passage, in West Antarctica, though intrepid merchants and explorers had already discovered the continent by the 1820s.

Joshua battled storm conditions and, as recorded in the ship's log, "heavy gales" around the tip of South America, with winds reaching forty knots or more for two days. The entire sea roiled with motion; belowdecks all Mary Ann could do was close her eyes and try to roll with the ocean. Reading in heavy seas was a sure recipe for seasickness. At the helm, Joshua ordered the sails made trim and small, with "Double Reefes," he noted, and, buoyed by the last of the currents that pushed along the coast of Patagonia, they finally passed through the Strait of Lemaire and made the turn at the southern tip of Argentina. The island of Cape Horn and its rocky headlands lay about 125 miles dead ahead and would require them to swing wide into Drake's Passage to keep sea room.

Then, when they came into the lee of the continent, expecting to run into the full fury of the gales, the winds instead fell suddenly around the headland. This was worse than a moderate gale for a sea captain. Strangely becalmed off the southern end of the South American continent, in the phenomenon known as "Drake Lake," Joshua could only curse as the currents drifted them backward. When captain's wife Susannah Weynton found herself off Cape Horn in conditions "not so severe . . . as we had anticipated," her only consolation was that the calm seas allowed the "luxury" of a warming fire in the captain's quarters. Even in summer this far south the nights were freezing.

To be in light breeze at the bottom of the world, though, was also a spectacular sight. At night, warmly wrapped and looking out to the far reaches of the Milky Way, Mary Ann could see the Southern Cross—the Southern Hemisphere's equivalent to Cassiopeia. Here, below 50° S, the constellation never dipped under the horizon. She could watch the solitary albatross hanging above her as it rode the airborne currents asleep with its head tucked under a wing. Mariners believed that they were the souls of dead seafarers, destined to wander. Life as a captain's wife was small and narrow. The galaxy was vast and brilliant. Mary Ann decided that, like the celebrated Eleanor Creesy, she would learn to read its secrets and to let it guide her.

Standing alone on the captain's quarterdeck at night, she practiced reading the stars and learned to pick out the constellations. At noon, she learned to measure the sun at its zenith. Below, in the captain's quarters, with Maury's charts and the captain's logbook spread out before her, she passed the long hours looking up calculations in the nautical almanac and scribbling sums in pencil on a bit of paper until she had mastered the art of celestial navigation. Joshua, looking down from the deck through the windows that lit the cabin, could see her dark hair where it curled at her nape and her head bowed over her notebook.

**Celestial navigation is** the place where math seems to dissolve into magic. There is a sense of awe that remains undimmed across the centuries. As long as you know where in the sky the stars (among which, of course, our sun is numbered) and moons and planets are and know their phases of coming and going in their revolutions, all provided in a series of mathematic tables in a nautical almanac, you can determine your place in the world—your latitude and longitude—with just two pieces of equipment: a timepiece and a sextant. If you can find where you are in the world, then, as long as you have a chart and a compass, you can find your way home from anywhere. And finding their way home was what Mary Ann wanted.

The calculations are not simple. It requires a basic understanding of trigonometry, the mathematics of angles, and a decent head for numbers. But Mary Ann, thanks to the Sunday School lessons the Old North Church had afforded the Brown children, was good at numbers. The hardest part, in fact, is simply holding the sextant to the sun or the stars and learning to take precise and accurate solar readings without blinding oneself. Sun blindness and cataracts were occupational hazards, and some historians have proposed that this may be the reason pirates wore eyepatches.

Navigation was the responsibility of the captain and his officers, but some captain's wives had become famous for their skills with a sextant. Joshua was proud of Mary Ann's cleverness and encouraged her to double-check his numbers. She was becoming, he could see, an able, steady-footed mariner. Had she been born a different sex, she might have had the makings of a captain. But no woman had ever taken the helm of a clipper as her master, and certainly not around Cape Horn in the world's most fearsome waters.

# 7

# Westward Ho!

> The whole country . . . resounds with the sordid cry of 'gold! Gold!! GOLD!!' while the field is left half planted, the house half built, and everything neglected but the manufacture of shovels and pickaxes.
>
> —*The Californian*, May 24, 1848

The lull as *Neptune's Car* came 'round Cape Horn was short lived. The next day, thankfully, a steady, brisk wind picked up. The race was still on, and they were on track to make a hundred days to San Francisco, if only the wind would stay with them.

Joshua, now more cheerful, ordered the sails set, and they made sure and steady progress past the archipelago, "doubling" Cape Horn and passing back north of 50° S on the other side of the continent fifty-six days out of Sandy Hook. As they passed the Cape, in the distance Joshua made out two masts belonging to the brig *Governor*, also bound for San Francisco, and as they slipped along, exchanged signal flags with the captain. The next day, March 12, the boy high in the masts spotted two clipper ships in the distance, and with the spyglass Joshua tracked a bark that he recognized as the *Diego Ramirez*.

It was impossible to make out the signal flags of the clippers from the distance. Was one of them Captain Hussey and the *Westward Ho!*? From the vantage point of the quarterdeck, Joshua strained to catch a glimpse of Captain Hussey's ensigns from the telescope, but the clippers on the horizon were too far away to make out the flags that identified them to each other. It was a strange race, this one, in which one could see neither one's destination nor one's competition.

*Neptune's Car* had been lucky this time, and Joshua knew it. They had rounded Cape Horn, having never gone beyond 57° S, and they had got off lightly with winds in the twenties. One couldn't count on this kind of good fortune in Drake's Passage, and they were making astonishingly good time. Spirits were high. This was the kind of sailing everyone onboard wanted.

Two weeks later, Drake's Passage was a memory. They were in the open ocean again, with no other vessel in sight, on a course thousands of miles off the coast of Peru. The temperatures crept back up into the pleasant midseventies. They crossed back over the equator on April 3, 1855, at 112° longitude. Then: nothing.

For eight days they were again plagued with light winds. Becalmed and bored, the crew scanned the horizon. Still nowhere did they see Captain Hussey or the *Westward Ho!* despite a keen lookout. Joshua had no way of knowing if this was a race he was winning or losing, and light winds in a race could make a clipper master short-tempered.

Joshua was known for being slow to anger, but captain's wife Hannah Rebecca Burgess confided to her journal the year earlier that her husband was not quite so sanguine:

> *I do not like a calm for it makes the Capt. so cross, if for no other reason. You can quickly perceive the influence it has upon him.*

*Everything acts contrary and wo! to the person who crosses him then. Well it is taxing a Ship Masters patience a great deal, to encounter head winds and calms.*

Joshua was no less frustrated, and Mary Ann could see the strain when they dined together at the captain's table in the evening. Light winds were a financial danger and could jeopardize their dreams. They had been making rapid progress, and now all that was being lost as they floated on a glassy ocean. Time was, in the clipper trade, quite literally money. Joshua could see their good fortune slipping away with every day they bobbed and floated. It was a race against the clock as much as a race against Captain Hussey.

They suffered until April 13, watching their chance of profit and fame diminish, until finally a brisk northeasterly breeze came up. Joshua wrote in relief in his logbook that evening: "Neptune's Car doing a little better." From there, they pressed on as quickly as Joshua could manage. If they could clear the Golden Gate in a hundred days, it would be an internationally newsworthy achievement.

To understand how rare a passage from an Atlantic port around Cape Horn to San Francisco in under a hundred days was, consider that in the entire history of the clipper era only twenty-two times did any captain ever achieve that feat of seamanship and good fortune. Joshua Patten had nearly done it on his first Cape Horn transit. Nearly.

Because on April 24, at 4:00 P.M. the clock ticked over to day 101, and they were still dozens of miles off the coast of San Francisco. Joshua could claim a remarkably swift passage, but it would not be one for the record books. All he could hope for now was to at least beat out Captain Hussey.

**San Francisco Bay** was and remains another notoriously hazardous harbor, and *Neptune's Car,* at 216 feet long and 40 feet wide, was a large ship, with little ability to maneuver in tight spaces or light winds.

As one approaches from the south, thirty miles offshore, a captain runs the gauntlet past the stony Farallon Islands—known in the 1850s to sea captains simply as the "Devil's Teeth" for what they could do to a hapless vessel. The islands are often shrouded in fog year-round, and here more than four hundred ships have floundered. Joshua approached the islands at midmorning, passing through thick kelp beds in cloudy weather.

By one o'clock on April 25, they passed the islands, and Joshua would not attempt to go much farther unaided. There were more reefs and shoals ringing the harbor. Ten miles off the coast, Joshua ordered the men to send off the flares that signaled to the pilot boat. In the watchtower on Loma Alta—renamed Telegraph Hill after the transcontinental cable was connected—the harbormaster would signal to the merchant community what kind of ship was arriving, and merchants expecting the arrival of a particular vessel would begin scanning the horizon for the company ensigns to meet their consignment in the harbor. An hour later they had taken onboard the pilot.

It was now two o'clock in the afternoon. Mary Ann was glum. Joshua was short-tempered as they looked out in the distance to the Marin headlands. Several miles ahead of them lay the entrance to the harbor, the "Golden Gate" that would not boast its iconic bridge until a century later. The race would end on the other side of the gate, when they broke free into the harbor and dropped anchor.

Joshua castigated himself: He should have pushed them harder in the Atlantic, he should have flown more canvas rounding Cape Horn. He should have done like Captain Samuel Samuels and remembered that it was hard sailing at night that made the difference in the time of a passage. He had not understood how every minute counted. And they still had no idea whether they were ahead of Captain Hussey or behind him.

Joshua eyed the chronometer and looked out at the waters. They would not be able to enter the harbor on an ebb tide. On a strong flood, the pilot assured him that it was a fast approach but not reckless. This was Joshua's first approach to San Francisco; these were not familiar waters. For those also not familiar with those waters, the Golden Gate is another narrow tidal passage. When millions of gallons of water rush out of the harbor twice a day, especially on a large tide, the currents can run up to six knots against an incoming vessel and the strong upswell can make a ship uncontrollable. When Lieutenant Manuel de Ayala became the first non-Indigenous captain to enter San Francisco Harbor in 1775, he recorded in his logbook that the current on the ebb side was so strong that his ship appeared to move backward. A captain could spend all day sailing in light winds against a six-knot current and never pass the same spot on the headland.

On a strong flood tide, although the waters flowed in a ship's direction, the passage through the headland could be turbulent and hair-raising. Joshua decided to risk it, and they rode the flood past the Marin Headlands just after five o'clock; by 6:20 Joshua's men had dropped anchor off North Point. And there, riding her anchor gently, sat the *Westward Ho!* and Captain Hussey, who had beaten Joshua by hours.

They were soon surrounded by small boats eager to unload rich cargo and thirsty seamen. As Joshua recorded wryly in the captain's log: "Pilot left and Pirates came on board and commenced their work. So ends this Passage by J. A. Patten."

**San Francisco harbor** on the evening of April 25, when Mary Ann first saw it, was a forest of masts.

Gold had transformed San Francisco. In 1847, eight years earlier, only three sloops arrived in that harbor in a year, still a remote trading outpost. Gold was discovered in 1848. By the spring of 1849,

17,000 men had arrived in San Francisco to find their fortunes. By 1850, that number had grown to 63,000 annual arrivals, and ships entered the harbor daily. "Not since the Crusades had such a large assemblage of people gone to sea," the newspapers reported. Mary Ann had been the only woman aboard ship for months, and on shore in California she would not find ready female companionship either. Less than 10 percent of the non-native population of San Francisco that spring were women.

The city should have been a dazzling sight, but Mary Ann was down. They had come by sea nearly 13,000 miles. They had lost the $2,000 bonus by twenty-six hours. And then, there had been the great indignity of Captain Hussey's gloating. What could she possibly say to console her husband? There weren't any words she could offer. But they didn't need words between them either. In the flush of love, a wry smile and a squeeze of the hand would be enough to say: next time.

Captain Hussey had brought the *Westward Ho!* to anchor off Shaw's Wharf, at the end of what is today modern Filbert Street, at 2:00 A.M. the night before, on the slack tide, "bringing a large cargo of general merchandise." Because she had arrived one hundred days and eighteen hours from Boston, the *Westward Ho!* could also not claim the international glory. But the experienced Captain Hussey, for whom San Francisco Harbor held few mysteries, had slipped through in darkness.

**Despite the disappointment** of missing the bonus for a run of a hundred days or fewer and the chagrin of losing out to Captain Hussey, it was a remarkably good run. A hundred-and-one days was not a record, but it was fine sailing. Joshua's reputation as a crack sea captain was growing.

Just how celebrated Joshua was becoming is apparent in a newspaper article that appeared a bit later that year, following the arrival of the clipper ship *Herald of the Morning* in San Francisco in May 1855 in ninety-nine days, pilot to pilot, under Captain Otis Baker. *Herald of the Morning*, renowned for a bowline cut "so sharp as to take the form of a razor," had made the fastest run of the year, and on her best day had traveled more than fourteen knots average. She had been built in Medford, Massachusetts, and apparently the intense rivalry between New Yorkers and their northern cousins dates back until at least the 1850s, because, as one Boston reporter noted, "some of our New York neighbors . . . have been crowing over the passage of *Neptune's Car*." And the *Herald of the Morning* had accomplished what *Neptune's Car* had not managed.

It is a strange newspaper commentary, but it's easily explained by a controversy that had been brewing in San Francisco for months already. A great debate had started on the docks almost the moment Captain Hussey and Captain Patten brought their ships to anchor.

The hotly contested argument on the docks and in the public houses of California was: Had Captain Patten or Captain Hussey really won the race? It depended on how you counted, didn't it? *Neptune's Car* and *Westward Ho!* had shipped from different ports, one leaving from New York City and the other from Boston. How was that, the crew of *Neptune's Car* asked indignantly, a fair contest? Their captain and their ship were the better.

In fact, it's not entirely clear how Captain Hussey's departure farther north, in Boston, gave him any decided advantage, but the crew of *Neptune's Car* insisted boisterously that their master was the victor, on the grounds that New York City was a less-advantageous harbor. As the debate raged on, the fact that maritime circles in the city were "crowing" about the prowess of Captain Patten was a mark of his growing international reputation.

Samuel Hussey was indignant when he learned from his crew that his victory was being discounted. He was a competitive man.

He enjoyed winning, and obviously Boston was farther from Cape Horn than New York City. Seamen could debate forever which port was best suited for a fast passage. He had beaten Captain Patten to anchor fair and square, and it was not even a tight margin.

To settle the matter like gentlemen, however, Captain Hussey proposed a rematch, and this time he wanted a rematch for money: a wager not just for bragging rights but for stakes. Hussey offered to bet anyone a thousand dollars that he would beat Captain Patten from San Francisco to Hong Kong, on the onward leg of the around-the-world journey. This time, it would be port to port, a race of apples to apples. In fact, Captain Hussey proposed that they keep on racing as long as the two ships were continuing in the same direction.

The San Francisco bookies weren't willing quite yet to take that kind of a risk on a twenty-eight-year-old sea captain, no matter how impressive his first few voyages. Captain Hussey and Captain Patten would see who could make the best time from San Francisco to China, but Captain Hussey would have to settle for the only stakes being bragging rights and honor.

**With the race** on and the summer trading season approaching in China, Joshua and Mary Ann stayed in San Francisco just long enough for the cargo from *Neptune's Car* to be unloaded at the Pacific Street Wharf (today, Pier 40) and to see family. Joshua's stepbrother and cousin, the thirty-five-year-old sea captain Lemuel Bailey, had arrived in San Francisco sometime in early 1855. By the time *Neptune's Car* dropped anchor, Lemuel had established himself in the city as a merchant master mariner. His young wife, Mary Ann Waterman Bailey, who did not fancy the life of a clipper captain's wife, remained at home in New England with their small children, so Lemuel had checked himself long-term into one of the city's premier hotel establishments.

They had lost the $2,000 bonus but Joshua and Mary Ann would make good money from the sale of their private cargo in California, and their percentage of the profits from the commissioned cargo would add nicely to their nest egg.

Goods arriving "ex-*Neptune's Car*" were advertised for sale in the local newspapers, and it is for this reason that we know that among the items Joshua had ferried around the bottom of the world included two hundred boxes of candles, a hundred cases of "Shaker's Catsup," one hundred half casks of American brandy, 150 cases of French champagne, five thousand pounds of Kentucky leaf tobacco, and a load of building cement and plaster that conveniently did double duty as ballast. These newspaper advertisements hint, too, at how important speed was in the clipper trade and how outrageous the prices were. Supply was short, and the profits were straight-up price gouging. Coffee and tea sold in San Francisco in the 1850s for sixty dollars a barrel. Sugar for twelve dollars a pound—in 1855 dollars.

How much are all these figures in modern dollars? Multiply any price in US dollars in 1855 by thirty-five and you get a pretty good rough historical price comparison: That's over $400 in today's values for a pound of sugar. For Captain Hussey's proposed $1,000 wager, read: a $35,000 gamble. A $2,000 bonus was worth at least $70,000. A profit of $10,000—the amount Joshua and Mary Ann might reasonably have cleared on the leg from New York to San Francisco—was today's $350,000. A $100,000 competence was $3.5 million.

But a gold rush miner could also make $1,000 or more a day prospecting, and it generally burned a hole in his pocket. As one historian notes: "No modern bootlegger would dare to hope for such prices as were freely offered in San Francisco. . . . If [a ship] could get there quickly before the market broke, she could make fabulous profits." The first leg of the journey around Cape Horn had been, despite the personal disappointment for Joshua as a racing captain, a financial success for them. A couple could begin to dream.

**Loading for the** next leg of their journey, though, was a conundrum, and Joshua was frustrated. The clipper trade was not neatly triangular, and it was hard to accept that some legs of a circumnavigation were going to be all risk and no profit.

There were fortunes to be made bringing cargo and passengers from the East Coast to San Francisco at the height of the gold rush. There were fortunes to be made on the other side of the Pacific, carrying Chinese luxury goods—especially tea, opium, and paper—back to Britain and America. But opportunities between San Francisco and China were thin on the ground. Beaver pelts and fir trees were, apparently, not coveted by the residents of the Far East, especially not in China, which boasted a remarkably self-sufficient and sophisticated economy in the nineteenth century.

Part of Joshua's job as captain was to take onboard freight for the ship's owners, from which he would take his commission, and he dutifully sent out a call for cargo delivery. There came back only a disappointingly small number of consignments. Seeing that there was only a limp export market among the merchants of San Francisco, he wasn't willing to risk their savings on private cargo when he didn't understand the Hong Kong market. So *Neptune's Car* would sail for Hong Kong loaded with rocks in her hold as mere ballast. This leg of the journey would lose him money, and there was no pretending that wasn't a disappointment.

They did carry aboard one other necessary cargo, though it was certainly not stored anywhere except the safe in the captain's quarters: Shipowners needed to transport across the Pacific sometimes large sums of "specie"—cold, hard cash, generally in the form of silver dollars. Some of the money earned in San Francisco needed to find its way to the tea markets in China, and only part of that transaction could take place using notes of credit and letters of exchange, though, increasingly, the speed at which an extreme clipper could deliver those financial instruments and the usurious rates charged for doing so was part of how a ship's owners made their profit.

But great financial opportunity lay ahead of them in China if they could cross the Pacific Ocean safely. On May 13, 1855, in a race with Captain Hussey to Victoria Harbor, Hong Kong, *Neptune's Car*, loaded with stones and apparently without any passengers, passed back through the Golden Gate toward open water.

**This time, they** would cross at the slack to ebb and ride the tide out to sea. The sailed on the same tide as Captain Hussey, so that this time there could be no debate about the starting line. By 10:00 A.M. they had slipped past the Golden Gate. By 11:00 A.M. they were underway with, as Joshua recorded in the logbook, a full roster of "all white" seamen, something unusual enough to be noteworthy at a time when mariners in the international merchant maritime trade came from home ports that spanned the globe and often included men of various national and ethnic origins.

Stalled in light winds, they slipped south of Kona Island, Hawaii, a month later, on June 14. They passed through the Philippine Sea and into Hong Kong sometime in the last days of June or in early July. Without good wind, they drifted there for days; as races went it was uninspiring. Joshua was glad that he had not gambled any of his own money on this passage. With a small fortune in silver dollars in the captain's cabins and no ability to take evasive action in light and baffling winds, Joshua fretted about the risk of pirates off the coast of Asia, ordered a sharp watch, and kept his pistol loaded.

They finally made Hong Kong after fifty days at sea: a slow and expensive leg of the voyage. Joshua could at least take some satisfaction that Captain Hussey, becalmed, would take eleven days longer. It was a good thing for Samuel Hussey that that no one had taken him up on his offer to bet a thousand dollars.

**The island of** Hong Kong as Joshua and Mary Ann encountered it was nothing like that teeming metropolis of the present. In the region of Hong Kong in the 1850s, there were three areas of the coastline that were important to clipper captains and ship's owners: the port of Canton, some eighty miles up the Canton River; the island of Macao to the south, at the mouth of the river; and the island of Hong Kong to the east of the harbor.

Joshua and Mary Ann were arriving in a pause between the two opium wars that would define the economy and geopolitics of this area. The first of those wars, between the British and the Chinese from 1839 to 1842, brought an end to the Chinese "factor" system of restricting foreign trade to the single port of Canton and restricting foreign men to a sealed compound of warehouses and dormitories outside the city walls known as the "factory" or the "Golden Ghetto." Until the end of the first opium war, foreign women were forbidden to step foot on the Chinese mainland, a law intended to discourage any permanent foreign colony. Women could live only on the island of Macao, controlled by the Portuguese government as a colonial outpost.

The problem with opium was, in part, precisely the problem of onward cargo and capital outflows that Joshua had found so frustrating in San Francisco. The British were mad for tea and, especially before the development of tea plantations in its Indian colonies, mad for tea from China. Ships left China loaded with expensive cargo of teas, but the British were required to leave behind a great deal of silver as payment for this luxury commodity. The British solution to this capital outflow was to search for a commodity that the Chinese would purchase, so trade was conducted in a circulation of goods rather than in a one-way depletion of the national treasury. Unfortunately, the Chinese had little interest in buying British goods. When they had silks and teas and fine bone china, why would they want wool tartan or Lancaster cottons?

What the Chinese consumer would purchase, if it were smuggled in from the poppy fields of India, was opium. The result was an epidemic of addiction that dwarfs even the modern plague of fentanyl. American merchants, capitalizing on the trade, soon followed the British lead, smuggling opium into the only legal port for foreigners, Canton, and bribing customs officials to accept opium as payment for tea and silk. Because of their speed and ability to evade custom agents, clipper ships were the prized vessels.

When the Chinese emperor attempted to crack down on this illicit trade and ordered thrown into the sea a fortune in opium seized from British merchant ships, the British prime minister, as outraged by the dumping of opium in Canton harbor as by the dumping of tea in Boston some fifty years earlier, sent the navy to blow up coastal fortifications and to force China to pay restitution for the value of the drugs and to open up trade to other harbors. The result was that, after 1842, Hong Kong became a new center of international trade in opium. By the 1850s, the trade in Hong Kong was divided more or less equally between inbound opium from Calcutta and outbound tea from China, as different sets of clipper merchants peddled one in exchange for the other.

Joshua was not trading in opium, at least not inbound. *Neptune's Car* had arrived from San Francisco, and the trade in opium came from India and not from California. The sea captains who worked the opium trade—captains like Samuel Bancroft, living with his family in Calcutta—traveled the route back and forth between Calcutta and Hong Kong or Canton as part of a regular circuit.

But in Hong Kong, Joshua's instructions from the ship's owners were to take on whatever freight would earn the highest premium, and to do business at all in the China trade was to accept that opium was part of the international currency in the region. Deep local resentment of this fact made shipping in these waters a risky undertaking.

**The main port** in Hong Kong was Victoria, a natural harbor on the north side of the island, and mountains rose up above a coastline dotted with small, white houses. There were no wharfs. *Neptune's Car* dropped anchor in the harbor in early July, and Mary Ann watched as a flotilla of young boys in small boats jostled for position off their stern end, offering to ferry her to and from the shore. As one British resident remembered it in the 1840s: "In Hong Kong harbour on a moonless night you seem to be in the midst of a fairy scene. All the bay is bright with lights on hundreds of ships and boats; and every dip of oars into the water is followed by splendid phosphorescence." At night, lamplit boats decked in flowers floated past the ships on anchor. It took Mary Ann a moment to understand: floating brothels.

When Joshua and Mary Ann slipped into Victoria Harbor that summer, Hong Kong, like San Francisco, was also no longer the remote outpost that it had been a decade earlier. The entire population by 1855 had grown to 75,000 people. The permanent European population on the eastern side of the island, though, remained small and isolated, somewhere well under two thousand civilians, of which again only a tiny proportion were women.

Joshua knew the captains of the other ships that dotted the harbor. There was his fellow Masonic brother Captain Michael Gregory on the *Sunny South*, with its strange figurehead of a deep-sea monster glaring from the bow. She had arrived in Hong Kong with the unsettling mixed cargo of two hundred bags of potatoes and the remains of ninety-four Chinese laborers being returned home for burial. Captain Ebenezer "Eben" Linnell, a famous clipper-race master, arrived on July 10, anchoring the *Eagle Wing* alongside *Neptune's Car* and boasting of a record-breaking passage of eighty-three days, twelve hours from London to Hong Kong. But there were no other captain's wives, and, for whatever reason, despite their proximity in age, Mary Ann seems to never have visited Captain Hussey's daughter, Melissa.

They had arrived at Hong Kong in ballast, and unloading the useless cargo of stones was Joshua's first task once they had cleared their arrival. Joshua set out a call for cargo, and they would have to wait to see what their next destination would be. It might be India or Peru or Britain. They had arrived just as the season for clipper ship arrivals from the United States was opening, and brokers could choose their ship and their captain. Joshua was relieved when *Neptune's Car* was quickly chartered to deliver a shipment of "first-flush" tea from Foochow to London. A commission to Peru would almost certainly have meant sailing with indentured human cargo.

There were two areas of China famous for the teas in the British and American markets, and connoisseurs speak in a language of terroir that rivals that of any oenophile. The finest souchong from the Wuyi Mountains was rarely exported. Young hyson tea (the tea of choice at the Boston Tea Party) fetched the greatest prices, and the black teas from the Min River plantations weathered the ocean voyage with the least damage. The best teas were those harvested from the first spring growth, where they were roasted, dried, tossed, and rolled according to ancient traditions, and then packed for export into brightly painted or paper-appliqué tea chests, made of light wood but lined with pounded lead to keep out moisture. Those who arrived in London with the season's first teas could command astronomical prices that rivaled the price gouging of the California Gold Rush.

They would be making the run back up the coast to Foochow—modern Fuzhou—the "tea district" of the China trade, to load black tea from the Min River plantations, destined for the British market. Before they could load a cargo as fragile and as expensive as tea, all the cargo holds of *Neptune's Car* would need to be thoroughly scrubbed and fumigated.

This was the most lucrative part of the circumnavigation, and Joshua and Mary Ann would bring back tea as part of their private cargo allocation to sell in London to the brokers and auction houses. They were risking their capital, but, if they made it safely to London, if the tea were in perfect condition, if Joshua had selected the quality astutely and had gauged the consumers' preferences correctly, they might end this journey with substantial progress toward their competence.

It was a lot of "if's," though, and, for a young captain who had never purchased tea before, the risks were enormous.

# 8

# All the Tea in China

> Last Night 3 Cargoes of Bohea Tea were emptied into the Sea. This Morning a Man of War sails.
>
> —John Adams, December 17, 1773

The tea commission meant the end of their round-the-world race with Captain Hussey.

Joshua, whose experience with the Atlantic emigrant packets had soured him on transporting even willing passengers, eschewed the trade in the other commodity in China that could make a sea captain a fortune: the transport of indentured "coolies." These were the men whose remains Captain Gregory returned as cargo.

Captain Samuel Hussey had made his competence many times over. The captain's quarters of the *Westward Ho!* were a public testament to those riches, with crystal chandeliers, polished wood, and gleaming rich silver. During the years when he and his wife, Sybil, resided in Calcutta, they lived in opulent colonial splendor. Some part of Captain Hussey's wealth came from the transportation of forced labor, and that was true now, on the next leg of his onward journey.

A "coolie" in 1855 was not necessarily a Chinese person. A coolie was any day laborer sold by indenture, sometimes as debt slaves, sometimes as part of clan violence, sometimes by trickery or in sheer economic desperation, and the trade flourished throughout the British Empire, especially in China and India and especially after the abolition of the British slave trade in the 1830s. The year that *Neptune's Car* arrived in Hong Kong, the center of the coolie trade was on the nearby island of Macao, and, in the words of one early maritime historian, "There is no chapter in all sea history so sickening as that of the coolie trade." Terms of indenture ranged from two years to as long as eight, with the laborers sometimes branded on the back, and systematic rape of women from India was disturbingly common.

The *Westward Ho!* would sail, alongside Captain Gorham of the *Winged Racer*, to the port of Swatow (modern Shantou, China) and—contrary to the direct "official" command of their ships' abolitionist owners in Boston—each loaded a cargo of six or seven hundred indentured men for labor transport to the Chicha Islands off the coast of Peru, where guano—dried seabird excrement—was mined under the lash, in air poisoned with ammonia, for trade as fertilizer, most of it destined for the cotton plantations of the American South that fueled the textile mills of Britain.

Up to 40 percent of these laborers would not survive even the voyage to the Chicha Islands or to the Caribbean. Aboard the clipper *Waverley* in 1855, the men were caged below decks until 251 of them died of suffocation. The following winter in Peru, more than three hundred desperate Chinese laborers would simply commit mass suicide by taking hands and walking together into the ocean. And, because the Chinese had a cultural tradition of satisfying honor with vengeance, clipper ships in Far East waters were frequently attacked and crews massacred, because in the opium smuggling trade "only about two-thirds of a crew . . . had ever been to sea before; the rest were hill coolies, bullock drivers, and other landsmen, who had either been caught in the crimp's net . . . or owed him money." While some of those sea captains probably merited their fate at the end of a cutlass, it meant that masters generally had a hair trigger and discipline aboard these ships was violent.

The indenture trade was just one part of the increasingly fraught question of slavery that by 1855 was already forcing Americans (and Britons) to reckon with the relationship between the luxury commodities being bought and sold and transported and the forced labor that underwrote the global economy of the so-called Anglosphere. The problem had been deferred since well before the Missouri Compromise of 1820, which admitted Maine to the union as a free state, in exchange for Missouri entering as a slave state, to keep a precarious political balance. The admission of California as a free state in 1850, coupled that same year with provisions in the Fugitive Slave Act, which required citizens in free states to return escaped enslaved people to their masters, had made further deferral all but impossible, especially after the electrifying publication in 1852 of Harriet Beecher Stowe's novel *Uncle Tom's Cabin*, written during her residence in Brunswick, Maine.

It would be another decade before all this would spill over into the secession of the southern states into a Confederacy and the Civil War in America, but the long fuse had already been lit, and clipper ship captains, whether they engaged in this trafficking or not, were part of a lucrative global trading system confronting an international labor shortage.

In Victoria Harbor, that reality pressed in upon Mary Ann and

Joshua, and perhaps they heard how, in "one of the innumerable sampans" in Hong Kong that summer, Captain Hussey purchased for his daughter, Melissa, a young Chinese boy, whom he named, apparently without irony, Tom Jefferson, as an indentured household servant.

Melissa would have to wait to travel to Calcutta. Her father's ship was destined for South America from Hong Kong. In fact, she would never make it to India. After delivering hundreds of indentured servants to the islands off Peru to harvest guano, the *Westward Ho!* would next deliver a cargo of that manure to Alexandria, Virginia, to fertilize the cotton plantations. There, Melissa would become engaged to marry a young Virginian gentleman. Ownership of Chinese Tom was among the wedding gifts that Captain Hussey left behind in port along with his daughter.

**When** *Neptune's Car* was prepared and ready to set sail back up the coast of China at the end of July for the tea plantations and Foochow, there was another woman onboard ship for the first time.

Eliza Chamberlin Gibson was the twenty-five-year-old wife of a young Methodist missionary named Otis, and the couple had traveled east as passengers aboard the clipper *R. B. Forbes*, commanded by Captain Ballard, in the spring of 1855. The Gibsons were on their way to tea country to meet up with several other missionary families, intending to open a boarding school for Chinese students. They were also coming, in particular, to meet up with some friends: a serious Dr. Erastus Wentworth, his eager young second wife, Anna, and his motherless fourteen-year-old son, Jimmy, who may not have been entirely enthusiastic. Both families' tales mixed tragedy and love story.

Eliza and Otis Gibson were newlyweds, only married in early 1855, and they had wed over the strenuous objection of Eliza's family, who did not consider their daughter traveling to China a desirable outcome. But they were in love, with each other and with their mission, and the couple were leaving everything behind to start a new spiritual and marital life together in China.

They looked to heaven for their happiness. The United States was in the midst of what historians have called the Second Great Awakening, an enthusiastic Protestant revival, and, for the devout, choosing to become a missionary in the Far East was an undertaking that, in fact, did demand an absolute faith in one's salvation. The chances of perishing in the first few years were, optimistically, fifty-fifty. "[M]issionaries in China are made to feel how close they are to eternity," one church worker quipped grimly of the number of casualties. While the missionaries were greeted by the local population with what one of their members acknowledged was an "attitude of decided hostility" and while there were occasional acts of violence when local exasperation spilled over, the real problem was the disease and sickness.

There was already a small community of Methodists established in Foochow, but the numbers had been depleted recently. The winnowing would be a constant problem. Justus and Sophia Doolittle had arrived before the Gibsons and opened the first missionary school in the winter of 1855. They were already poorly. Sophia Doolittle would be dead within a year. Mr. and Mrs. Francis McCaw had arrived in Foochow as missionaries on June 15, 1855, around the time of Mary Ann and Joshua's arrival in Victoria Harbor. Both of them would be buried before Christmas.

And, three days after the arrival of the McCaws, Erastus and Anna Wentworth—the Gibsons' dear friends—had landed in Foochow. That was also not going to be a happy story, though it started out with promise. Because the Wentworths were also newlyweds and in love.

Erastus Wentworth was a middle-aged philosopher and theologian who thought that life's passions were long behind him. He had watched his first wife, Mary, die a lingering and painful death from tuberculosis. Unwilling to delay his mission to China—his real priority—and aware of the practical need for him to have a wife on his mission (as well as a mother for the teenaged Jimmy), he proposed, without much thought of anything except form and convention, marriage to Anna, a bookish, religious young woman devoted to music, good works, and charity. Anna, her eyes on heaven and not Erastus, accepted. To both their surprise, they found themselves aboard ship from Boston to Hong Kong falling deeply and unexpectedly in love. By the time the Wentworths had arrived in Hong Kong at the end of May, Anna was six months pregnant.

Now, from Victoria Harbor, the Gibson family needed to find a way to join the Wentworth family in Foochow to regenerate the mission. "There was no regular line," Eliza Gibson recalled, "and we must rely on a chance ship. After 3 weeks in Hongkong we heard of a ship going to Foochow to load with tea." So, as Eliza continues the story:

> Mr. Gibson went to see Capt. Patten. He was on shore and the mate told him to see Mrs. Patten. He told her of his dilemma. She said Josh would not take passengers, and moreover every stateroom was filled with cargo. He remarked how disappointed Mrs. Gibson would be. She said, 'O, is there a Mrs. Gibson? I have not seen a white woman for over five months. Why, yes, Josh can take you as well as not. I'll have a stateroom cleared out right away.' We sailed on the "Neptune's Car" for Foochow.

By the time Eliza Gibson arrived in Foochow on August 12, 1855, after a "delightful trip" of two weeks in Mary Ann's daily company, Anna Wentworth's baby daughter had been safely delivered. Anna, however, like so many others, had not fared well in her first few months in China. She had contracted almost immediately on arrival a parasitic dysentery that would destroy her liver; she would be dead by the beginning of October and, like the McCaws, buried well before Christmas.

While missionary work was hazardous, so was being a captain's wife. These were the realities of global travel in an era before modern pharmaceuticals or vaccinations. The average life expectancy in the United States was thirty-nine in the first half of the nineteenth century. In India or China, that figure fell into the midtwenties. An unexpectedly heartbroken Erastus Wentworth, upon sober reflection, would soon send both his son, Jimmy, and baby Anna back home to America alone, on a returning ship, to be raised in his long absence by Anna's parents.

Mary Ann, lonely and aware of how easily any of them might succumb to fever or infection, had liked Eliza Gibson. She felt deep sorrow for Eliza's friend Anna. Anna's fate might belong to any of them.

**Foochow, located several** dozen miles up the Min River, had no wharfs for huge sailing vessels like a China clipper. The port had only been open to Western trade since 1844 and access remained contested.

Joshua anchored alongside the other British and American sea captains farther downriver, about a dozen miles to the east of Foochow, at the very beautiful spot simply known, because of the picturesque temple on a mid-stream island, as the Pagoda Anchorage. On this little island were all the amenities required by the international clipper colony, including a busy depot with two chandleries, where captains could put in for repairs and provisions.

On August 18, 1855, Joshua cleared customs with the American consul.

From here, traveling upriver to Foochow to load the vessels was a slow and tedious business. Joshua would need a local pilot to guide *Neptune's Car* through the narrow gorges and past the hidden sandbanks on the last part of the voyage.

Captains made this difficult trip upriver simply because it was lucrative. Foochow was another dozen miles, but the tea plantations could be a hundred miles up the river. No clipper would or could travel that far. The toasted and rolled fresh tea leaves were floated downstream in shallow-bottomed sampans. But, because the tea leaves were harvested two months earlier along the Min River than in the other regions of China, they could be loaded in time for the captains to beat the monsoons and to arrive in Liverpool before the competition.

Joshua was already arriving midseason. The first of the British tea clippers had set sail for London in early June, and the fastest of them could make the run from Foochow to London in under a hundred days. *Neptune's Car* arrived two months into the season in mid-August. It would take another month or more to have the tea brought downriver and carefully loaded. *Neptune's Car* was commissioned to carry, from Foochow to Britain, $96,100 worth of tea—a cargo worth $3 million in today's values. A 5 percent primage alone was worth nearly $5,000, not including Joshua's private allocation, and, as Mary Ann attested: "[E]very stateroom was filled with cargo."

Mary Ann and Joshua, waiting for the tea delivery, had a little time to tour Foochow and the surrounding areas, as part of Joshua's interest in learning about the tea plantations. Selecting their private cargo wisely and profitably required judging a tea's value and quality. For Mary Ann, however, making her way to shore was almost as complicated as bringing chests of tea downriver. Ladies had to be swung off the stern of clippers in wicker contraptions known as "gamming" chairs and lowered down by rope into tippy sampans.

Mary Ann's fashionable dress did not make the operation simple or safe. Like all other British and American middle-class women, even in August in China, she wore stiff crinoline and horsehair underlayers of billowing petticoats that made her full skirts, decorated with fussy fringes and braided trimmings, stand out for feet on either side of her. While the wire cage crinoline would not become the rage until 1856, the stiffened petticoats of the early 1850s posed plenty enough challenge.

A lady had to get these stiff skirts over the edge of a boat, into a wood-and-wicker swing, and down twenty feet or more, over the side of a vessel, without somehow showing more than an ankle. Indeed, stiff skirts had an unfortunate tendency to tip over entirely or catch the breeze, making for some unfortunate exhibitions. Thanks to laced corsets and tight-fitting bodices, encumbered by drooping, flouncy "Pagoda sleeves," and half-blinded by a frilly bonnet, a lady had to perform this exercise constrained and constricted and without a great deal of oxygen to assist her. And this was all assuming the crew didn't dunk or, worse, drop her. A captain's wife had to be brave to attempt it. Mary Ann almost certainly did not know how to swim, but, if she had known, it would not have mattered if she ended up in the water. The weight of her skirts would have sunk her.

They may have traveled as far up the Min River as Wuyi Mountain, where the finest teas were sourced, to see the picturesque temples and waterfalls. They would certainly have visited the Kushan Monastery, carried from the river to the temple in sedan chairs, where the air was cooler in the summer and picnics were a popular pastime among the British and American residents and merchant-tourists. It was a brief pause, and then, by September 15, they were loaded with tea. Joshua was consumed with organizing and logging cargo and with carefully cramming tea into every possible nook and cranny.

On September 29, the winds shifted. The season was already late as *Neptune's Car* set sail again, destined for the tea exchange in London.

Their route this time took them back south, past Taiwan and Hong Kong, and into the South China Sea, between modern-day Vietnam and the Philippines, where Joshua set men aloft to keep a sharp eye out for the pirates that routinely and ferociously attacked merchant ships making the transit. They slipped past the dangerous coral reefs of Pratas Island and were spotted by another ship reprovisioning in the Port of Anyer on the island of Java in early November. It may have been here, in Indonesia, that Joshua bought for Mary Ann the gold-and-coral earrings that were among her most prized possessions thereafter. She would not have needed Joshua to explain to her the significance: Coral was to keep you safe and close to the heart, more ocean amulet than gemstone.

It was a journey of months, and they were slowed by light winds as they came into the Indian Ocean. Joshua's log of their voyage from China to London and then back to New York City does not appear to have survived; only about 20 percent of the ship's logs from this period in our history are extant. But their route onward would be, as their route thus far had been, entirely predictable, and other captains on the tea run reported particularly difficult weather that autumn. They were sailing a veritable maritime highway. From the Indian Ocean they had ahead of them another treacherous transit around the Cape of Good Hope, at the bottom of Africa, and they would have skirted their way back up from the South Atlantic to the North Atlantic, riding the trades past the Azores, then up the coast of western Europe, before tucking into London, where they arrived on January 22, 1856, after 115 days at sea, to offload their rich cargo of tea from China.

The entrance into London also required a river journey up the Thames with a pilot. By the time they rounded the Isle of Dogs and passed Greenwich and the 0° meridian, Mary Ann could see the docklands of the metropolis ahead of her. Mary Ann had seen New York City, which in 1850 had a population of somewhere around 500,000 residents. Her view of London was something entirely different. London in 1850 was the largest city in the world, more than five times the population of Manhattan, with more than two and a half million inhabitants.

At the bend around St. Katherine's and Wapping, they were towed into the deep canals and basins on the west side of the London Docks, in the shadow of the Tower of London, where in 1845 the city had constructed new warehouses, large enough to hold 120,000 chests of tea. Behind the basins and the jetties of the London Docks ran the warren of twisting lanes that were the heart of the world tea trade. As much as 80 percent of the global trade passed through this quarter of the city, and Joshua would have heard on arrival about the new £500 prize awarded to the first clipper each year to arrive with spring tea from China. It was the talk of all the sea captains.

On the streets of London, the sights and sounds and especially the smells were like nothing else Mary Ann had ever experienced. Horse-drawn omnibuses ferried residents from one district to another, leaving behind mountains of manure for the street cleaners. On Saturday nights, as one resident described the city in 1851:

> [T]he sights, as you elbow your way through are . . . multifarious. Here is a stall glittering with new tin saucepans; there another bright with its blue and yellow crockery. . . . After this

is the butcher's shop, crimson and white with meat . . . A little further on stands the clean family, begging; the father with his head down as if in shame . . . One minute you pass a man with an umbrella turned upside down and full of prints; the next you hear one with a peepshow.

The year that Mary Ann first saw London, the novelist Charles Dickens described the river Thames as a "deadly sewer." The drinking water, too, could pose a danger, resulting in a strong and rather reasonable preference for alcohol among many residents; in September 1854, 616 residents of the district of Soho died of cholera in a two-week period after drinking water from a well drilled too close to a cesspool. The risks of disease, after all, were not confined to Hong Kong or Calcutta.

In London, Mary Ann had the opportunity to refresh their wardrobes and purchase bits of finery for her sewing, while Joshua was busy ensuring that the tea aboard *Neptune's Car* was carefully unloaded and sent to auction. They would be given only six weeks at the docks to unload their cargo and be gone, because punitive wharf charges would be levied that could wipe out a captain's profits. The docks were too busy for a ship to sit idle taking up moorage.

Until 1837, the tea trade in London had been a government monopoly controlled by the East India Company; the year that Joshua and Mary Ann arrived in London, the tea markets were a furious open competition for the first time, and auctions were held weekly by brokers on Mincing Lane, in the heart of the city of London, and known in 1855 simply as the Street of Tea. And, fortunately for Joshua, tea was an easy commodity to broker in the London market. Within a week or two, the tea, including their private cargo, had been sent to auction.

That season, the best-quality teas were fetching eight dollars a pound, an astonishing sum of money. Joshua did not have the capital to buy enough tea to fill up the entire allocation of 56.5 (short) tons of private cargo: 113,000 pounds of China tea would have required a captain to gamble an entire competence, though the profits might have been spectacular. But even an investment of a thousand pounds of tea would have been a substantial windfall.

Outbound again, the return leg to New York City and home would be less profitable, though they would not have to return, as they had traveled from California to China, with rocks as their main cargo. They would carry this time finished retail and textile goods destined for New York City and, ultimately, San Francisco.

By February 26, the final cargo was being put in place to make them sail-ready. Because there were not the same returns on private cargo between London and New York, Joshua sold the empty space in the staterooms this time to eleven paying passengers, earning them another several thousand dollars. Joshua prepared Mary Ann, too, for an unpleasant and trying voyage home. He knew this route well, and no one would be more glad to step foot back on dry land in Manhattan than the captain. Crossing the Atlantic in winter is a wet and windy business. One does it because the only thing less pleasant is crossing during the summer hurricane season. The winter storms in the North Atlantic are fearsome. But Joshua also had a personal reason for wishing them quickly back in Boston or Rockland. They had been living in cramped quarters for more than a year already, cheek by jowl with stewards and mates and, on this last run, passengers, and what young man would not look forward with a certain twinkle in his eye to a few weeks alone with his wife unaccompanied?

It was a predictably hard crossing. On March 11, one of their seamen, John B. Kearn, a native of New York, fell from the main topgallant mast in foul weather, struck the deck, and was killed instantly. Toward the end of March, they were caught in a fierce lightning storm at sea, and the fore-topmast was struck and shattered. Several more members of the crew were injured in trying to make the repair in bad weather. Mary Ann now pored over the medical books in the captain's library, trying to learn how to nurse the injured men until they could reach New York and a doctor, for which she earned a degree of affection and loyalty that would serve her well in what came later.

*Neptune's Car* finally passed Sandy Hook, with something of relief, and they took aboard the pilot on April 5, 1856. By the time Mary Ann and Joshua landed back on shore on the Eastern Seaboard, they had been at sea for fifteen months and had circumnavigated the globe.

Mary Ann was now nearly as skilled a navigator as Joshua. The captain's wife was also a favorite among the crew of *Neptune's Car*, who no longer thought she was unlucky. They had earned for Foster & Nickerson an excellent profit and for themselves a fine addition to their nest egg of capital.

They would not earn their $100,000 competence on this trip. But they may have cleared as much as a quarter of that amount. If fortune were with them, they might earn enough in just a couple of trips around the world to imagine building a home in Maine on the banks of the Weskeag River and starting a family.

It was all so nearly in their reach that they were blind to the dangers.

**Joshua and Mary Ann** were not in New York City long that spring.

Abel Foster was a busy man, but, when Captain Patten arrived in his office with the ship's papers, reviewing the ledgers was a pleasure that he took time to savor. Captain Patten had made a tidy sum for Foster & Nickerson. He had acted with sensible efficiency and good judgment. Here was a man one wanted sailing one's clippers.

Foster promptly offered Joshua a new contract. Captain Patten would take *Neptune's Car* on a repeat voyage, heading to San Francisco with mining equipment and groceries and arriving in Foochow for the tea season to the London auctions.

This time, the ship's owners wanted the leg from New York to San Francisco to be part of a five-way clipper race. The race would be open to public betting and covered in the newspapers. Captain Patten had nearly made San Francisco last time in a hundred days, and New York City journalists had crowed about his passage. Now, any number of punters were willing to gamble good money that Captain Patten could drive a ship faster and harder than anyone. These informal clipper races were the nineteenth-century equivalent of fantasy football, except the betting was more ferocious, and everyone had a favorite clipper captain.

The competitors would be *Neptune's Car*, the *Romance of the Seas*, the *Intrepid*, the Maine-built clipper *Snow Squall*, and one other vessel, likely either the *Fleet Wing* or the *Silver Star*.

The master of the *Snow Squall* that season was Captain Lloyd; at the helm of the *Intrepid*, on her maiden voyage, was Captain Gardiner, an old salt and the favorite to win, who as the master of the *Comet* a few years previously had shattered records on the Cape Horn transit. Commander of the *Romance of the Seas* was the experienced New Englander Captain Henry.

*Neptune's Car* would be loaded on this voyage out, according to the insurance records, with $350,000 worth of cargo from New York City, worth more than $12 million in today's values. Even if his primage was only 5 percent—a very low contract figure, especially for a now-seasoned master—Joshua's cut for the first leg alone might be as much as $17,500, plus his salary of $3,000, plus private cargo for which Foster & Nickerson would loan him the capital, plus a $2,000 bonus for any trip under one hundred days in transit. They stood to clear, in modern terms, a sum of well over a million dollars if this circumnavigation went well. It would put them in grasping distance of their dreams for a house on the river and a family.

There was one catch. The season was early. *Too* early. Foster & Nickerson wanted Joshua to depart by the end of June. That meant transiting the tip of South America at the end of winter in the southern hemisphere, when the risks were perilous. This time, Cape Horn would show them the weather for which the headland was legendary.

**Joshua agreed to** risk it and took the contract.

He and Mary Ann remained in Manhattan in May and June, preparing the clipper for her next circumnavigation. Joshua and his first mate supervised repairs and reloading. Mary Ann laid in provisions of books, dress patterns, and supplies for needlework and sewing. They may have traveled by steamer up to Boston to see her family for a short time in April. Mary Ann was particularly close to her older brother, George, twenty-six in 1855, and to his wife Margaret, and she wanted to see how much little George Patten Brown had grown since his christening. There was probably not time for Joshua and Mary Ann to have traveled up to Rockland. Mary Ann would have to rely on letters with her mother-in-law, Sarah, for news about their little house and the Maine family.

During the last week of June, loading was underway in lower Manhattan, and each day some new commission arrived, requiring careful attention to the storage of cargo. As race day approached, New Yorkers came to the wharves to view the contenders and place their bets. Joshua planned to cast off the lines and start the clock for *Neptune's Car* on June 30.

On June 29, however, disaster struck. There was a shriek of agony and a mighty crash from the forecastle. Crew rushed forward to find that the first mate, the captain's trusted right-hand man who had sailed with Joshua and Mary Ann on their last circumnavigation, unaware of the open main hatch, had stepped forward into empty space, for one long moment fallen, and now lay twisted among the cargo. Someone yelled to a ship's boy to run and fetch the doctor, but no one needed to wait for the physician's arrival to diagnose the obvious. The first mate's mangled leg was broken.

A first mate with a broken leg could not sail, and not having a trusted first mate was a very serious problem. Departure would have to be postponed.

**The first mate** was a high-ranking position aboard a clipper and a hands-on one. Only the captain had more authority. Even a captain deferred, by convention, to his first mate as an officer and a gentleman. The first mate dined with the captain, might live in one of the staterooms near the captain's quarters, and was a master's most trusted officer. He was one of the few people to whom Mary Ann, as the captain's wife, was permitted by those same conventions to speak.

If we think of a clipper ship as a company—and clippers were, above all, a business—the ship's owners were the controlling shareholders, the ship's captain was the CEO, responsible for the high-level executive decisions, but the first mate was the president, responsible for overseeing and executing operations. Aboard ship, the first mate reported to the captain. But in port, as a system of checks and balances, the first mate also had a direct and confidential line of communication with the ship's owners. As Richard Dana wrote in 1841 in *The Seaman's Friend*, his follow-up publication to his bestselling *Two Years Before the Mast*:

> [T]he law looks upon the chief mate as standing in a different relation to the master from that of the second mate or

the men. He is considered a confidential person, to whom the owners, shippers and insurers look, in some measure, for special duties and qualifications. The master, therefore, cannot remove him from office, except under very peculiar circumstances, and then must be able to prove a justifiable cause. . . . The law also makes the chief mate the successor to the master, in case the latter should die, or be unable to perform the duties of his office; and this without any action on the part of the crew.

The journey ahead was dangerous, and Joshua and Mary Ann were placing their lives in the hands of a first mate for large parts of the voyage. A first mate was utterly essential.

Joshua considered. The second mate, William Hare, was a good sailor and conscientious. He was in his midtwenties, just a bit younger than his captain, and both Joshua and Mary Ann knew and liked him from their first circumnavigation. But Hare had one serious deficiency: He couldn't read. That meant that he couldn't keep the logbook or read the almanac tables required to navigate, and that meant he wasn't really qualified at all to stand as an officer. Only the shortage of crew and his popularity with the seamen—a fact that stemmed from his willingness, in general, to look the other way when it came to discipline and rations—could account for Hare's promotion to second mate. There was no way to move him into the first mate position.

The third mate, George Kingsley, was competent enough at sea but a mean-spirited and violent thug of a man, with a murderous temper, already known aboard ship from the last voyage as a bully who took pleasure in being cruel to the young boys on their first few runs as seamen. He was not a man Joshua was keen to promote, and, anyhow, he wasn't qualified either.

From there, of the twenty or so crew who sailed with *Neptune's*

*Car* on the outbound voyage, we only know the names of three other sailors: Hallock, McDermott, and one of the youngest crew members, a lad named Thomas Jones. We know their names because they would all testify to Kingsley's violence at a murder trial in San Francisco.

There was nothing for it. Joshua could not sail without a first mate. He told Abel Foster that the voyage would have to be delayed. *Neptune's Car* place in the race would have to be forfeited.

# 9

# Cape Horn

Below 40° S there is no law; below 50° S there is no God.
—Sailors' maxim

Abel Foster said no when Joshua told him. He refused to consider a withdrawal. Captain Patten would sail as contracted, or he would replace Captain Patten.

The captain *did* need a first mate. The first mate reported to the owners. Abel Foster could see that was going to have to be solved. That same afternoon, he located a new first mate for Captain Patten. He was, admittedly, scraping the bottom of the barrel to find someone on a few hours' notice, but in the clipper business time was money. Captain Patten would have to manage. If a man couldn't control his officers, he had no business being a sea captain.

The new first mate, William Keeler, was twenty in 1856, a hotheaded, violent, and duplicitous mariner from Philadelphia, and he was unemployed that afternoon, it would turn out, for good reason.

Joshua had no choice but to accept the decision of the ship's owners, and they would have to make the best of it, but he returned to the docks with a sense of foreboding.

There was no starting gun on a clipper race, even a public one. No hats were thrown down. Each vessel would leave when their cargo was ready, and each of the captains planned to leave in the last days of June or in the first week of July for San Francisco. The race for each vessel started the moment they cleared Sandy Hook and released the pilot. It would end, as with Joshua's first race, the moment they cleared the Golden Gate and dropped anchor in San Francisco.

The *Romance of the Seas* was towed out of New York Harbor on June 30. On July 1, a day behind schedule, *Neptune's Car* cast off her lines. Captain Gardiner on the *Intrepid* left the wharves just behind her; Captain Lloyd followed a few days later.

Mary Ann stood on the quarterdeck. What a spectacle: The wharves were lined with crowds of people who had turned out to watch, who jostled with the merchants and stevedores carrying on their business as usual. The gardens of Battery Park slipped past first. The steeple of Trinity Church disappeared from view as they were tugged toward the Narrows. It was hot and muggy in the city, but there was the first hint of a cool ocean breeze when they finally cleared Sandy Hook and left the pilot behind just before midday.

Joshua called all hands on deck and gave the captain's traditional pep talk to his crew. A race around the Horn was something a winning crew could take pride in, along with a captain. It would take all their cooperation and discipline.

The ship would be divided into two watch crews. Mr. Keeler, the new first mate, would supervise the starboard watch. Mr. Hare, as second mate, would take the larboard. Like a nineteenth-century version of schoolyard gym class, Keller and Hare chose their watch crews sailor by sailor. Each day was divided into five four-hour watches and two evening dinnertime half watches of two hours each—the "dog watches"—which ensured that the overnight hours rotated between the crews. When a crew was on watch, it was their job to ensure the safe and fast running of the clipper.

Joshua, as captain, did not stand a watch. The captain came and went as and when he pleased, and in all cases the navigation and command of the ship was his sole prerogative. At sea, nothing mattered as much as that one principle.

A first or second mate might make some small independent adjustments to the sailing of a clipper. They might direct the crew to trim or adjust the sails to maximize their speed. They could exercise, as well, their own punishments. But no officer could make any decision about the command of the ship or her navigation. To reef a topsail or adjust course required an officer to call the captain to the quarterdeck. Only the captain could make such commands. The gentleman's agreement was that the captain gave those directions to his officers to implement and that if the captain had a criticism of an officer, he gave it in private. In exchange, the mates were authorized at sea to stand in place of the captain and granted immense power over the lives of the other seamen.

They turned their bow toward the open Atlantic in light winds. A day at sea began at noon, when the sun was at its zenith and the captain could take his first sightings with the sextant to set their geographical position. Joshua squinted into the sunlight. He turned to the slate board and recorded in chalk his data. Mr. Keeler—for the captain and his wife would only refer to the officers with such civilities—would later ink these for the captain into the log as the ship's official record. A correct meridian reading set the entire journey off with a good reckoning. Knowing one's position at sea as accurately as possible was key to making time to San Francisco. Without a fix on their position, Maury's charts were useless.

Captain Hussey had beaten him by less than a day in a journey of thousands of hours last time to California. Joshua was determined this time to fight for speed every mile of the voyage. To win the race—and to earn the prize money and commissions that would give him and Mary Ann their financial freedom—he meant to take advantage of every puff of wind and to run with every scrap of canvas. He and Mary Ann for weeks had pored over Maury's tables, considering and reconsidering wind and temperature and position. Joshua had no doubts about his wife's good judgment as a sailor.

This was Joshua's command to his new first mate: They were going to fly as much sail as the vessel could sustain in good winds, especially at night, and they were to fight from the helm for every gasp of breeze in light weather irrespective of the hour. Joshua wanted every watch, all the time, to be looking for wind and some advantage. It meant a great deal of work for the crew and the officers, who would have to be making constant adjustments. He was not going to lose again by being careless in the early weeks of a race. Mr. Keeler's job was to ensure that happened, but he was not happy about it.

**The days at** sea passed quickly. Mary Ann was now an old hand at ocean voyages. When Joshua was at the helm, Mary Ann joined him with the second sextant and confirmed his readings. She continued to practice the arts of navigation. She had learned, as well, "the ropes" and how the complex sails were managed. She was a captain's wife, but she was also a seaman's daughter.

Mary Ann had nothing of the rebel in her. Unlike Mrs. Bloomer, who was much in the news in the mid-1850s, Mary Ann did not expect to wear the pants—or the pantaloons known as "bloomers" that were popular in some progressive New England circles. Like the sea captain's wives whom Nathaniel Hawthorne admired, she was good-natured, cheerful, quietly religious, and deeply and simply loved her husband. No captain's wife gave up the comforts of home except for a love story. Joshua reciprocated with tenderness, passion, and admiration for a wife in whose intelligence and good nature he delighted.

So, when she saw how things were unfolding with Mr. Keeler, at first Mary Ann said nothing. At dinners in the captain's cabin, waited on by the steward, Mary Ann listened to Mr. Keeler and took his measure. There was something brutish and ugly, she felt, in the first mate's character. Many sailors thought that a woman aboard a ship was bad luck, and Keeler, a barrel-chested man with an outsized swagger, made no secret of his contempt. Mary Ann was the only woman aboard the ship. The snide remarks about women at sea would only have been aimed in her direction. Mary Ann shrugged off the first mate's incivilities, but she was definitely going to keep her eye on Keeler.

Mary Ann was also keeping her eye on Joshua. Joshua worried her, if anything, more than Mr. Keeler. He was suffering from crippling headaches, and he had a lingering cough that frightened her and reminded her of her father. George Patten Sr. had been failing quickly in Boston, and Mary Ann knew that he might not be alive when she returned from this circumnavigation. It was a sober and tearful subject, and nineteen is a young age in any century to contemplate losing a father.

Joshua dismissed her worries about his health. Fit as a fiddle. He'd been butting heads with Mr. Keeler since they'd left Sandy Hook, and the winds were fickle, and that was a trial for any captain. Mary Ann might have nodded. But she was not persuaded.

**In retrospect, it** is hard to know if William Keeler was incompetent, hopelessly lazy, simply malevolent, or deliberately trying to sabotage

*Neptune's Car* and throw the race because he'd been paid to do so by a competitor. The betting stakes on clipper races were high enough to have made a bribe an attractive option, and, in retrospect, it seemed curious to Joshua and Mary Ann that he'd fallen into Abel Foster's line of sight at just that moment. The circumstantial evidence certainly suggests that he may have been paid by someone back in New York to make sure that Captain Patten did not arrive first in San Francisco. Joshua didn't like to think that any captain would debase himself with a bribe in what was, essentially, a contest of honor. But a competing ship's owner, looking to grow the reputation of a clipper and along with it his profits, might be sorely tempted.

The first mate seemed determined to have a confrontation with Captain Patten from the outset. About a week out of Sandy Hook, the problems with William Keeler boiled over and put the second mate, William Hare, in a terrible predicament. When eight bells rang for the 4:00 A.M. change of watch, Mr. Hare found the starboard crew on deck but the sails mismanaged and the first mate, Mr. Keeler, happily catnapping.

To be caught sleeping on watch was a serious infraction for a member of the crew. A young man named Clarence Ray, who shipped out as an apprentice on the *Cutty Sark* as a seaman, wrote in a letter home: "if we go to sleep in our watch on deck, they make us ride the grey mare—that is sit up on [the saddle atop] the upper topsail yard for the rest of the watch," swaying a terrifying hundred feet or more above the ocean. No one nodded off on that saddle. Not if he wished to live to see breakfast.

For the first mate to be caught sleeping on watch was unthinkable and unforgivable: a dereliction of duty of the first order. The pecking order was brutal among the officers and the crew. Ratting out another officer to the captain was a loathsome prospect. But Mr. Keeler napping put them all in danger, and, if the crew followed his very public example on watch, it would be the end of all discipline and order.

Mr. Hare reluctantly but dutifully informed the captain.

Joshua was incandescent. He reprimanded his first mate in private, because that was the protocol, but he did not mince words with the young officer. William Keeler's response was hot-tempered and insubordinate. Joshua brought his officer to heel with a blunt reminder of what it meant to be the captain. Mr. Keeler backed down this time, sullenly.

Over the next few weeks, Mr. Keeler looked for every opportunity to undercut the captain and to show his disdain for Joshua. At first, it was little things, like the first mate not putting on sail aggressively, losing them speed and momentum. Letting the crews do work shoddily. Making "accidental" transcription errors in the logbook. Troublesome, infuriating, passive-aggressive: but not enough for Joshua to do something about as the captain, except to reprimand his first mate in private. He could not demote a first mate, especially not one handpicked by the ship's owners, without very serious evidence of dereliction.

But the frequent reprimands meant that, behind closed doors, the relationship between William Keeler and Joshua was growing outright combative in the captain's quarters. Mary Ann was sure that she had caught looks between the first mate and the third mate, George Kingsley, a loutish thug who respected only the threat of the lash, and she was careful now to lock the door to the captain's cabin when Joshua was at the helm. When Mary Ann and Joshua spoke in quiet, it was with a growing concern that William Keeler was trying to stir up bad feeling against the captain—the first step toward mutiny.

They hit the doldrums on August 1 and passed through the quietness in good time. A week later they crossed the line, with all the accustomed revelry and the arrival of Poseidon and with Captain

Gardiner and the *Intrepid* not far behind them. Soon they would hit the southern trades. Another two weeks, and they would be down the coast of South America.

Even in bed in the captain's quarters, to catch a few hours of sleep between change of watches, Joshua was alert to the motion of *Neptune's Car* as she sailed through the night. Pulling on his oilskin overcoat one night with the equator just behind them, he went up on deck unannounced in darkness. The motion of the ship was not what he expected. Something felt wrong to him as captain. It was the starboard watch. William Keeler should have been on the quarterdeck. But the first mate was nowhere to be seen. Joshua found the third mate, Mr. Kingsley, commanding the ship. The alarm in Kingsley's eyes told the whole story. Joshua felt for the loaded pistol at his waist. Kingsley's eyes grew wider.

Joshua was a calm man and an even-tempered captain, but all he could see was red. He demanded of the first young man he saw to know where he could find the first mate and ordered the second mate awakened. A quavering hand pointed the captain toward the cook's quarters. There, Mr. Keeler was not only catnapping this time but was tucked up sleeping through watch near a warm fire. Joshua sacked his first mate on the spot in front of the crew and demoted him back down the ranks to seaman. Mr. Keeler would bunk with the rest of the low-ranking sailors in the fo'scle at the front of the ship, and he would work alongside the ship's boys on their first journey, doing menial tasks that even the able seamen thought beneath them. Humiliating, to be certain, but, considering the magnitude of the offense, this was a restrained punishment. Joshua was within his rights to have Keeler whipped. It must have been tempting.

Keeler had no respect for the captain and was an intemperate and stupid young man. When Joshua ordered him to the forecastle, he spat out words threatening revenge and violence against the captain. Joshua calmly leveled his pistol and ordered Seaman Keeler taken below to the brig and put in leg irons if that was how he wished them to manage this.

Joshua immediately promoted Mr. Hare to first mate and Mr. Kingsley to second, but, while that restored order aboard *Neptune's Car*, the grave problem was that Mr. Hare still could not read and, so, still could not navigate. Joshua would need to stand watch with the new first mate, at least intermittently. This meant that, for the remainder of the voyage, Joshua, still suffering from a cough and blinding migraines, would sleep only fitfully throughout the night and, even then, only when weather conditions permitted. In a storm, no captain slept in more than snatches regardless of who was on watch. Joshua would need to remain on deck as well during the daylight hours, to ensure work aboard the ship was being done, especially in these crucial weeks before they came into Drake's Passage and faced the fury of Cape Horn. He was grateful once again for Mary Ann and her skill in celestial navigation, because she could fill in for Mr. Hare by taking sights and updating the logbook.

Few men would have the endurance to survive the sleepless nights and battering storm conditions this was going to require of Captain Patten, and, by the middle of August, six weeks out of New York, the situation was beginning to alarm Mary Ann. She could see that Joshua was more than simply exhausted from weeks of not sleeping properly. The fevers that came and went now burned hotter, and his eyes shone too brightly. Sometimes he seemed to her a little delirious. Her father already had tuberculosis. He'd had it the last time she and Joshua had seen her family in Boston. She began to suspect that Joshua did too. She knew that without rest and a doctor it would be a death sentence.

Alongside Maury's books and the pilot charts, Mary Ann again pored over the medical books in the ship's library, as she had done trying to aid the seamen injured crossing the Atlantic on their last crossing. She flipped through books like Dr. Ritter's *A Medical*

*Manual and Medicine Chest Companion: For Popular Use in Families and on Ship-Board, for the Treatment of the Ordinary Diseases of the Human System* (1847). She studied the jars with their little paper labels in the medicine trunk in the captain's quarters.

She wasn't reading those medical books only about consumption and fever. She was reading up on a certain queasiness in the morning that was *not* seasickness. Mary Ann had begun to suspect something else these past few weeks. She also looked up one other section in those medical books: What to do if a lady at sea on a long voyage were pregnant.

Mary Ann was two and a half months along, nauseous, excited, and a more than a little bit frightened—and she was sailing with an unreliable first mate and a sick husband, right toward the world's most dangerous waters.

## 10

# The Tempest

> Now would I give a thousand furlongs of sea for an acre of barren ground: long heath, brown furze, any thing. The wills above be done! but I would fain die a dry death.
>
> —Shakespeare, *The Tempest*

They struggled along another week with Joshua taking turns on watch and returning to the cabin in the small hours of the night, chilled and breathless. Mary Ann could see the toll it was taking.

Then, on August 24, in the "roaring 40s," it went from bad to much worse. *Neptune's Car* slammed into a ferocious *pampero*, a wild polar windstorm, south of Buenos Aires. With waves mounting forty feet high before they crashed over the bow, sending a shudder through the white oak planking of the clipper and knocking seamen off their feet, Joshua would not leave the quarterdeck in these conditions.

When the *Snow Squall* ran into that storm system a short time later, it would take Captain Lloyd out of the competition. A topmast was torn off in heavy seas, whipping wood and sails across the decks. Partially dismasted, the *Snow Squall* and her crew survived only by making a sorry retreat to the port of Montevideo, on the headlands off Buenos Aires, where Captain Lloyd, disconsolate, sat in dock for more than two months watching his seamen and his fortune slip away to other, more fortunate vessels. A captain would move heaven and earth to avoid ending up stranded in a foreign port on a Cape Horn voyage.

By the end of August, a week later, Tierra del Fuego Island was less than thirty miles ahead of them to their starboard. Somewhere ahead, to their port side, was the mountainous Staten Island.

If you are not a nautical type, "starboard," Anglo-Saxon for "steorsbord" or the "steering-board side," is on the right side of the ship as you are facing forward, a throwback to a time when rudders were not routinely in the aft-center. The right was the steering side because most skippers are right-handed. The "port" side is on left, which is to say it is the side on which you dock your vessel, because, if you are a Viking and your steering board is on the right, you don't want your gear smashing into bits on the rocks, do you?

Staten Island to the port, Tierra del Fuego to the starboard, then. You're heading south and running a gauntlet. Between these two rocky shores is a narrow channel, twenty miles wide, with powerful currents and infamous fogs: the Strait of Lemaire, a graveyard of shipwrecks. Mary Ann and Joshua had been here once already. On the other side of the Strait of Lemaire is the bottom of the world and the fury of Drake's Passage.

If they were going to turn back, this was their chance to head to Buenos Aires and join Captain Lloyd in his misery, but Joshua did not entertain any thoughts of abandoning their journey or his cargo. He was a sea captain, a young man in his late twenties, with a wife whom he adored, a dream for the future—and, although he probably did not yet know it, a baby on the way.

Mary Ann would have been hesitant to add anything to Joshua's stresses. She was already deeply worried about his health and growing exhaustion. No, all things considered, this was definitely the kind of news that was best celebrated on the safe side of Drake's Passage.

Joshua would have scoffed at such fussing. Sailing was a profession, storms were to be expected, especially around Cape Horn in winter, and his instructions were to set a course for Drake's Passage and to sail as fast as possible.

By September 1, 1857, though, Joshua has stood at the helm and fought the sea for eight days and nights. He has misjudged not his sailing but his fortitude and his illness. That morning, there is no fight left in him. He slips to the deck and lets the darkness take him.

Mary Ann in the captain's quarters looks up through the window. She sees a face contorted with fear and excitement. The eyes meet her own. Something is urgent. She hears the cry: "Captain!" Mary Ann knows: Joshua.

She throws on an oilskin, but on deck her hair whips wet against her face, and cold rain drips between her shoulder blades. Joshua is limp, unconscious. The seamen are carrying him gingerly toward her, and the ship moans with the force of the storm that is all around them. Or is it Joshua moaning?

Mr. Hare, the first mate, looks at her. He has taken the helm already. He is a fine mariner and will hold them steady. But he cannot read, and he does not know where they are headed.

On the bed, in the wood-paneled cabin's quarters, Joshua's forehead burns, but she does not think he hears her. Mary Ann only knows that Joshua is alive because she can see his breath rising and falling.

And the situation is grave for all of them. They are caught in a terrible storm between two dangerous headlands, and the worst—Cape Horn—is ahead of them. This time, it will show her no mercy. She lets her head fall for a moment on the cool bedsheets, and she is not sure if she is thinking or praying. She is nineteen. She wants to go home. She wants to see her parents. She wants once more to see her father. She wants Joshua and their baby and a farm on the Weskeag River where a salt marsh flows into the Atlantic.

But she knows that, first, they must get to San Francisco. Before that they must reckon with Cape Horn. Mr. Hare cannot command the ship. When they come around the corner of the southern tip of the South American continent, they will need to chart a new course to the West and face the force of Drake's Passage. Someone will need to navigate and order that new heading, and she will have to do it.

**In the salon,** at the great wooden table, she lays out the charts of Drake's Passage. She turns the little gold key that opens the rosewood box and carefully takes out Joshua's chronometer. She will need to know the "mean" time far away in Greenwich.

In front of her rests *The Nautical Almanac and Astronomical Ephemeris for the Year 1856*. She does a quick calculation in her head and thumbs to the page in the almanac for September 1.

But until the sky clears, her sextant is useless. She will need, until then, to guess their position on the ocean, to "dead reckon."

She has to hand a leather-bound volume, and the letters printed on its spine read: *Explanations and Sailing Directions to Accompany the Wind and Current Charts* (1851). She needs, once they turn the headland into the full fury of Drake's Passage, to know where they should go, where the currents and winds will let them make headway out of this danger. She remembers their last voyage.

She turns to the section on Cape Horn and reads Lieutenant Maury's guidance:

> Cape Horn navigators should not forget that the prevailing winds encountered in doubling the Cape are westerly winds; that the Andes, which in fact terminate only with the continent, stand up as a barrier to these winds, and consequently these winds come around the Cape in violent sweeps, puffs, and gales.

Once they turn into the open expanse of Drake's Passage, they will be beyond the protection of the mountains.

Mary Ann continues reading:

> [T]he strength of these sweeping winds is probably felt with more force near the Cape than it is at a considerable distance off, and out of the influence of land. Therefore, I would advise navigators in doubling the Cape, first to pass through the straits of Le Maire, if practicable . . . [then] to hug the Cape as closely as the winds on one hand, and the rocks on the other, will allow, and so make westing down there when the degrees are short, as fast as without fighting adverse winds and weather they may do, until they cross—if bound to California—the parallel of 50 South, between the meridians of 80 and 90 West. But,

and here Mary Ann paused:

> if after getting through the straits, and before doubling the Cape, a westerly gale strike them in the teeth, then instead of stopping there off the pitch of the Cape to fight against it, with intention of holding their own till the gale abates, or

wind slants so as to let them get round, I think the chances would be altogether in their favor, by sticking her away South, under the expectation that they would soon get out of the strength of the winds which, eddy-like, come sweeping around Cape Horn, sometimes at one distance, sometimes at another, according to the direction of the gale. But even in doing this, the navigator who is desirous of making a quick passage, will not fail to take advantage of slots. He will always prefer, until he doubles the Cape, the tack upon which he can make the most westing.

Mary Ann's heart sank. The conditions in the Strait of Lemaire had been ferocious for a week and showed no sign of abating. The strait was sheltered water. They were driving full force into a mighty storm as soon as they passed the headland off the tip of Argentina. She would need to plot a heading that took them south, far into Drake's Passage. She would try to keep them, if she could, north of 60° S. They would plot a line diagonally southwest across the passage, keeping the winds to their starboard. Somewhere halfway to Antarctica, they would make a great turn, and head northwest toward the Pacific Ocean, with the wind to port. If a "slot" allowed, they might tack once or twice along the way to gain a little ground westward. But tacking a mighty clipper in a gale was a dangerous business, and already the seas mounted up around them.

She worked quickly with the stub of a little lead pencil.

**First mate William Hare** was at the helm. His face was taut with tension. Mary Ann spoke. They would need to make the turn. She had charted the direction and gave the heading.

Would Mr. Hare, she asked, help her bring *Neptune's Car* to port safely? He would be her first mate. He would direct the men and command at the helm. He would keep the watch and work with Mr. Kingsley. He would attend to the sails and order the men aloft. She would navigate and command their direction.

In short, she asked Mr. Hare, would he accept her as the captain? Mr. Hare nodded. She gave the bearing and coordinates.

**Belowdecks, still in** shackles, Mr. Keeler has been busy. The weather is foul. It is raining ice, and they are battling now the full force of Drake's Passage. The ship rises and falls as the waves lift and then drop them. Word has passed among the men about this extraordinary thing: The captain's lady is navigating their clipper. Mr. Keeler is indignant and vengeful. He has been stirring up the crew against Mary Ann and against Joshua.

He has been saying that the captain's wife, a slip of a girl, is not their master. No woman is his master. He has been saying that command of the ship belongs, in right, to him as the first mate. That Captain Patten had no right. That Mr. Hare does not know how to do a reckoning and that without him they will all be shipwrecked and will perish. He has been pressing the cook and the crew to release his bonds, and he can see, as the storm rages, their resolve softening. When he is in command of the ship, then the captain will understand what it means to trifle with him. He thinks about the captain's pretty little wife.

For a time, the crew are unpersuaded. One day, two days, three days, Mary Ann and Mr. Hare struggle on without opposition. But on the fourth day, the wind and waves are overpowering them; they are running just to stand still. The waves sweeping across the icy bow are fearsome and deadly. The crew begins to doubt. Mr. Keeler seizes the moment.

He demands pen and paper. He can read and write. He can do sums and navigate. He writes to the captain's wife. He says that he will take command of the ship and demands that he be released from shackles. He reminds her that the coast here is treacherous and that she is in unfamiliar waters. In his letter he is firm and angry. He is the first mate. It is his right. He alone can save them from danger.

When the letter is taken to her, Mary Ann sits and considers.

Mary Ann knows that the calls for mutiny are growing. She can see it at the helm now with Mr. Hare. She can see the glances.

Mary Ann also knows that if Mr. Keeler takes command, she and Joshua will be ruined, perhaps murdered. Keeler is a violent man. He and Joshua have already come near to blows, and he has been chained belowdecks for insubordination for which, when they come to port, he will have to answer. Mr. Keeler is looking at a prison sentence. It's a mighty incentive to dispatch a captain.

She considers the alternative. Even in the best of circumstances, Mr. Keeler takes them into port somewhere along the coast of Chile, perhaps Valparaíso. Perhaps he turns back to Argentina. There, the crew will abandon ship. They will disappear into the port and easily find other ships eager to hire them and take them anywhere around the globe they wish. Without crew, they will be trapped in port. The wharf fees are ruinous, and within weeks, gone with the seamen, will be any chance of a profit. With Joshua unconscious, perhaps dying, there will be no one to broker the sale of the cargo—the captain's wife cannot, on land, be given that authority. It would need to be sold off at a loss. Already, Captain Lloyd is watching his good luck slip away in Montevideo.

And Mary Ann considers another thing: Joshua. He needs care and a doctor. She has pored over the medical books in the ship's library to try to know how to help him. He is delirious and incoherent. Sometimes he moans with the headaches that blind him. Other times he is taken with seizures and falls insensible. She reads that to treat brain fever, "the head should be shaven as soon as possible, and kept moist with napkins wrapped round it dipped in cold vinegar, or equal parts of water and the neutralized solution of ammonia." It's a delicate operation in heavy seas, but she has wrapped the cool cloths around him. The patches she has missed look wretched.

But he's still burning, and she knows she must get him to San Francisco.

Soon, someone, she knows, will take Mr. Keeler's part and release him. Then there would be mutiny. Mary Ann decides that there is no alternative. On September 5, she asks Mr. Hare to order all hands on deck. The captain's wife wishes to address them. This, in itself, is extraordinary. Captain's wives do not address crew members. It is an unspoken rule of the sea. But Mary Ann is not addressing them as the captain's wife; she is addressing them as captain.

She orders that Mr. Keeler be brought to the quarterdeck to listen. Under her oilskin she has carefully wrapped Joshua's pistol close to her body. She does not think that the crew yet can see how it is swelling. She holds out Mr. Keeler's letter to show these demands and begins to speak.

**What exactly Mary Ann** said in that dramatic moment was never recorded, but later there were men aboard *Neptune's Car* who recounted parts of what they remembered on the wharves, and in pubs, and to eager newsmen. In 1857, when this voyage was over, one awed young undergraduate turned those collected recollections into a romantic poem, read as far away as London. Whatever Mary Ann said, it must have been one hell of a speech, and it went something like this:

Mary Ann said that she had received Mr. Keeler's letter and understood there was some dissatisfaction.

Keeler interrupted, spitting with fury, saying something to the effect that command and respect was due to him. He had been humiliated by the captain's wife. And he would not forgive it.

Mary Ann acknowledged that, in the natural order of things, command should pass to him as first mate in the event of the captain's incapacity. Then, growing herself angry now, she recounted one by one each of Keeler's accumulated failings. How he had slept on watch. Repeatedly. How he had lost them wind in their sails. His insubordination, his threats, the occasion of his incarceration.

"My husband did not trust Mr. Keeler," she told the crew, and, looking to face each of them, plainly said, "I shall not reinstate him." The captain's decision was to demote Keeler. That demotion stood.

She pointed out that Joshua had collapsed with exhaustion because he was doing Keeler's job. The captain had ordered Mr. Keeler in irons. Mary Ann dared any of them to countermand him. The captain, she reminded them, was yet alive and might soon recover from his brain fever. And, in any event, the captain's orders were the captain's orders, and she would see that they were followed. Tears streaked her face as she gave her impassioned speech, but with each moment her voice grew clearer and stronger.

Mr. Hare, she said, was the man her husband had made first mate. As first mate he would continue. Until her husband was able to resume command, which she hoped would be soon, she would stand in the captain's stead and navigate.

There was a long pause. Mr. Keeler glared at her and looked around at the crew as if to ask them whether this was credible.

Mary Ann then turned to the crew and simply asked them not to mutiny. She asked them to accept her command and Mr. Hare as her first mate. As *The New York Times* later recounted this moment in her speech: Mrs. Patten "explained to them the helpless condition of her husband, at the same time appealing to them to stand by her and the second mate." She would leave them to discuss and make their decision. She nodded to Mr. Hare, then she turned away from the crew to make her way back to the captain's quarters and Joshua. If the crew refused, she would lock herself in the captain's quarters with Joshua and stand guard with the loaded pistol as long as she was able.

The crew who witnessed this astonishing event remembered later how small and childlike the captain's wife seemed that day. She was barely nineteen, less than five feet tall, and, as they certainly all knew by the end, pregnant. She was a girl, they remembered thinking.

But she was also the captain's wife, and Joshua was not the only one who understood that the captain's wife was an exceptionally fine navigator and able mariner. Some of them, who had come around Cape Horn with Captain Patten on their first voyage, remembered, too, how Mary Ann had nursed the sick seamen and had showed the crew uncommon kindness and compassion.

Before she had taken more than a few steps, a crack split the air and then a cry.

Mary Ann stopped, her heart racing.

It took a long moment for her to understand that the crack was the crack of palms clapping. The crew was applauding. No one had meant or planned it; it just happened. Then, they were all calling out, as one, "Captain Patten."

It took her a moment more to understand that it was her and not Joshua they were naming. The younger seamen later recounted how the old salts among them had tears in their eyes.

Mary Ann in that moment, on September 5, 1856, was acclaimed captain. They told reporters later, "each man responded by a promise to obey her in every command." Never before had any woman been acclaimed captain of a merchant clipper.

She would have to be, as well, the first woman to do what she would have to manage next. She would have to take them around Cape Horn in a terrible gale without shipwrecking them off the coast of Tierra del Fuego or among the icebergs of the great Southern Ocean.

# 11

# The Land of Mist and Snow

How a Ship having passed the Line was driven by storms to the cold Country towards the South Pole . . . and of the strange things that befell.

—S. T. Coleridge, *The Rime of the Ancient Mariner*

What came next was one of the worst storms off Cape Horn in several seasons, a veritable blizzard at sea.

It would go down among the sea captains as an unusually hard winter. As one maritime historian put it, ships "staggered into port frozen masses of ice, sailors sick and dying in the forecastles, and often without sufficient man-power to let go the anchor." Nowhere would that be truer than in Drake's Passage.

Mary Ann, in the days that followed, did not have the leisure to record in any journal what slamming into hurricane-force winds looked like at the bottom of the world, but other sea captain's wives and passengers who survived the passage in those decades of the mid-nineteenth century left a harrowing record. No one who had done it once ever forgot it.

Sea captain's wife Susannah Weynton was caught in a storm with hurricane-force winds in Drake's Passage in the autumn of 1849 aboard a ship bound for the West Coast, and as she recalled:

> The immense length of wave, at times rolling almost mountainous high and at top the curling foam of the breakers, is an awful experience, especially to watch the abyss between each rolling wave . . . My dear Husband and many others on board say that they had never before experienced such a terrific night. From the violence of the wind eleven men were detained aloft about an hour taking in the main top sail. One small sail called the storm sheet was all that could be carried. To retire to rest was out of the question, it was indeed a fearful night, the terrific raging of the sea and roaring of the wind and the violent tossing of the vessel caused us almost to fear that we should be a wreck or be engulfed beneath the awful depths, ere the morning dawn . . . Death seemed to be near, and death at sea is very awful.

When *Neptune's Car* came through the Strait of Lemaire, the waves were so tall that, as those out in the storm that night remembered, they broke over the deck "masthead high."

How high was a masthead high? Somewhere out in the storm sailing with them was *Romance of the Seas*. Her first masthead was fourteen feet above deck, and her freeboard—the amount of hull that rode above the level of the water—was at least twenty. A wave breaking across a deck at masthead tall meant waves more than thirty-five feet high crashing all around you. It meant the force of a hundred tons or more of water knocking your feet out from under you and sustained winds at fifty knots or greater. These storm conditions swept sailors out to sea.

By September 7, the second day of the storm, with Joshua still swinging from delirium to stupor, the winds had reached sixty knots, driving snow and sleet that turned the rigging to ice. Waves fifty feet tall pummeled them, seemingly from every direction.

As long as they could keep control of the helm and not take a wave broadside, as long as they could ride the crests of the waves and not have those waves break on deck across them, *Neptune's Car* had a theoretical limit of surviving waves up to seventy feet high without being knocked down sideways or dismasted. But the waves were coming far too fast. They were breaking over them. And that meant that everyone aboard *Neptune's Car* was in mortal danger, not just a feverish Joshua.

In the captain's quarters, Joshua remained lost to her in a brain fever, and when Mary Ann came below for a half an hour of rest, shivering and wet, eating anything hot was impossible. As Hannah Rebecca Burgess, aboard the *Challenger* in 1854, remembered: "away flies everything moveable . . . all of a sudden, your Soup is ruining your clothes, or some hot tea upset." Some hard bread. A bit of wine. Just enough to keep the body and the spirit going. A quick glance at the charts, a few markings in pencil which might be their position, and Mary Ann shrugged back into her soaking weatherproofs and trudged again to the helm in darkness.

On September 8 or perhaps 9, three or four days into their ordeal, one of the boys came from the lookout. They had spotted another ship in the distance, among the towering waves. She was "lying a-hull."

In great storms at sea, there are a few ways to try to save a ship from wrecking.

Taking in sail—because wind plus sail is power—is simply the most critical and obvious among them, though for a captain caught unawares it meant sending seamen up into icy rigging barefoot and gloveless. Any slip could be deadly.

You can throw an anchor off the stern to drag behind you in the water in an attempt to slow your drift and keep your bow toward the wind.

You can "heave-to," stopping the motion of the ship by counterbalancing the forces of wind so that it blows into your sails from forward and backward, to find calm in a tempest.

And, if things are really very, very bad, if you have no other choice and are at risk of perishing in the kind of fifty- or sixty-foot waves where you are quietly praying only for survival, you can choose to "lie a-hull," with your helm lashed to leeward and your hatches "battened," to ride the seas powerless and bare-masted. There is a saying among ocean sailors that a seaworthy vessel is almost always able to withstand more than her crew. Sometimes, you must trust her and ride out the storm with her.

With the helm hard to the lee of the wind, the ship will point into the wind or "windward," and that is what you want most now, because all that matters this night is not taking the sea too hard on your beam and making that terrible roll toward the water. A sailor in a great storm "a-hull" expects a knockdown: a partial roll, where the mast touches the sea, and the long, dreadful wait to see if the weight of the keel is enough to right her.

Mary Ann asked the watch boy: Had he made out the ensign or the inverted Stars and Stripes that signaled mayday on an American vessel? It would not be until 1859 that pyrotechnic signal flares would be patented and purchased by the US Navy from its inventor, another intrepid Boston woman, Martha Coston.

They squinted. Everything was wind and sleet. Mary Ann couldn't make out signal flags and the spyglass bounced about the horizon wildly, but her heart sank as she found them for a moment. The vessel was, indeed, a-hull and riding the current backward. They could only have been in dire straits, but there was no way in such heavy seas to attempt to help them. Two ships near each other in waves such as this would be a disaster. She hoped for them all for a long, silent moment. Then, *Neptune's Car* fell through space as the wave beneath them crested, the spyglass bounced, and she lost sight of the ship and the horizon.

The newspapers would later report that the hapless vessel had been the clipper ship *Rapid*, commanded by Captain Phineas Windsor. "Probably no ship that ever doubled Cape Horn ever had that kind of misfortune to an equal extent, in addition to the usual hardships, that the Rapid has had on this present voyage," Captain Windsor wrote in his logbook of that passage. They had been at sea since May, put in for expensive repairs in Brazil, where Captain Windsor's financial prospects had been ruined. Some of his crew had deserted. A good part of the rest of his crew had suffered through two bouts of deadly smallpox.

By the time Mary Ann spotted them in this maelstrom, Captain Windsor had already tried to take down sail in desperation. Up went one young, fresh seaman. He had lost his grip on the ice-covered ropes and fallen to his death on the decks below with a sickening cry. Up went another seaman. Another seaman was lost to the sea.

Ten times Captain Windsor sent up men. Ten of them perished. Getting down the sails that threatened to overwhelm them was a matter of life and death for them all, but it was a dreadful spectacle.

Captain Windsor had a crew of twenty-four. Ten were dead. Half a dozen lay, as one historian puts it, "absolutely helpless in the forecastle" from disease and seasickness. Hunched over the helm, his arm aching from the strain, his hair frozen stiff, as he remembered it, "like so many needles," with only six crew remaining, Captain Windsor turned just in time to watch a wave break over their bow and to see his much-loved young nephew, a cabin boy, swept away overboard into the waters.

Too shorthanded, too heartbroken to carry on westerly, Captain Windsor lashed the helm and wept. He then ordered his handful of remaining crew to turn the ship around and let the currents and the storm carry them back eastward toward Rio de Janeiro. Somewhere out there, in the mountainous waves of water, rushing backward that day through Drake's Passage, Captain Windsor spotted *Neptune's Car* and signaled. Mary Ann and her crew were powerless to help him.

There was no sight in Drake's Passage of the other ships, their competitors. But Captain Gardiner of the *Intrepid* and Captain Henry of the *Romance of the Seas* were out there somewhere in the maelstrom.

When night came again, they rose and then plummeted through the sea in darkness. At sea, in extremis, ships become eerily quiet. No one panics. No one speaks. There is this watch, this wave, this moment. But the crew, changing watch in the small hours of the morning, remembered later seeing Mary Ann below, through the window to the captain's quarters, hunched over by lamplight, bracing herself against the bolted table, checking and double-checking the pilot charts and the reckonings, her brow furrowed. Joshua was lashed into bed so he could not tumble.

**The tempest was** too strong.

Storm watch changed every thirty minutes. They had tried everything.

Mary Ann was wet and inexpressibly tired. A white line of salt came halfway up her skirts. She had not changed her clothes since September 1, nearly two weeks earlier, the day Joshua had slipped into his coma in heavy seas.

"How Mrs. Patten fought that ship" in that last day, one account notes, "is a story that has no parallel in fiction." Although Joshua was universally considered a fine captain, it was said that "few shipmasters then living could have excelled his wife, in seamanship or as a navigator," and neither Mary Ann nor her crew aboard *Neptune's Car* would never again experience anything like it. Hour after hour, one death-defying wave after another, living only to survive the next moment, they tried to battle forward.

There is that loose hierarchy of storm tactics at sea, depending on the particulars of conditions: reefing, heaving-to, lying a-hull like the *Rapid*. But there reaches a point where the wind and waves are too strong, where they will crush a ship or swamp it or break it upon the sea into pieces. In those moments, fighting the forces of the sea and the wind are futile.

At that point all that is left is to turn your helm and hope that, if you can find the correct angle, the rotating gyre of the storm will furiously expel you. Mariners still today are taught that, gripped in an offshore low-pressure cyclone, sometimes the only way to survive is to follow the curve of the wind out of the storm system and abandon any idea that you are in charge of where nature will take you.

How to know where to point your helm in a tempest? Scientists know the phenomenon today as the Coriolis effect, the result of inertia and how Earth's circular rotation spins the currents of air in one direction or another. Sharpshooters know that it's the reason to adjust their aim slightly off-target. Golf professionals adjust their long drives to account for it. We are on a spinning planet, always in motion.

Mary Ann, though, knew how a storm worked at sea simply from experience, and they had reached, she knew, the point where *Neptune's Car* would break to pieces.

She stood on deck with William Hare and remembered. If, in the southern hemisphere, you stand with your back to the wind and point your arm straight out to your right; there, where your finger points, is the center of the storm system, once the front has passed you. Storms in the southern hemisphere rotate clockwise around their center. Your goal now is to keep the wind not on your bow but behind you, pushing you. You are turning tail and running from the storm system.

That was now where Mary Ann decided they would have to let the weather take them. She ordered a position to the outside quadrant of the system. They would need to skirt the storm and try to come around the back side of it.

Running away from a westerly that is turning clockwise in Drake's Passage means letting a tempest carry you east and south: straight into the Southern Ocean.

**They were heading** toward polar regions. These were—and remain—among the world's most unfamiliar waters.

Antarctica, at its farthest end, long known on maps as "Terra Australis Incognita," or the "unknown land to the south," was only dimly known in 1856 even to sailors who traveled this maritime highway around the tip of South America. When Samuel Taylor Coleridge wrote *The Rime of the Ancient Mariner* in 1797, the southern polar regions still seemed fantastic.

It was the Dutch explorer Jacob Le Maire, who named Cape Horn in 1615 and, in time, lent his own name to the terrifying strait between Tierra del Fuego and Staten Island where Joshua had sunk to the deck delirious, who first discovered these frozen lands. It was not until the 1770s that Captain Cook aboard the *Resolution* traveled south of 66°30′, below that line where summer is endless sunlight and winter is perpetual darkness, or until 1819 that the British merchant sea captain William Smith first sighted land in the South Shetland Islands.

For the thirty-five years that followed, the continent was partially mapped by a handful of sealers, whalers, and British geographers. The first systematic charts of the region were published after

1842, when Lieutenant Charles Wilkes successfully returned to New York from a four-year expedition, but only with Ernest Shackleton's journey—more than sixty years later, in 1917—did Antarctic exploration capture the broader imagination.

**Mary Ann's tactic worked.** The storm hurtled them southeast, and Mary Ann could hope to slip south of the tempest and pick up the winds as they turned again westward.

When the waves came less relentlessly, she dared to sleep for just an hour. Watching Joshua breathing more easily, she might have dared to hope that his fever, like the storm, would break soon also. He was still desperately sick. But he could sip warm broth now sometimes and could open his eyes for a few moments.

When she awakened, the horizon was still dark. Dawn came late at the end of the Antarctic winter. The ship, she realized with a start, was no longer being catapulted from wave to wave. A strong, brisk breeze was blowing. She had slept in her dress for weeks, and she did not bother now with changing.

She came on deck in the gray half-light and greeted the crew on watch. Her crew. There might have been as many as two dozen of them all told on the passage. The ship's insurer would later write that Mary Ann had "exercised a proper control over a large number of seamen . . . by her own skill and energy, impressing them with a confidence and reliance making all subordinate and obedient to that command," and that was never truer than on this morning.

Her crew later would put it more simply: After what they had witnessed, they had only wanted to match the courage of Captain Mrs. Patten. Every man was doing his best now to win this race and bring them into San Francisco safely and to get Captain Patten to a doctor. Every man except Mr. Keeler, still fuming and plotting belowdecks in leg irons.

They might have had a few moments that morning to relish the relative calm on the other side of a mighty Drake's Passage hurricane, but, now that the skies had cleared, Mary Ann could take the first sextant sighting in days. They needed urgently to figure out their precise position. They had been blown southeast. God only knew how far or how quickly. They needed to make westerly.

Dead reckoning in the tempest had meant that Mary Ann, working at night over the flicker of the lantern, had been estimating their current position based on the knowledge of a last known position—their "fix"—and some complex guesswork to account for how many knots one had traveled and how much one had drifted through wind or currents.

One of the important tasks aboard a clipper, even in a storm such as they had just survived, was to try to capture information on their speed, precisely because knowing one's position when the blow passed was such a critically important factor. Speed was measured by throwing a weighted line off the stern of the ship and measuring by hourglass how many "knots" in the line were spooled out in thirty seconds. The space between the knots was measured out in equal fathoms, and on some nautical charts today depths are still measured out in those six-foot intervals.

*Neptune's Car*, like all clippers sailing around Cape Horn from East Coast ports like New York or Boston, passed through the Sargasso Sea and the waters around Bermuda on the route to South America, and you would not have needed to explain to anyone aboard ship what Shakespeare meant when he wrote in *The Tempest* of a great storm at sea and a shipwreck in the Sargasso:

> Full fathom five thy father lies:
> Of his bones are coral made;
> And those are pearls that were his eyes:

Nothing of him that doth fade,
But doth suffer a sea-change.

Every man aboard that ship had known someone lost as sea. They knew they were lucky to be alive this morning. They knew, too, how to count in fathoms.

Speed was just one factor in taking a calculation from dead reckoning. To try to formulate their current position, Mary Ann had also needed to try to account for drift: how far and how fast they had been pushed forward or backward or sideways by wind and ocean currents.

Mary Ann's best guess was that they were somewhere just a bit north of 60° S, a hundred or so miles to the northwest of Captain's Smith's South Shetland Islands, the volcanic archipelago standing as a last barrier between the tip of South America and the Antarctic mainland. Mary Ann was not only the first woman to captain a vessel in these waters. In 1856 she was still among a small number of clipper captains to travel this close to the continent of Antarctica. Captains did not do it willingly. Of the million or so people who have ever in human history ventured south of 65° S or stood on the continent of Antarctica, the vast majority of them have traveled there since the turn of our millennium.

Now that the sun was visible at last and the winds had calmed, Mary Ann could go on deck and take a noontime reading, and she would no longer need to guess. With her readings, she could pinpoint their location for the first time in more than a week of heavy weather and set them fresh on a new heading.

Instead came a cry of "Sail to port!" from the crow's nest. Had another ship outrun the storm and been blown so far off course with them? One of the young seamen had been sent aloft to keep a lookout on the horizon, and something white shimmered there. Mr. Hare would need to fall off to avoid striking their fellow vessel.

Then came the gasp of realization: It was not a sail but an iceberg.

On deck now it was chaos. Mary Ann called for all hands. Nimble young men, some rubbing sleep from their eyes, scrambled up the ropes. They would need to turn the ship into the wind to come to a standstill. Striking an iceberg would be fatal. One wrong move and *Neptune's Car* would be lost. They would sink into icy waters.

The sight of the iceberg was both fearsome and awesome.

Mary Ann knew from reading Lieutenant Maury that below 55° S they were among Cape Horn's many hazards. Occasionally mariners encountered icebergs as far north as 50° S as they drifted up from the continent, and, while the days were growing progressively longer, they were still more than three months away from the summer solstice in the southern hemisphere. At 60° S in winter, they were not unexpected so much as deeply unwelcome.

One captain's wife, who recorded the first appearance of an iceberg at sea off Cape Horn, wrote of sighting an iceberg the following season: "The magnificence of the scene far exceeds any language at my command. A portion of the first one appeared like a little gothic church with a huge something in the rear, which one might fancy a grave yard. As we approached nearer, it assumed a blueish appearance & as the foaming waves dashed over it, the scene was truly sublime." The blue is what anyone who has traveled in the Southern Ocean and sees those icebergs remembers.

One thinks of ice as white or colorless. It is not. That is perhaps the most shocking thing about icebergs. The ancient ice there is an almost an electric, neon blue. Seeing ancient ice for the first time, to put the experience in resolutely modern terms, is not unlike seeing Times Square at night as a novice, as incongruous as seems that metaphor. One does not think of these as nature's colors.

Those dazzling colors and their otherworldly beauty masked a terrible danger for sailing vessels.

In 1854, the Rockland-built clipper the *Red Jacket* had been trapped for four days in an ice field and had only narrowly avoided the fate that famously befell Ernest Shackleton and the crew of the *Endurance* many decades later. Also in the spring of 1854, the *Medway*, with passengers bound for Australia, was caught among ice floes as far north as 56°57' S, less than a hundred miles off Cape Horn and in the main sailing channel. "The dreadful apprehensions that assailed us yesterday, by the near approach of the iceberg, were this day most awfully verified," wrote one captain:

> About 3 P. M., the iceberg came in contact with our floe, and in less than one minute it broke the ice; we were frozen in quite close to the shore; the floe was shivered to pieces for several miles, causing an explosion like an earthquake, or one hundred pieces of heavy ordnance fired at the same moment. The iceberg, with awful but majestic grandeur (in height and dimensions resembling a vast mountain), came almost up to our stern, and everyone expected it would have run over the ship.

The crew now heard everywhere the cracks like gunshot: morning light on the ice fields. They floated on the current and waited. As the horizon grew more light it became clear that their problems were greater than they imagined. There were icebergs all around them.

**The logbook of** this journey aboard *Neptune's Car* has never been found, though Mary Ann is sure to have diligently kept one, so all that is known for certain is that for another three sleepless days, from September 10 to September 13, 1856, they crept their way slowly under an easy sail, taking constant soundings, past mountains of ancient blue crystal that were sometimes more than two hundred feet tall and stretching for a mile, through deep fogs that turned to ice on the riggings, in search of open water. At moments, beating their way carefully northwest, they skirted the edge of the ice fields, through slushy seas that might trap them. When Mary Ann closed her eyes for a moment on the bed beside Joshua, listening to his breathing, when she placed her hand now on her womb and hoped to soon feel her child's first "quickening," the familiar rocking of the clipper was her assurance that they still had sea room. To stop moving now was to stop breathing.

The ice fell away at last on September 14, and then they were back—with relief—in the heavy winds and roiling seas in Drake's Passage. But this time, the gale was nothing that *Neptune's Car* and her crew couldn't weather. Mary Ann ordered sails unfurled and a westerly heading. They were in a race, she reminded Mr. Hare with a grim smile. They had lost ground, and the currents were still against them. In heavy seas, they passed Cape Horn far offshore, and by September 18 they had finally "doubled" the Horn, passing back through 50° S on the west side of Chile, into calmer weather.

Now, Mary Ann's eyes were only on San Francisco—and, as fast as they could, a doctor for Joshua.

And their miraculous escape from polar waters had also brought something else wonderful. Joshua's fever had passed. A few days later, by the third week of September, Joshua was still too weak to stand, but from bed he could work the charts and resume command of the vessel from an armchair.

Joshua could see for the first time how exhausted Mary Ann was—and understood now for the first time that she had taken the ship around Cape Horn in an eighteen-day gale and put down a mutiny. It may have been now, too, that Mary Ann leaned over to whisper something to him. She had been keeping a happy secret.

Joshua was still too weak to whoop, but he could grin and kiss his wife even from an armchair.

**William Keeler, still** in leg irons, was contrite now that the captain was improving and looked likely to survive the voyage.

Keeler was in a bad spot. He had disobeyed the orders of his captain and attempted to stir up a mutiny. He was guilty of serious and repeated dereliction of duty and insubordination. Under maritime law, those were grievous offenses. And Keeler's problem was that Joshua could decide, more or less with impunity, what the consequences would be for this conduct and betrayal.

Ask an old merchant marine today, and none of them can believe that William Keeler wasn't keelhauled somewhere back in the North Atlantic. While historians believe keelhauling—the extreme form of punishment that sees an insubordinate mariner dragged along the bottom of a barnacle-encrusted ship in a public spectacle—was, like marooning, a rare occurrence in the nineteenth century, it looms large even today in the imagination of every merchant seaman.

Joshua, in fact, did not even flog Mr. Keeler, though that might have been expected. Flogging on deck with the leather flail known universally as a cat-o'-nine-tails was ubiquitous in the 1830s and 1840s and would have been the accepted minimal punishment for Mr. Keeler not even a decade earlier. In the early nineteenth century, the US military listed thirty different offenses for which flogging was appropriate, and those offenses included smuggling a little private flask of brandy aboard a ship contrary to a captain's instructions.

What complicated matters for Joshua was the fact that, on September 28, 1850, bowing to a decade of public outrage that had branded the practice as "degrading, barbaric, and despotic" on the part of a government against its citizens, the US Congress had banned flogging for enlisted mariners in the Navy—but not corporal punishment in general and not for the merchant service. This ambiguity put civilian sea captains in a quandary throughout the 1850s.

Joshua had been given command of *Neptune's Car* precisely because his predecessor had been too liberal with the lash; he wanted to be respected as a fair and decent captain. He had done everything he could to work with Keeler, but attempted mutiny was a bridge too far for even the most mild-mannered master. Keeler understood that, in San Francisco, there would be consequences.

Quitting was not an option for Keeler. In the "articles"—the voyage contract—Keeler and the rest of the crew had signed on for a circumnavigation. Nineteenth-century law did not permit a mariner to leave a ship mid-contract. No sea captain took onboard men to sail with him only as far as California. That captain would be left without crew to sail the ship any farther. The terms of Keeler's contract would not end until they returned to New York City. And, in fact, the captain's authority as the "master" was not entirely dissimilar to the plantation system. Merchant mariners who deserted ship, even in port, could be arrested and imprisoned. Even in port, the captain remained a sailor's master. Joshua could forbid Keeler shore leave or "liberty" when they arrived in San Francisco. He could keep Keeler in leg irons. Joshua *could* order Keeler flogged or place him on short rations. The merchant service was not the Navy.

American law followed British Common Law, and under the common law, "the master has authority over all the mariners on board the ship, and it is their duty to obey his commands in all lawful matters relating to the navigation of the ship and the preservation of good order." The Supreme Court of the United States found in 1849 that "In the discipline of the merchant service, where an act of disobedience is persisted in, and endangers the due subordination of others, the captain is justified, not only in punishing personally but in resorting to any reasonable measures necessary to produce submission."

Keeler, demoted to common seaman, was in for a long year or two ahead of him, and he approached Joshua now with humble entreaties and promises of good service. Joshua knew that he was still weak. He could see that Mary Ann was exhausted. Mr. Hare, despite his heroic service in those eighteen days around the Horn, still could not read or reckon, and the fact was that Joshua needed a first mate able to navigate until he was strong enough to be above deck himself. Joshua reluctantly reinstated William Keeler to his position as first officer and chose to believe his promises of reformation.

Mary Ann was silent. She had her doubts. She saw the look in Mr. Keeler's eyes. He was biding his time and waiting for vengeance. She was going to watch Mr. Keeler very carefully.

## 12

# The Long Way Round

From California to the New York island. From the redwood forest to the Gulf Stream waters.

—Woody Guthrie, "This Land Is Your Land"

For a time, with the gales of Cape Horn behind them, *Neptune's Car* sailed on smoothly, picking up light but steady winds that carried them northward into the South Pacific Ocean. Above, Keeler and Hare, on alternate watches, sent down readings from the sextant and the speed log and provided compass bearings and sail conditions. Below, propped up with pillows and wraps and gaining a little strength each day, Joshua charted their course and issued instructions to his officers, once again in command as captain.

Mary Ann was uneasy. Quietly, from the private confines of the quarterdeck and below when Joshua was resting, Mary Ann was double-checking Mr. Keeler. She tapped her pencil and looked again at the charts spread out in front of her. It was no good. By the end of September, just a week out from Cape Horn, she knew.

Keeler was not following Captain Patten's navigational headings. He was steering them off course.

They should have been staying offshore up the coast, making a beeline for the equator. Keeler, when he was at the helm, was adjusting the course and heading them straight toward Valparaíso, about sixty miles west-northwest of Santiago, Chile. He was sending down false readings for the logbook, so they would chart the wrong position, and it was only because Mary Ann was taking surreptitious double sextant readings that she knew for certain.

In 1856, Valparaíso was a cosmopolitan port city built into the terraced slopes of the surrounding hillsides, with sprawling docklands and wharves along its beachfront, and, until the opening of the Panama Canal in 1914, at the nexus of global trade. One nineteenth-century Englishwoman who visited there described it as a "long straggling place" in the shadow of the snowcapped Andes. Perhaps Keeler was trying still to throw the race for one of the other ship's owners and had been promised a payday. More likely, however, Keeler's motivation was simpler and more self-centered. He had every reason to want to jump ship and disappear in a foreign port to escape the maritime justice that would be waiting for him in California, and, between Cape Horn and San Francisco, Valparaíso was his best option.

Mary Ann knew what landing in Valparaíso would mean. They would be ruined financially. There would be a delay of months in getting Joshua home to rest and a doctor.

If Keeler took them into port by trickery, he would disappear into the crowded port. The rest of the crew would disappear, too, first to the public houses and brothels and then, tempted by higher wages, to the ships of other desperately shorthanded captains. There would be no inflated gold rush market for the goods they were transporting, only delays of months while Joshua waited for letters to travel back and forth from Valparaíso to New York for new instructions, and crippling port charges and duties and paperwork that would ensure that, even if they managed to carry on with a new crew to San Francisco, there would be no profits. The personal losses on their private cargo would be staggering.

Mary Ann was not going to bury her husband in Chile. She was going to get them both back to New England. She was going to get Joshua to a doctor.

When Mary Ann presented him with her suspicions, Joshua was aghast. The first mate was trying to ruin them, and this was tantamount to a second mutiny. He was mending but was still too weak to spend more than short period of time on deck at the change of watch without returning to his quarters exhausted. There was no way he could stand watch at the helm with Keeler to monitor what he was doing. And, as he explained to his impatient and furious wife, whose mood was not improved by being at sea and pregnant, without absolute evidence of Keeler's duplicity, maritime law did not allow him to sack for a second time his first officer.

They would need, Joshua said slowly, to catch Mr. Keeler in the act. Mary Ann nodded. She was already thinking about how she could make that happen. If she could arrange for Joshua to see the heading for himself when Keeler was at the helm, would that be enough to confirm that the first mate was countermanding the captain's directional orders? Joshua agreed. That would be more than sufficient.

Waiting until the starboard watch, when Keeler and his men were off duty in rotation, she sent the steward up on deck to position the "tell-tale"—a little strip of light fabric or string that fluttered in the winds and signaled their relative direction—near the raised window of the captain's quarters. Below, hauling furniture into position and propping Joshua up on a mountain of pillows, she found the line of sight that would allow him to see the headings unseen and while resting.

The confirmation was immediate and so were Joshua's instructions. Keeler was ordered back down into the brig, back into leg irons, and Captain Patten would not be offering him any third chances.

The problem, though, was the same as in the Atlantic. Down a first mate, the captain would have to stand his watch, and Joshua's health, though improving, was precarious. Joshua insisted on remaining on the quarterdeck during the starboard watch, because, as captain, it was his responsibility. Second mate Hare still could not read or navigate, so Joshua would also need to be awakened during his watches to make decisions. He needed to show his crew that their captain was well enough to command, even if all the men knew that it was the captain's wife who was holding the pieces together in the chart room.

For a few weeks, Joshua staggered on, but Mary Ann saw that the fevers were returning. At night, in snatches of sleep, Joshua moaned and coughed, tangled in wet and sweaty sheets. By the time they crossed the equator on October 17 at 115° W, he was suffering again from the blinding headaches and the returned brain fever. Three days later, on October 20, in light northeasterly winds that were carrying them toward the northern tip of Mexico's Baja Peninsula, Joshua collapsed on deck for the second time. This time, the fever affected his optic nerve, rendering him blind as well as delirious.

The crew did not need to consider who would take command of the ship. They turned immediately to Captain Mrs. Patten, who had already earned the loyalty and respect that would take them the rest of the way to San Francisco. "The men manifested their sympathy by the greatest alacrity in obeying her orders," as *The New York Times* later put it.

And they flew up the coast of California in strong northwesterly winds. The only race that mattered now was the race to get Joshua to a doctor. She could not know that Captain Henry was already mere days out of San Francisco, not quite two weeks ahead of them.

But Mary Ann and the crew of *Neptune's Car* also could not know that they were ahead of all their other competitors.

**On the approach** to San Francisco, the wind disappeared.

For ten maddening days they were becalmed in the Pacific, fewer than a hundred miles off the continent. The crew searched for any puff of wind that would let them make headway.

Belowdecks and in the captain's quarters, Joshua's fever would not break, and, still blind and delirious, he slipped in and out of consciousness. Only now, with no winds to carry them anywhere and helpless to do anything else, did Mary Ann change her dress for the first time.

She had worn the same gown, day in and day out, since they left the Straits of Lemaire on September 1 and slammed into the winds of Drake's Passage in part simply because it was her loosest day gown, the everyday workwear of a fashionable woman of the 1850s. Mary Ann was six months pregnant by the time they arrived off the coast of California, and, until she had the time to unpick the pleats and tucks of another gown and loosen the bodice, there was nothing for her to change into.

Now, sitting next to Joshua's bedside, she picked up for the first time her sewing needle and painstakingly made the alterations. A captain's wife had a role to play in any port or harbor, and coming into San Francisco, especially in such extraordinary circumstances, Mary Ann intended to be dressed for it. She already knew that she would need to explain herself to the port authorities and underwriters.

Toward the end of the second week of November, a breeze sprang up at last, and *Neptune's Car* sailed the last several dozen miles to the

Golden Gate headlands. On November 14, they made it past the Farallon Islands, where Mr. Hare signalled to the harbormaster the incoming arrival of a great clipper, and then ran up the ensigns. On the slack tide just after noon on November 15, 1856, with Mr. Hare at the helm as first mate and Mary Ann in command as master, the 216-foot extreme clipper was brought into the harbor.

**Before** *Neptune's Car* came to rest, there was a splash and mighty commotion at midship.

The thuggish third mate, George Kingsley, though wise enough not to challenge the captain or the captain's wife at sea, had nevertheless conspired to release his friend William Keeler from the brig. Knowing that arrest and rough frontier justice awaited him on shore for actions at sea that had placed all their lives and hundreds of thousands of dollars of cargo in peril, Keeler had literally "jumped ship" and fled on one of the numerous small boats that came alongside arriving clippers to entice arriving seamen to their saloons, boardinghouses, and brothels.

The rest of the crew—with the exception of George Kingsley, now making a great show of being as surprised as anyone—looked on in disgust. The captain was desperately ill, probably even now dying, and, throughout their shared ordeal, the men had developed a deep admiration and sense of protectiveness toward Mary Ann. She had been a fine captain. She had taken them safely to port and accomplished what everyone from the youngest seamen to the saltiest graybeards among them recognized was good seamanship. At work, as they passed near the skylights that illuminated the captain's wood-paneled quarters, they had all seen her working late into the night, bent over the charts or studying the bottles in the medicine chest to care for her husband. No one doubted that Captain Patten was alive because of their own Florence Nightingale.

She was a slip of a girl, who, anyone could see, was deeply in love with her husband, and who, out of devotion and loyalty to him, had shown immense courage and strength of purpose. Every seaman aboard wished for a wife like Captain Mrs. Patten. She was, they told any reporter later who would listen, "a wife worth having." To a modern ear, that encomium may not sound sufficiently enlightened. In 1857, it was the highest praise to which a woman like Mary Ann could possibly aspire, and it was part of how everyone in the mid-nineteenth century understood and interpreted the story of her leadership and courage. The past, as they say, is also foreign country.

**They had passed** through the Golden Gate headlands and into San Francisco Harbor 137 days out of Sandy Hook, a long and hard voyage, and were brought to a wharf off Rincon Point, at Folsom Street, near what is today the Mission District. There, Mary Ann passed command to Mr. Hare, asking him to make *Neptune's Car* secure for unloading.

In the days that followed, there would be business to tend to and letters to write. She told Mr. Hare she would return to discuss them as soon as possible. She would need to write to New York City and ask the ship's owners at Foster & Nickerson on what terms the cargo should be sold and whether Mr. Hare could be deputized as master. Until she received instructions, back on dry land neither William Hare nor Mary Ann had the authority to dispose of the cargo. She would need to ask about finances and letters of credit. She would need to think about how to pay the doctor.

*Neptune's Car* would wait nearly two months before she was unloaded. Even selling their own personal cargo would be a challenge for Mary Ann. The law in the state of Maine had permitted a married woman to enter into contracts and dispose of property as a "sole trader" since only 1844. Since 1821 and 1835, respectively, Maine and Massachusetts had carved out narrow exceptions for instances in which a husband was incapacitated. But no law granting a legal right to married women over property was passed in California until 1872. Until then on the frontier it was all a gray area.

She would need to reckon with all this. But, first, she needed to get Joshua into bed and find a physician who could help them.

As *Neptune's Car* was secured and the gangway lowered, the solemn procession began. Four seamen gingerly lowered an unconscious Captain Patten down to the wharf. The crew gathered to stand at silent attention and watched as Mary Ann followed behind her husband's cot, dressed in her best gown, and, one likes to think, wearing those gold-and-coral earrings she cherished. She carried a small satchel of their most valuable possessions, all the money they had onboard, and the ship's papers.

Although a horse-drawn wagon stood ready, the planked streets of San Francisco were rough, and the captain could not be jostled. The men insisted they would carry Captain Patten up the lane to one of the city's dozens of boardinghouses. On the busy afternoon streets, strangers stood aside and stopped as they passed, and some of them must have noted that the drawn, pale young woman following behind the stretcher was visibly pregnant.

Once Mary Ann and the captain were out of sight and earshot, the silence was broken with a dozen questions from all directions. By evening, the story of what had taken place on *Neptune's Car*—how the captain's girl of a wife had taken the command and brought them safely around Cape Horn and through icebergs in an eighteen-day howler—was known up and down the waterfront.

Joshua's stepbrother, Lemuel Bailey, is listed in the San Francisco directory for 1856 as keeping rooms at the Rassette House, "a first-class hotel, well-known in the city," and, though there is no known record to confirm that Lemuel stepped in to help Mary Ann and Joshua, that now seems likely. The Rassette House Hotel was a couple of thousand feet from the docks off Folsom Street and stood opposite to Dr. Cooper's Eye, Ear and Orthopaidic Infirmary for the treatment of the blind.

Someone who was a fellow Mason quickly alerted the local lodge to a brother in trouble, and the San Francisco Masons arranged for one of their members, Dr. Harris, to see Joshua and assess his coma. This Dr. Harris may have been the well-known pioneer physician Dr. Stephen Harris, whose offices were on the southeast corner of Clay and Dupont Streets and who boarded at the Oriental Hotel.

Joshua lay propped on crisp, white sheets, but the room was dark and the heavy drapes had been drawn in the sickroom. Mary Ann leaned quietly against the wainscoting while Dr. Harris examined Joshua. She had been at sea four and a half months, and it would be a day or two before the world seemed to stop rocking.

Dr. Harris's news when he turned was not reassuring. Joshua was suffering from meningitis, brought on by advanced tuberculosis. There was no cure for tuberculosis: The disease is bacterial, and antibiotics would not exist until the twentieth century. It is because of diseases like this that physicians today are so perturbed by the specter of antibiotic resistance.

Some with tuberculosis survived. Most did not. Her father, George, had lingered with the illness for several years already.

Whether one lived or died depended largely on the fortitude of one's constitution, the climate, and "rest cures." The prognosis, though, was poor once the infection moved to the brain. Joshua's blindness and the seizures would be permanent. He was twenty-nine years old, at the peak of his profession, and Joshua would never command another clipper, whatever else happened. There were no blind sea captains.

It was the end of their dreams, and Mary Ann could hardly bear the blow. But Dr. Harris told her things might be worse than this, even. He couldn't tell yet whether Joshua had suffered massive brain damage.

**Mary Ann's only** goal that autumn was to save what she could and to get them back to Boston and her mother's help as soon as she could manage. Perhaps if Joshua could rest, he would somehow still recover. It was not impossible.

Mary Ann's letters home to her family have not survived, but they must have been heartbreaking. All we know is that her older, devoted brother, George, and Joshua's dearest friend, a young fellow sea captain named Judah Berry, living in New York City in the 1850s, promised that the day she landed, they would be there at the dock to meet her.

Unraveling the business concerns and trying to secure their own financial future with Joshua incapacitated was a harrowing and tiresome business. The ship's owners in New York would have to be reached to give instructions, and the mail took weeks in each direction. Forty days was average, and they came by steamer and rail over the isthmus at Panama. There was no telegraph yet. That would not connect San Francisco and New York City until 1861, and, even then, one of the stages would be by Pony Express. The railway in Panama had only existed since 1855—a year earlier.

By early December, determined to unload the cargo, the ship's brokers in the city appointed William Hare to take temporary command of *Neptune's Car*. Hare, however, could still not read or navigate, and there would have to be a different solution before there could be any onward voyage. The brokers could not make any decision about the captain's salary. That was a matter for the ship's owners in Manhattan. Their personal capital was held by Foster & Nickerson, too, and the owners would need to be persuaded to release it to anyone other than the captain. Until there was some solution, Mary Ann was without ready financial resources. Either Lemuel Bailey or the San Francisco Masonic lodge paid for the hotel bills and their return ticket.

By spring, the issue of Captain Patten's missing salary payment would set off an international public relations disaster for the ship's owners, because, though no one in San Francisco could yet know it, by late December 1856, the story of Mary Ann's voyage was already being reported breathlessly in the newspapers.

**It had started** on the docks on Folsom Street the day that Joshua had been carried by his seamen through the commercial district. News of Mary Ann's great maritime skill and Captain Patten's desperate illness spread throughout San Francisco, and curious onlookers went to the waterfront to view *Neptune's Car* for themselves and to marvel at the feat. Because it was an astonishing feat. There is a reason that even today, some 170-odd years later, the United States Merchant Marine Academy still teaches its young cadets the story of nineteen-year-old Mary Ann Patten taking *Neptune's Car* around Cape Horn and has named its campus medical building the Patten Health Care Clinic in her honor—though one confesses to wishing for a great sailing ship or a mighty destroyer.

For the onlookers in San Francisco in 1856, for whom disasters at sea were a fact of life, it wasn't just that *Neptune's Car* had survived her voyage around the bottom of the world in a terrible storm either. Mary Ann had brought the clipper into port looking neat and, in all respects, "shipshape." She had not come in with a ragtag crew or the vessel looking the worse for wear. That would have been a sign to anyone who knew merchant sailing—and everyone in San Francisco did—that morale had been low or her command had been sloppy. Maintaining a great wooden ship requires constant, daily maintenance by many hands. "Those who saw her enter the harbor," the newspapers reported, "say no vessel ever came into that port looking better in every respect."

That *Neptune's Car* had arrived gleaming and polished told the whole silent story: Here was a vessel brought into port by a commander whose crew had worked diligently and cooperatively. It was the sign of a highly effective captain, one who had earned the respect of a crew and had acted as a disciplined master. Captains were universally referred to in the forecastle as "the old man," irrespective of age. It was a testament to the great affection that Mary Ann's crew had for her as their captain—not a dismissal or a disparagement—that they called her "the little woman."

From Folsom Street and San Francisco, the news quickly traveled south and then east, as fast as the mail boats themselves. Word first arrived in the form of private letters written by merchants and bankers giving report of happenings in San Francisco. Reports of Mary Ann's heroism reached New York City toward the end of December. *The New-York Daily Tribune* applauded itself for having "published [at that time] the only account of this remarkable instance of female fortitude which had been given, in an extract from a commercial letter to the owners in this city."

Because many of these letter writers were relying on word-of-mouth information and hearsay on the docks and in the hotels, the details as the story grew tended toward the romantic and melodramatic. One newspaper turned Mary Ann into a "delicate blonde [with] soft blue eyes." Yet, in the daguerreotype of Mary Ann taken in 1857, it is clearly a woman with ebony hair and dark eyes who looks out at us. This same eager reporter was the first to circulate the mistaken story that "Mrs. Patten was born . . . of wealthy parents."

Other reports made out that, under her command, the passage of *Neptune's Car* was faster and more impressive than the facts strictly warranted, to make a more gripping story. About the general facts, however, all agreed: Mrs. Patten was a heroine and was likely soon to be, as well, a young widow. As one letter writer in early 1857 explained to a correspondent, "The matter has excited a good deal of interest here, and, independent of other considerations, all are anxious, for her sake, that the Captain should recover."

Mary Ann, however, would not have any inkling of her celebrity until she was en route back to New York City.

## 13

# The Iron Embrace of the Isthmus

*We rovers bold,*
*To the land of Gold,*
*Over the bowling billows are gliding:*
*Eager to toil,*
*For the golden spoil,*
*And every hardship biding.*

—Herman Melville, "Gold"

The journey ahead of them was full of dangers, even if Joshua had been healthy. And he manifestly wasn't.

By mid-December, *Neptune's Car* was being unloaded and her cargo dispersed to merchants in the city, and Mary Ann couldn't wait any longer in San Francisco with Joshua faring so poorly. He needed specialist care and months—perhaps years—of recuperation, and the best place for them was Boston, with her parents, and then their little house in Rockland. Mary Ann already knew there would never be a farm on the Weskeag. But Mary Ann was also now seven months pregnant. Traveling with a newborn across Central America would be dangerous, perhaps fatal, and she also wanted to be back in Boston before the baby's arrival.

There were only two ways to travel east in 1857, over land or by sea, and Joshua could not have survived the rigors of horseback or stagecoach. The alternative was the steamer mail "packet" that departed twice a month from San Francisco to Panama City, Panama. From there, Mary Ann would need to travel overland across Panama, before connecting on the other side with another steamer bound for New York. The first tickets she could arrange were for the steamer on January 5, 1857.

A doctor would need to travel with Joshua if he were to have any hope of surviving the journey. A "respectable" middle-class woman in the 1850s—and a captain's wife was squarely in that category—did not undertake that kind of voyage solo either. Even walking the streets of San Francisco alone during those six weeks in California had been an intimidating experience.

In 1849, the ratio of men to women in San Francisco had been fifty to one, and nearly all of the women were what was known as "the fairer sex in full bloom," a euphemism for prostitution. By the winter of 1856, when Mary Ann arrived, the ladies of "polite society" in the city—those not "in full bloom"—numbered in the hundreds but not in the thousands, and the distinction was not always recognized immediately. Even walking unaccompanied the handful of blocks to a Ladies' Ordinaire, a women-only tearoom, exposed her to leers and propositions. She certainly would not have been able to have dined in the hotel's restaurant unaccompanied.

Mary Ann passed a lonely and quiet Christmas, waiting for the steamer. From the hotel window, she watched as a rare snow dusted the city and the streets filled with children throwing snowballs in excitement. The winter of 1856 was exceptionally cold in California, and, on December 30, San Francisco was blanketed with snow, an event so unusual that *The Daily Alta California* newspaper reported that "The oldest inhabitant was about the streets yesterday, freely expressing his opinion that he had never seen such a day before in San Francisco." She could see the carriages pass on their way to winter entertainments as the lanterns lit up the streets in the evenings. When the thick drapes fell away from her hand, Mary Ann turned back toward Joshua's sickbed.

**Finally, the day** of their departure arrived. On the morning of January 5, the streets wet and clear, Dr. Harris arrived early, but San Francisco was already buzzing with excitement. The doctor, one of Joshua's fellow brother Masons, would make the journey home with them.

"Steamer days" in San Francisco were the 5th and the 20th of each month, and the arrival and departures of the steamers were an occasion. Crowds gathered at the docks to be the first to read the New York papers and to be reunited with family who had traveled thousands of miles to join them. Bills were due on steamer day, and letters were delivered to the mailbags. Gold dust was weighed and consigned onboard, for transport back to the banks on the East Coast.

A carriage waited on the street to transport Joshua, blind and frail, to the Vallejo Street wharf where the steamer was loading. Getting Joshua aboard was a slow and careful business.

Mary Ann and Joshua would be traveling out on the SS *Sonora*, a wooden sidewheel steamer, her immense paddles—thirty feet or more in diameter—fueled with coal-fired boilers belowdecks. These black-hulled steamships, burdened with heavy mechanical engines and loaded with a hold of coal to feed the fires, were notoriously unstable in heavy weather. They carried upward of five hundred passengers and their baggage. Boiler breakdowns were common. So were shipwrecks.

Lemuel Bailey may also have traveled home on the steamer with them. There are no records to show that he accompanied Mary Ann and his stepbrother home, but he was family and a fellow Mason, and he disappeared from San Francisco sometime in early 1857. According to the directory of residents, Lemuel was living in the city in 1856. He is not listed as a resident in 1857. He was unquestionably back in Maine with his wife and children by 1859, because he died that year in Rockland and was buried in the Patten family plot. It is difficult to imagine that Lemuel's departure that year did not coincide with Joshua's crisis.

The steamer left the docks at 9:00 A.M. sharp, and they had left the hotel just as the sun was rising. There was the bustle and the waiting until their tickets were taken and the stewards led Mary Ann to their stateroom, with Joshua helped aboard under the watchful eye of Dr. Harris. There was no way Joshua would survive the trip in steerage, and reserving a stateroom passage had added to Mary Ann's expenses and worries.

The cabin-class steamer ticket from San Francisco to Panama City and then on again, after a journey overland in Panama, from Colón to New York City could run anywhere from $250 to $300 per person, and they would need another $25 per person for the train ticket to take them across the isthmus from Pacific to Atlantic. Mary Ann would have to account for hotel costs during delays between arrivals and departures. It might cost as much as $1,000 for them to return to New York, money that Mary Ann did not have on hand. All their money—not just Joshua's outstanding salary—was tied up in the account books with Foster & Nickerson, including their personal capital. When the books were settled in New York, their finances would be less desperate. But, until the settlement, Mary Ann was working on a tight budget and relying on the kindness of friends and family.

The *Sonora* was operated as part of the Pacific Mail fleet, and, even for the hundred or so passengers booked in the first-class cabins, it was not a luxurious experience, though the first- and second-class passengers had roomy staterooms and access to reasonably private bathroom facilities. Those who traveled in steerage slept crammed into canvas bunks, from floor to ceiling, in single-gender dormitories that were airless, hot, and crowded.

No matter the class, the meals onboard were famously unpalatable, the bedsheets were often unclean, and the staff were generally unenthusiastic, unsurprisingly, especially when it came to cleaning up after nearly constant seasickness on a rough voyage. One irate passenger recorded in his diary: "The passengers were fed like hogs. . . . Some of the hard bread was of good quality, some moldy, and much of it was infested with black bugs. . . . If the bread was bad, the pork was worse." Cholera and malaria were common, though Mary Ann and Joshua were traveling in the winter season, when the diseases were not so virulent. Joshua would not survive an additional infection, and many travelers returning east went with a group of trusted friends, often accompanied by a doctor, in hopes that they would survive any illness on the long voyage.

Joshua's chances of surviving the next forty days of travel were not great, though by the time they departed San Francisco, Mary Ann at least dared to hope. He was conscious and calmer now than he'd been since summer. He was both blind and mostly deaf as a result of the brain infection, but he smiled when Mary Ann stroked his hand and talked about their baby. It cheered her to think that the seizures came less often.

**Mary Ann, having** taken a clipper around Cape Horn in a gale, did not suffer from the seasickness in those first days of the voyage that left many of the passengers retching over the rails or vomiting into buckets. She had to acknowledge, though, that a mail steamer on the open Pacific was not the most comfortable sailing she had ever experienced, especially when one was now quite heavily pregnant. She could not let out her dresses much further; by all rights she should have been at home, with her feet up, in "confinement," waiting for her baby's arrival.

Their first stop would be about a week out of San Francisco, when they would reprovision in what was then still the small coastal village of Acapulco, some 1,500 miles south of San Francisco. In 1857, the village was an important military fortress and staging post, and the *Sonora* anchored in a crescent bay of sandy beaches, with straw-roofed huts and some whitewashed stucco buildings rising up to the coastal mountains. Acapulco was also a raucous frontier town for the two or three days when the steamer was in port. Young men frequently went ashore for betting, drinking, cockfights, and "senorettas"; there was nothing onshore Mary Ann needed.

They set out again, and, four or five days later, the steamer arrived in Panama City, an American colonial outpost, which one traveler in that decade described as "dingy and antiquated, [its] dilapidated walls crumbling into the sea, somber-looking rows of houses with red-tiled roofs, numerous old churches, the tall towers of the Cathedral, whose lofty spires glisten in the sun with a coating of pearl-oyster shells."

They again anchored in the bay, now sometime in the third week of January, and this time they would have to disembark for the overland voyage. Passengers and baggage were ferried to shore by canoe at the cost of $2. Those who wanted to be lifted from the canoe and deposited on dry land to save wet shoes and damp petticoats (or stretchers) could hire a local for an extra charge of fifty cents, and Dr. Harris paid another dollar each for a hand truck to carry them into the city.

The American government controlled the port and the fortress; the local Panamanian population was largely impoverished and resentful. Panama City had a dangerous reputation, and everyone in San Francisco knew the stories long before departure.

The previous spring, tourists had been murdered while more than a thousand of them were milling around one of the barrios waiting for transportation onward. On the evening of April 15, 1856, local Panamanian grievances had erupted over the refusal of an intoxicated tourist to pay for some (allegedly rotten) watermelon from a street vendor. The vendor demanded payment. The tourist retorted "kiss my ass," and, pulling a gun, intimated that this was how he planned on making payment. The watermelon vendor pulled a knife. A bystander paid for the watermelon hoping to resolve the altercation. By then, matters had already escalated among the onlookers. Another bystander reached for the tourist's gun, tackling him, and in the tussle the gun went off into the crowd of locals. Some of the American men attempted to retrieve the pistol and began chasing the gun-toting bystander, at which point, as one witness put it, "the row then became general."

Several hundred working-class local men and women, angry about the arrival of the railway, the lost jobs for the mule drivers who previously had transported passengers and baggage, the high rates of unemployment, the Americans' preference for Jamaican immigrant servants, the rampant land speculation driving them out of their homes, the drunken tourists bringing cholera and yellow fever, the lack of direct economic benefit to the inhabitants, and the complicity of wealthy Panamanians in all this commercial exploitation rioted, yelling as they went, "Carajo Americano!"—*damned American.*

All this could have been foreseen. When the San Francisco newspaper *The Daily Alta California* reported on what came next, the reporter noted:

> The Panama Company did not seem to reflect that, previous to the location of the [rail]road, thousands had crossed on foot and by conveyance provided by natives, and that no

disturbances occurred. They did not consider why this was so, and how they might preserve the existence of a kindly feeling between the population and the Americans in transit. . . . at Panama passengers are hurried into the cars and boats with scarce an opportunity of procuring a drink of water. The natives see through the aggrandizing scheme, and have long been nursing a black idea of being avenged, and the massacre of the 15th of April was its first general expression.

Sometimes, there were as many as two thousand travelers waiting for steamer tickets to San Francisco, and the mob next went into two of the hotels, the Pacific and the Ocean, where scores of women and children were waiting while their "menfolk" arranged tickets. The vigilantes murdered the waiting travelers indiscriminately, stoning them, beating them to death, and even beheading small children. Terrified tourists fled to the railway station, where the mob and now the local police followed them. The police, coming under fire from the panicked tourists, joined the mob, killing more huddled civilians and destroying railway infrastructure.

By the time the riot ended the following morning, put down by the arrival of armed railway employees under the command of a former Texas Ranger known as Randall "The Hangman" Runnels, fifteen tourists and two Panamanians were dead, and more than four dozen Americans had been maimed or wounded. The incident sparked a major diplomatic crisis and outrage in the East Coast papers when word reached New York by the outbound steamer. The US government responded by invoking an article in an 1846 treaty that permitted them to occupy the isthmus, and the event hastened plans to complete a canal in Panama so passengers and trade could pass between oceans without having to engage in direct contact or trade with the local population.

Mary Ann and Joshua and everyone aboard the *Sonora* were walking into a tinderbox, and all anyone who arrived in transit wanted was to get out of Panama City as fast as possible.

Mary Ann was resigned. They would need to spend one overnight in one of the expensive and shoddy tourist hotels, where guests were jammed onto canvas cots dormitory style. The locals smoked cigars outside the windows, and returning gold diggers swaggered off to get drunk and visit the numerous brothels. There was a long wait while their trunks were unloaded, and then another long wait for the railway tickets they would need to travel onward.

Panama City was not, however, the most dangerous or exhausting part of the journey. They would next need to cross the mountains that divided the Atlantic from the Pacific and make their way through forty-seven miles of jungle.

**In late January 1857,** Mary Ann, Joshua, Dr. Harris, and Lemuel, if he was indeed with their party, were among the first generation of voyagers to cross the isthmus by train.

The Panama Railroad made its first journey two years earlier, in January 1855, the result of a private enterprise that exceeded all cost estimates, including the cost in human lives to complete construction. It was celebrated back in New York as a feat of industry and engineering: "American enterprise has stretched its iron arms across the hitherto impenetrable Isthmus of Darien, which bring together in one embrace the Atlantic and Pacific," wrote one traveler the year it opened.

Before 1855, the journey had taken days and required travel by mules over the mountains. Now, they could cross in two and a half hours, enjoying cane-bottomed seats for a scenic trip past mountain peaks, jungles with tropical birds, mangrove swamps, and bamboo hut villages.

The trouble was that the railroad was hastily built and hotly contested. Matthew Maury had foreseen as long ago as 1849 that the effect of building a railroad across Panama would be to make uniting the two oceans by a canal inevitable. "The railroad would soon be found insufficient," he observed, "and a ship canal would be the result." For a temporary solution, hundreds of lives would be laid down in the construction.

Dozens more lives would be laid down because that construction was done poorly. In the spring of 1856, a year after its opening, with more than five hundred passengers aboard, the train had jumped the tracks as it approached a curve coming down a hillside, resulting in a gruesome wreck and "monster accident" that left forty-three passengers dead and hundreds maimed. This—added to the unrest of the riots, the industrial action, the disease in the jungle, the furious local population—meant that calls for another route, a canal through Panama, were growing, just as Matthew Maury had predicted. "Another route is demanded now more than ever. . . . to save the future passengers by the Panama route from massacre and slaughter" wrote the editors of the San Francisco daily paper.

As they took that last turn, passengers' knuckles whitened. The jungle had swallowed up all evidence of the wreck the year before, and they made the turn safely. The sigh was general. The last seven miles of the journey sped them through marshland, until the train rolled into the little station in the town of Aspinwall, then named after the American industrialist and de facto military commander of this transportation hub outpost and today known as Colón. The "Company . . . has power of life and death on the isthmus without appeal," was the frank assessment of Robert Tomes, who made the voyage in 1855.

When they arrived, Mary Ann saw at once that all the warnings, here, too, had been sadly accurate.

**Aspinwall was a** miserable port town, and Mary Ann paid outrageous prices everywhere she turned. The entire population—described derisively and, to a modern ear, somewhat shockingly by Robert Tomes as an international mix of "Half-naked negroes, turbaned Coolies, and pale, livid white men, in Panama hats and linen jackets"—was dedicated to defrauding powerless travelers of as much money as possible. When Ulysses S. Grant visited Aspinwall in 1852, his wry comment was to wonder "how any person could live many months in Aspinwall, and wonde[r] still more why any one tried."

Aspinwall was the worst kind of tourist trap, in every way seedy and insalubrious, and tropical diseases and fevers plagued the city. All anyone wanted on arriving in Aspinwall was to leave as quickly as possible, and Mary Ann was no exception.

She was afraid that she might be trapped for weeks. Joshua's health had taken a sudden and deadly turn in Central America. The trip from San Francisco to Aspinwall had been too much for him. For a week his life hung in the balance. As the weather warmed and grew more humid, the tuberculosis festered, and Dr. Harris was increasingly pessimistic.

But Dr. Harris was eyeing Mary Ann as well with growing concern now. She was showing signs of fever, which he thought was probably malaria. He needed to get both his patients out of Panama as fast as possible.

It took Dr. Harris a week to secure staterooms. Finally, they arranged tickets aboard the immense oceangoing steamer the *George Law*, with a scheduled departure of February 5, and on the day of embarkation some local young men carried Joshua by litter from the hotel to the ferry. Mary Ann, still feverish, was able to stagger aboard, exhausted. The *George Law*, anchored out in deeper waters, bellowed out a black banner of smoke and waited to receive as many as 650 passengers and their cumbersome trunks and satchels destined for Manhattan. In the stateroom cabins were "returning Californian bankers, merchants, and tradesmen . . . Aged matrons, youthful expectant mothers," such as Mary Ann. She was, by now, eight months pregnant and weak from malaria.

Loading a delirious, deaf, blind, and half-conscious Joshua onboard the steamer was harrowing. Small harbor boats ferried passengers out to the steamer, where a staircase attached to the side of the vessel rose and fell with the swells. The *George Law* was more than 270 feet long, and 40 feet wide, with two immense red side-paddle wheels and a copper-sheathed wooden hull that sparkled in the sunlight. Behind the front mast was the wheelhouse, from which Captain William Lewis Herndon gave his orders. Passenger accommodations were on the second and third decks; the upper decks were lined with wooden benches where passengers could get fresh air or handle more delicately the effects of seasickness.

An African man named Dick came forward to introduce himself as the chief steward and asked Mary Ann if she needed anything. Dr. Harris continued to press her to take quinine tonic until they were sure she was recovered. Aboard the *George Law*, in the first-class cabins, that tonic came with a "refreshing plateful of crystal ice, fresh from Rockland by the last steamer." Maine and the banks of the Weskeag River must have seemed like a dream she'd once had in some tropical fever.

**In addition to** hundreds of passengers, the *George Law* on each trip also carried gold—huge amounts of gold—being transported from California back to Wall Street. The amount of treasure onboard ranged from a low of $800,000 to a high of nearly $2 million of bullion in 1857 values. Today, that cargo would be worth as much as $70 million. In fact, the *George Law* would carry from 1853 to 1857 a full third of all the gold transported back from California. It carried the "species" earned by Foster & Nickerson from San Francisco back to Manhattan.

When the *George Law* had departed Aspinwall on December 4, 1856, the month before Mary Ann's passage, aboard had been $10,000 in gold and silver, commissioned by Foster & Nickerson, much of it presumably the sale of the cargo from *Neptune's Car* in November.

Before the year was out, *George Law* and the gold she carried would change the course of history and the course of Mary Ann's life, though Mary Ann that winter could not yet know it.

**The next nine** days at sea aboard the *George Law* were terrible. As they passed the southern coast of the United States, Joshua slipped back into unconsciousness. Mary Ann's headaches were crushing. Sandy Hook came into view on February 14, 1857.

They had come full circle, around the world, fourteen months after they had departed, back to New York City, but this time everything was different, and their future was in ruins. This trip had been meant to secure their financial future and to let them return to Maine to build the home of which Joshua had dreamed. Instead, *Neptune's Car* remained in San Francisco, without her captain, and they were returning cash-strapped and dependent. They slipped through the lower bay and the Narrows. Looking out toward Governor's Island, ahead of Mary Ann were the old lazar houses and quarantine barracks, and then the spire of Trinity Church and the masts of dozens of ships on the wharfs off South Port.

They would come in on the Hudson River side of Manhattan, docking off Warren Street, a few blocks from what would become the site of the World Trade Center and is now the memorial to September 11. Mary Ann did not have the money to pay for even a hotel when they landed. The Masons, thanks to Dr. Harris, had seen them safe back to New York. Her brother, George Jr., and their friend, Judah, were on the dock waiting as promised.

George and Judah had brought with them a contingent of Manhattan Masons, who were also at the wharf, ready to carry Captain Patten by litter to the Battery Hotel, as far as Greenwich Street, where a local physician was waiting to meet a weary Dr. Harris and take over care of his patient. At the wharf, there were large crowds meeting the steamer, waiting for returning forty-niners rich with gold and the mail with news of California. They parted silently at the sight of a man so desperately sick as Joshua.

Their plan was to return to Boston as quickly as possible, but the doctors agreed swiftly that Joshua was too ill to be moved that week. They would need to wait at least several days in the hotel until his situation improved enough to move him and until the foul winter weather settled.

Her brother broke to Mary Ann another piece of news from home, too. There was no purpose in delaying. Their father, George Brown Sr., was gone. He had died of tuberculosis during the year of their voyage, and the family had slipped back into poverty in Boston. The 1860 census records show his widow, Elizabeth Patten, as having a personal estate worth a mere $500—something under $20,000 in today's values.

The entire Brown family had counted on Joshua to move them all into the middle class. Instead, Joshua was returning from sea blind, deaf, and helpless. And 1857 was not going to get any better for either the Brown or the Patten families.

## 14

# A Mighty Pretty Woman and a Heroine

Let them be sea-captains, if you will.
—Margaret Fuller, *Woman in the Nineteenth Century*

The arrival of Captain and Mrs. Patten back in New York City was news eagerly awaited in Manhattan by readers of the local newspapers, though Mary Ann had no idea of the stir her return had created.

They had arrived on Saturday.

On Wednesday, February 18, *The New York Times* ran its first story, reporting that:

> Among the passengers from California, who arrived by the steamer *George Law* . . . there was an invalid who had to be

borne from the vessel to his hotel upon a litter. By his side, superintending every movement, was a young lady, of prepossessing person, but with a countenance care-worn and anxious from long watching. . . . his wife, who had previously accompanied him on two voyages.

As the reporter went on to note for the city's readers, "She is a native of Boston, a mighty pretty woman and a heroine."

*The New-York Tribune*, having sent a reporter to interview Mary Ann on Tuesday morning, was less restrained and far more indignant in its coverage on behalf of what all of New York City now agreed was the much-wronged Mrs. Patten. On Wednesday, it also ran a feature article on Mary Ann, with the headline A HEROINE OF THE SEA, announcing:

> Yesterday we received a note from our ship-news collector, stating that Mrs. Patten and her husband were in this city. . . . We found them at the Battery Hotel, and obtained an interview with Mrs. Patten. She was assiduously attending her husband as heretofore, but his situation is such as to preclude all hope of recovery. . . .
>
> With that modesty which generally distinguishes true merit, Mrs. Patten begged to be excused from speaking about herself. She said that she had done no more than her duty, and as the recollection of her trials and suffering evidently gave her pain, we could not do otherwise than respect her feelings. Few persons would imagine that the woman who behaved so bravely, and endured so much for her husband's sake, is a slender New England girl, scarcely twenty years old. She is a lady of medium height, with black hair, large, dark, lustrous eyes, and very pleasing features. Her health is very much impaired from the hardships which she has undergone, and she is very

near the period of maternity. Yet she does not spare herself in the least, but is most faithful and constant in her attentions to her husband.

While the tale of Mary Ann's courage and feat of seamanship, combined with her youth, her prettiness, her pregnancy, and Joshua's desperate condition would have been enough to earn her the admiration and sympathy of any reader, the *New-York Tribune* reporter was also outraged to find that Mary Ann, a sea captain's wife, was broke and having to depend on family charity because her husband's pay and capital had not been released to her by the company.

The owners of *Neptune's Car* owed Joshua a $3,000 salary for having taken the clipper safely to San Francisco. More than that, he was owed his contracted percentage on the cargo delivery and the return on his private cargo sales, brokered by the company representatives in California. As was customary, though, his finances and the finances of the ship's owners were even more deeply entangled. Foster & Nickerson had loaned him funds to purchase his private cargo and held much of his working capital.

Joshua would never work again as a captain. As *The New York Times* reported to sympathetic readers, his "sight and hearing will never be restored," and that would render Joshua effectively unemployable. Their hopes for wealth and a competence were over. But once the final accounting with Foster & Nickerson was done and they were returned what was owed them, they would have a comfortable nest egg and enough to anticipate a reasonably secure and prosperous future. As long as Joshua survived, it would be a disaster but not a tragedy.

The trouble was that Foster & Nickerson were stalling. Some of the delays were the inevitable result of the slow mails and the complications of unraveling the inventory. But it was more than that. Captain Patten, the owners observed, had been unconscious for most of the passage and had not, in fact, delivered the vessel. They had no obligation to pay the captain's wife, who was, after all, not their employee and a woman. The ship's owners agreed to cover the costs of the return voyage from California to New York, so Mary Ann could settle those debts, but the rest of it would be a slow process, and the shipowners' reluctance to pay the contract salary placed her in a deeply embarrassing financial position for the moment.

In Manhattan, the newspaper readers and the merchant community were scandalized: "We have been informed," the reporter for *The New York Times* wrote:

> that she is in strained circumstances, and although she might and doubtless would shrink from assistance from others, yet it seems to me that this is a case in which our merchants may do themselves honor, by a liberal recognition of her heroic conduct. The Board of Underwriters, we understand, have voted or will vote her $1,000.
>
> Considering that the ship and cargo were worth nearly $350,000, and that to her skill and decision they are mainly indebted for its safety, under most severe circumstances—for the weather was unusually severe—we think, looking at the matter from a purely pecuniary point of view, the least they should have done would have been to give her a check for $5,000. Not only did she safely take the ship from Cape Horn to San Francisco, but both vessel and cargo were in better trim than any of her competitors when she reached port. Of course the owners of the ship will do handsomely by Mrs. Patten, but were the merchants of New York to make up a liberal purse it would prove highly acceptable to the widow (as she almost certainly soon will be) and her small family.
>
> .... Mrs. Patten and her brother will convey him to their home in Boston today by the steamer, if the weather will

permit. That she has the entire sympathies of this community in her trying affliction she may be fully assured.

For the owners of *Neptune's Car* and the investors at Foster & Nickerson, this was just the beginning of an international public relations disaster.

**Rough weather and** Joshua's fatigue kept them in New York until Friday, February 20, six days after their arrival. The delay only excited more press attention and for the first time began to panic the ship's owners, who were coming in for some considerable public criticism for their shoddy treatment of a national heroine.

Colonel Richard Borden, a wealthy Massachusetts industrialist and the owner of the Fall River Line, which ran a luxury packet steamer and connecting railway service from New York City to the Boston area, read about the plight of Captain and Mrs. Patten in the Boston papers during the second week of February. Since Mrs. Patten found herself unfairly embarrassed for resources, he immediately called in the newspapermen and announced that he had arranged for Joshua and Mary Ann to have free passage home to Boston. He directed the steward aboard the *Bay State* to show Mrs. Patten first-class service. The officers on the steamer, keen to show their respect for Captain and Mrs. Patten—because they, too, had read the papers—made "every effort to render their situation as comfortable as possible," *The New York Times* reported the following Tuesday.

When the *Bay State* steamer to Boston departed in thick fog and icy weather at 3:00 P.M. on February 20, onboard now with them was Captain John H. Nickerson, the son of one of the owners of *Neptune's Car*, and John Sullivan, one of the company clerks, determined to get ahead of the press coverage in New England, though Joshua's salary and the return of their personal capital was still in limbo. The press was having none of it.

*The New York Times*, still following a story that was quickly being picked up by newspapers across the nation, reported on the Saturday after their departure that "During the effort to remove [Captain Patten] to the boat, he suffered several convulsions, and Dr. Harris considered it doubtful if he reaches his destination alive. Several friends were present to see them off." Among those friends, the newspaper reported, "Mrs. P makes especially mention of Judah Berry, Esq., who met them at the steamer upon their arrival, and spent the day and night in watching the bedside of her husband." The nation now was waiting on tenterhooks to hear the fate of Captain Patten.

When the *Bay State* arrived in Fall River for the change to the train to Boston, Colonel Borden, determined not to stint on getting his fellow citizens home, ordered that a private carriage be added to the accommodation train so Captain Patten could recuperate in quiet and instructed the engineer to start and stop the train carefully "to occasion as little jarring as possible." Readers were delighted to learn that these kind attentions had made all the difference. "Capt. Patten spoke intelligently of what was passing," during his journey north, "and was evidently conscious that he was on his way home" the papers reported.

When Mary Ann and George arrived back in Boston, Joshua remained lucid and talkative, and Mary Ann dared to believe that he might still survive the illness. The Brown family lived on Salutation Street in 1857, a short, narrow lane, one end of which boasted the Salutation Tavern, the favorite drinking establishment of the local shipyard workers and where the Boston Tea Party had once been planned by "Samuel Adams, Josiah Quincy Jr., Joseph Warren, Paul Revere, John Adams, James Otis, and the North End ship caulkers." As they arrived at the Brown family home and Mary Ann embraced her mother, Joshua, on a stretcher cot, quietly gave the men some precautions about the staircase up to the bedroom. He was conscious enough to want to not be dropped down the stairwell. When settled into bed in their old room, Joshua took Mary Ann's hand. "This is home—this is home," he said, his voice breaking.

This touching scene, too, made the national papers.

**Despite the public** show of support from Foster & Nickerson on the trip to Boston, there had still been no decision to release to Mary Ann the captain's salary and no settlement of their capital.

In New York City, the Board of Underwriters, some of the city's most prominent and well-respected merchants, more keenly attuned to public sentiment and to the growing anger toward Foster & Nickerson in the city, not only released to Mary Ann a payment of $1,000—in recognition of the insurance losses that she had saved them by taking command of her husband's vessel—but advised the newspapers as well that they were making "some suitable testimonial to Mrs. Patten, on their private account."

Mary Ann's letter of acknowledgment, written on February 25, quickly found its way to the papers a week later:

> *Gentlemen: I received yesterday, your communication of the 15th inst., and it is with mingled sensations of gratitude and embarrassment that I leave my post as a watcher of my husband's sick bed to reply. I am sincerely grateful to you and to all those you represent for the very kind expressions of sympathy, and for the liberal inclosure which you have transmitted to me in their behalf. I feel very sensibly, gentleman, that kindness which has prompted you to commend the matter in which I have endeavored to perform that which seemed to me, under the circumstances, only the plain duty of a wife toward a good husband, stricken down by what we now fear to be a hopeless*

*disease, and to perform for him, as well as I could, those duties which he would not perform for himself, especially when it was to carry out his own expressed wish. But I am, at the same time, seriously embarrassed by the fear that you may have overestimated the value of those services, because I feel that without the good services of Mr. Hare, the second officer, a good seaman, and of the hearty cooperation of the crew to all our endeavors, the ship would not have arrived safely at her destined port. Be assured, gentleman, that through all the trials which may be before me, and while I live, your considerate kindness will ever be held in thankful remembrance. By yours very respectfully, Mary A Patten*

No one could help but be charmed by a letter this generous and as gracious. Mary Ann Patten in February 1857 was, quite simply, everyone's darling.

**The fame of** a heroine this winning was bound to spread, and at the end of that month Mary Ann was again called to public attention.

There was, in 1857, a public effort to raise the funds to purchase General Washington's estate at Mount Vernon as a national memorial, organized by the Mount Vernon Ladies' Association, and the two causes—the valor of Mrs. Patten and the valor of founders of the republic—quickly merged in the public imagination.

That United States in 1857 was at a cultural crossroads. The generation of men and women who had fought for the independence of the republic in the 1770s and 1780s were gone, and the nation turned to a kind of collective remembering and forgetting. Americans are bound by the stories of our national origins and the values inherent in those stories. Look through the pages of a US passport; it is a flipbook of our legends, including the legends of Old

North Church and the gold rush. In the 1850s, those foundational stories were still being written.

The United States, just at that moment, was also on the brink of a great unraveling. The tensions that would lead in 1861 to the outbreak of the Civil War had been simmering already for decades. And, while the question of the "peculiar institution" of slavery was one of the contested values, so was the issue of the civil rights of women and their legal and domestic subjugation. Abigail Adams had written to her husband, John, in 1776:

> *I long to hear that you have declared an independency . . . [and] in the new code of laws which I suppose it will be necessary for you to make, I desire you would remember the ladies and be more generous and favorable to them than your ancestors. Do not put such unlimited power into the hands of the husbands. Remember, all men would be tyrants if they could. If particular care and attention is not paid to the ladies, we are determined to foment a rebellion, and will not hold ourselves bound by any laws in which we have no voice or representation.*

The founding fathers made no such provisions.

Abolition and women's suffrage fifty years later seemed to many like two sides of the same coin. When the women of America finally proclaimed their liberty in 1848, at a political convention in Seneca Falls, the former slave Frederick Douglass would deliver one of the keynotes.

The battle for women's suffrage, as for the civil rights of African Americans, would be a long road. The Nineteenth Amendment to the US Constitution would not be ratified until 1920. But when suffragettes in the 1840s and 1850s imagined what the full political and economic rights of women might look like, they did not imagine, as we do today, girls who would grow up someday to be president; they said instead, as Margaret Fuller wrote in a treatise called *Woman in the Nineteenth Century*, "Let them be sea-captains!"

Women's suffrage in the 1850s was hotly debated and contested. Nothing about the political moment of the 1850s was straightforward or easy. At stake was the role of women not only in the nation but in the home. Much of America was more comfortable with the idea of women as domestic angels and caregivers, and the ladies of the Mount Vernon Ladies' Association cleaved to this respectable model. "If the men of America have seen fit to allow the home of its most respected hero to go to ruin," Louisa Bird Cunningham wrote to her daughter in 1853, "why can't the women of America band together to save it?"

And this was how, in February 1857 in Boston, the greatest orator of nineteenth-century America happened to be giving a fundraising speech for the Mount Vernon Ladies' Association and the inauguration of a new statue with the advertised title of *The Character of Washington*.

The orator was an elderly man named Ernest Everett. He'd been in his time the governor of Massachusetts, a US senator, a member of the House of Representatives, the US secretary of state, the ambassador to Great Britain, and the president of Harvard, and in 1857 he was a well-known public figure. Today, if he is remembered at all, it is as the man whose two-hour keynote speech at Gettysburg was eclipsed by a few pithy words of address by Abraham Lincoln.

Now retired, Everett was on a whistle-stop tour. To save Mount Vernon, the ladies of America needed to raise $200,000, and the audience was packed. His voice rose and fell in the clipped and melodic tones of a New England orator. When the ladies shifted on the pews, their crinoline skirts crackled. And shift they did, for this was not going to be a short oration on this battlefield either. Now and again came an appreciative murmur of approval. Everett was warming to his theme: the moral character of the nation's first president—and the national example that George Washington set for all who considered themselves American.

In 1857, what it meant to be American was still not entirely certain.

The war in the Crimea had just ended, making the intrepid English nurse Florence Nightingale famous. Florence Nightingale had argued passionately for the moral and intellectual capacities of women, railed against the social institutions that limited their scope of action, but also had said, "I am of certain convinced that the greatest heroes are those who do their duty in the daily grind of domestic affairs whilst the world whirls" around them, in recognition of the heroines all around her. America had been, officially, neutral in Crimea, but the war had, unofficially, once again placed Britain and her former colonial possession at odds with each other. At home, the Compromise of 1850, putting a ten-year pause on the question of slavery, had solved nothing. Mrs. Beecher Stowe's weekly magazine installments of the story of Uncle Tom and his cabin had gripped the North and infuriated the South and only entrenched strong feelings.

What did it mean, in the face of these cultural divisions, to be an American? Surely the answer must lie in that not-too-distant past of the great Revolutionary generation, with its heroes like General Washington.

Perhaps Reverend Everett guessed that his audience was growing restless. He'd been talking for quite some time now. Perhaps he guessed that the ladies in attendance, in particular, might be growing weary of his examples of civic virtues drawn from the lives of ancient Roman senators. Few ladies in 1857 had ever been permitted to learn Latin. Playing to the crowd, to warm popular sentiment, he urged them earnestly now to consider two heroic modern-day women, in the mold of General Washington himself:

"Witness," he intoned to the crowd, "that heroic, aye, that angelic vestal, Florence Nightingale, who, beneath the eyes of admiring Europe and admiring Asia, walked with serene unconcern, for more than a twelvemonth, the pestilential wards of a hospital." Here was a universal heroine. Only the most unfeeling among them would not pause to applaud this admirable British lady.

Everett waited. Now, playing to the hometown crowd, he went on:

> [W]itness our not less heroic countrywoman, Mary Patten . . . the wife of a merchant shipmaster—who . . . with no eye to witness and no voice to cheer her, when her husband was taken down by illness . . . took his place on the quarter deck of his forlorn vessel; took her observation every day with the sextant, laid down the ship's course on the chart, cheered and encouraged the desponding crew, arrested the thief mate—who was for creeping into the nearest port and who, poor young wife as she was, hardly twenty years of age . . . with a strong will and a stout heart, steered her husband's vessel, through storm and through calm, from Cape Horn to San Francisco.

The applause was ecstatic. For everyone knew the story of Mrs. Patten. She was no less celebrated in the winter of 1857 than Florence Nightingale or George Washington.

That fame was soon international. By the spring, the amateur poet William Attfield had published in London his epic poem *The Neptune's Car*, which he described as a "romantic little narrative, of a late adventure of a merchant vessel." While the verse is, admittedly, sophomoric, who could debate the sentiment when, like Edward Everett, he says of Mary Ann:

> *Steadfast alike—and bright, thy truth hath been;*
> *The diamond's brightness—and its core within.*

*Gone though it be—thy young life's fond romance,*
*Its nobler germ outlives all change and chance:*
*And written on memory's page shall be thy name—*
*One clear, bright page—aloof from vulgar fame,*
*Where grateful homage, with full heart, records*
*Deeds of thy sex, which pass the praise of words;—*
*GRACE DARLING, thine! thine, FLORENCE NIGHTINGALE!*
*And, gentle PATTEN, in the marble shrine*
*That hallows woman's worth—be place for THINE!*

Even Harriet Beecher Stowe was charmed with the story of Mary Ann Patten. Already, the author of *Uncle Tom's Cabin* was at work on another story that would come to be known as *The Pearl of Orr's Island: A Story of the Coast of Maine*. In it, she, too, would pay tribute to (and capitalize on the celebrity of) the celebrated wife of Maine sea captain Joshua Patten. "Why, I 'member goin' a voyage with Cap'n Eaton," one of her female characters says, in a Maine accent that, it must be noted, is about as nuanced as William Attfield's poetry:

> when I saved the ship. . . . Cap'n Eaton wasn't hearty at that time, he was jist getting' up from a fever, & it was when Marthy Ann was a baby, and I jist took her and went to sea and took care of him. I used to work the longitude for him and help him lay the ship's course when his head was bad, and when we came on the coast, we were kept out of harbor beatin' about nearly three weeks, and all the ship's tacklin' was stiff with ice, and I tell you the men never would have stood it through and got the ship in, if it hadn't been for me.

It is difficult to overstate, in fact, the fame of Mary Ann Patten in the late 1850s and into the 1860s. The speaker was right: She did represent, at that moment in time, something that seemed to many as quintessentially American. The America we wanted to be as a young nation, at the moment when the nation stood on the precipice of that terrible reckoning.

**In the midst** of all this fame, Mary Ann herself was nowhere to be seen. She and her brother, George Jr., the foreman at one of the local shipyards, accompanied by the two representatives of the shipping company, had landed back in Boston with Joshua sometime during the third week of February. She was still sick and feverish. Mary Ann was into the ninth month of her pregnancy.

At her mother's home in the North End, three weeks later, on March 10, 1857, a little boy was born and recorded in the parish register. Mary Ann named their son after his father: Joshua Adams Patten Jr.

It is possible that Joshua never held his infant son. Joshua's condition was serious. The bacteria that had caused the tuberculosis to infect his lungs had traveled to his brain and infected tissue. This had been the cause of his brain fever on their voyage and also of the blindness and deafness that was permanent. That inflammation had led to a buildup of cerebrospinal fluid on their passage across Panama. The pressure in the brain, however, also accelerated the deterioration of his mental status, and, because the disease damages nerve cells in the brain, the cognitive impairments were also irreversible. In the late winter of 1857, Joshua's condition would have looked to a nonspecialist something like the later stages of dementia.

Mary Ann had recovered from her bout of malaria by March, though she was still weak, especially having endured a long labor to deliver little Joshua Jr. Then, at the end of May, Mary Ann got sick again, this time with typhoid, contracted by drinking contaminated water. *The New York Times,* still following the story, advised its readers: "Mrs. Patten, the woman who so heroically navigated the clipper *Neptune's Car* into California, after her husband lost his sight, is now dangerously ill in Boston with typhoid fever—consequent upon the fatigues and exposure incident to the voyage, and her untiring devotion to her husband. Capt. Patten has lost both his sight and hearing." *The Rockland Gazette,* Joshua's hometown newspaper, published a letter from Dr. Clark, her Boston physician, who reported:

> *In regard to Mrs. Patten, you may state that she has been sick, for several weeks, with typhoid fever, and that she is now dangerously ill. Her husband has recovered his general health but remains entirely blind and deaf. Any further amendment in him, though not impossible, is, I think, not to be expected.*

And the shipping company had still not paid out Captain Patten's salary or settled on their capital, leaving them short on finances.

**The news that** the heroic Mrs. Patten was in need and sick in Boston opened the floodgates of sympathy among the women of New England, who were determined to show that, like Mrs. Patten and Miss Nightingale, they, too, were made of stern stuff and could rise to their duty and the occasion. Although no one, least of all these women, ever used those terms, it was a veritable ladies' revolution.

The $1,000 reward from the New York Underwriters in February had not satisfied Mary Ann's champions in the press. As a disgusted reporter for *The New York Times* reminded its readers on April 1, 1857:

> The captain of a large and valuable ship fell sick at sea. The wife seized the quadrant, in his dying condition, and steered the noble Neptune's Car and cargo in safety. Admiration for

her bravery stood on tip toe—the trumpet of Fame proclaimed her fortune—the tongues of rumor reechoed her praise—the underwriters gave her one thousand dollars . . . [and] it may sustain her whilst she nurses her husband and sends him packing into the grave, then perhaps she will find a workhouse, while her beneficiaries dine in the Fifth avenue on their profits.

Had she been a man, Mary Ann would not be in this unenviable position. A man would have received a handsome acknowledgment—and his promised salary. Some society women in Boston, prodding their wealthy husbands to open the purse strings, started the cause. *The Boston Post* picked up the baton and called on all its female readers to relieve the distress of their fellow citizen, Mrs. Patten. Readers, male and female, but especially female, responded to the paper's call from around the world as the story was picked up in one newspaper after another.

Two ladies gathered up their dress money and sent $20 to *The Boston Courier*'s office for the captain's wife, when a rival paper started its own subscription. Soon *The Boston Post* joined the action, raising $1,018 from donations. Children sent in letters with their Christmas savings. "A lady on Mount Vernon Street," one newspaper announced, sent a donation to "Mrs. Patten, whose courage and devotion entitle her to the esteem of all." The businesses of Boston, sensing a feel-good public relations opportunity, quickly followed the example of their customers.

Nor was it only the ladies of Boston. The *Rockland Gazette*, noting that "Capt. Patten is (or was) a citizen of our own place, and is a young man of worth and integrity who has many friends among us," called on the women of his hometown to meet the "needs and claims of their sister, who has so nobly exemplified that heroism, which, though not always or often rewarded by the world's praises, has shone brightly . . . from a thousand humble hearthstones." From a blind man in London arrived $100 for a fund for Mrs. Patten, along with a letter assuring Mary Ann that "Our journals have made all Europe acquainted with deeds which are appreciated as much in the old world as in your own native country."

The end of June, *The New York Times* was urging its readers to out-donate the New Englanders.

"The merchants of Boston have taken up her case, too, with proper spirit, and have resolved that she shall be provided for permanently," came the word from Manhattan. Captain Patten, they noted:

> can sail the seas no more, and the noble wife who braved for him the storms of the great deep, and the temper of mutinous men, must now meet the harder and wearier trials of a life of such labor as society offers to women, unless the community to which she belongs, and upon which her achievement will reflect so much permanent distinction, shall do itself and her the justice to adopt her into its fostering care.

Who could bear the thought of the heroic Mrs. Patten, a young widow, in penury with a small child, suffering the drudgery of a laundress or a charwoman? "When, in the years to come, the name of Mrs. Patten shall be made the theme of song and speech," *The New York Times* exhorted:

> let not any recollections be coupled with it which shall make our descendants blush for their ancestry. The Bostonians propose that the women of America shall at least be offered the opportunity of honoring their sex, in the person of this young wife. The proposition is most just—and we trust that no time will be lost in organizing such a subscription among

the women of the metropolis as shall have the loving labors of our Boston neighbors a generous superfluity.

Or, roughly translated: Let's show Boston! But the message was also serious: The options available to Mary Ann when—and it was now "when" and not "if"—Joshua died were hard and narrow.

All the newspapers reported these gifts as they arrived in the office, rewarding Mary Ann's benefactors with a glowing public mention, fueling new donations. "Any aid which has been or may be rendered on the part of our citizens to Capt. Patten or his noble and deserving wife," the editors of *The Rockland Gazette* assured its readers, "we shall be pleased to acknowledge through our columns."

**Joshua, on Salutation Street** in Boston, in that bed that had become his home, was already dying by the time that article was published on June 27, 1857, in Manhattan.

By the second week of July, the situation was hopeless. Mary Ann resisted until the very end. Her brother George broke it to her gently in the first days of July: Joshua would have to go into care sooner or later. Joshua's fits and outbursts were more than Mary Ann or her mother could safely manage. Institutional care for those addled in the mind meant now, as it had meant for Mary Ann's sister-in-law Ann Patten, the insane asylum.

On Friday, July 17, 1857, Joshua was transferred to the McLean Asylum for the Insane in nearby Charlestown, just across the Charles River, at the top of Cobble Hill, which, along with nearby Bunker Hill, had been fortified in the 1770s during the Siege of Boston.

The McLean Asylum had been named after its benefactor, a shipping merchant named John McLean, who had been forced to declare bankruptcy when a ship laden with a fortune in cargo was lost at sea; when the missing ship sailed back into Boston Harbor and McLean's fortunes were restored, he became a local legend. Most of that fortune went to fund the insane asylum. Today known as a mental health clinic for the rich and famous, in 1857, the patients ranged from wards of the state to private patients whose families could afford to provide them with better accommodations.

The process of declaring a person insane in the 1850s required certification of a physician and a writ with the state, and in Joshua's case the outcome was always a forgone conclusion. Their physician, Dr. Clark, was a renowned specialist in treating "ship fever" and infectious diseases, and a visiting surgeon at Massachusetts General Hospital from 1851 to 1875, which administered the McLean Asylum. Dr. Clark agreed with George Brown's assessment. Joshua required constant care for brain damage, and that care did not have any particular medical component.

The process in general, however, was subject to considerable abuse, and symptoms of insanity could include "intemperance, masturbation, overwork, domestic difficulties, excessive ambitions, faulty education, personal disappointments, marital problems, excessive religious enthusiasm, jealousy, and pride." In the landmark case of *Townshend v. Townshend*, the courts in Maryland considered whether setting free one's slaves was de facto evidence of lunacy, sufficient to set aside a will with a deed of manumission. The eighty enslaved people whose lives were at stake in the estate challenge were not awarded their freedom. In 1860, the public was scandalized by the forced incarceration at McLean of Mrs. Lydia B. Denny, declared insane by her husband for seeking to divorce him.

The decision to commit Joshua to the asylum, especially knowing the history of Ann Patten, who remained incarcerated in the Maine Lunatic Asylum as late as the 1870s, was a difficult one for the entire Brown family.

Joshua's experience, however, is likely to have been a caring one, for all the stories of the legal abuses that could lead some patients to these facilities. "Under the control of intelligent and liberal men, officered by persons of both sexes, chosen, as well for their humane dispositions and proper temperaments," the advertisements announced, "the institution has gradually come to share the entire confidence . . . of those who have been obliged to resort to [it on] behalf of suffering friends." For many of the working-class patients and wards of the state, the asylum was a far better option than the alternative: the poor farm. Joshua was placed, along with nearly two hundred other inmates, in what were in the 1850s undeniably crowded accommodations.

What Joshua's experience might or might not have been, in any event, was soon irrelevant. He entered the asylum on Friday. On Monday morning, at 2:00 A.M. on July 20, just three days later, Joshua Adams Patten died at the McLean Insane Asylum from the effects of tubercular meningitis. He was barely thirty.

**Mary Ann and** the Brown family buried Joshua at a funeral service at Old North Church on Tuesday, July 28, inside the cool stone walls where she and Joshua had married not five years earlier and where she had been a parishioner since childhood.

The reporters were here, too, apprising an eager public of how the story everyone had been following was ending. "The body," *The New York Times* assured its readers, "was enclosed in an elegant metallic case of a new plan and patent, upon the top of which, running the whole length of the casket, was a heavy French plate of glass divided into three sections, so that the entire form of the body would be seen without removing the lid." A modern reader can only shudder at our countrymen's and countrywomen's familiarity with death in the 1850s.

Someone placed the Masonic regalia and the Mason's apron belonging to Joshua on top of the casket. It had traveled around the world with them. When the mourners read aloud the words of the 23rd Psalm, "he leadeth me beside still water," there was a quiet murmur of approval. The words were a fitting end for a sea captain at rest.

After the service, as a commemoration of the occasion, Mary Ann, in her widow's weeds, allowed her portrait to be made at the studio of a local daguerreotypist.

Mary Ann looks out of that portrait at us, her cheeks watercolored to a blush, with dark eyes that gaze straight at the camera. Their look is penetrating. She is wearing the gold-and-coral earrings meant to protect her. She is also wearing at her heart a mourning brooch, with a lock of Joshua's fair hair. In the image, Mary Ann is small and plump and impossibly young. She was just twenty the day the image was captured, and she could not have imagined what would happen next. She had no clear idea yet of how gripped all of America had become by her story or how keenly the city around her was aware of Joshua's passing.

As the word spread along the wharves of the North End of Boston on July 25, 1857, that Captain Patten was being carried to his grave at Woodlawn Cemetery, the ships' ensigns in the harbors were lowered, and then came the chimes of the bells of the Old North Church, where Frederick Jewell, who would later marry Joshua's sister, rang out the captain.

Then the ships' bells of every vessel within earshot of Old North Church in Boston Harbor began ringing, first one, then another, in a poignant, echoing clamor. On the streets, people stopped to listen in respectful silence, thinking of the story of *Neptune's Car* and the young heroine, *their* young heroine, who was now a widow.

No one in that busy seaport needed the significance of the bells glossed for them. The sailors across Boston and his fellow captains were ringing Joshua out in the ancient ceremony known as Eight Bells, which tolls the end of watch at sea, when a mariner can finally stand down from duty.

## 15

# The Sea Captain's Widow

˞

> Who shut up the sea with doors, when it brake forth, as if it had issued out of the womb? . . . And said, Hitherto shalt thou come, but no further: and here shall thy proud waves be stayed?
>
> —Job 38:8, 11 (KJV)

What had started as news reports out of San Francisco and then New York City, applauding the courage of a woman who was "at once navigator, nurse, physician and protector of the property entrusted to her husband," had fanned out across the smallest towns in America and spread with the mail packets around the world to London, Liverpool, Shanghai, and Sydney.

The papers now reported on the death of Captain Patten, and the "legend" of Mrs. Patten grew that summer. She had been romanticized in the poetry of William Attfield not just as a heroine but as the modern-day incarnation of a queenly sprite from Sir

Walter Scott's bestselling novels, the otherworldly spirit protector of her family.

Some of the seamen who had been aboard *Neptune's Car* could be forgiven for saying, after a few pints down by the docks, where a good yarn, well-told, might see you stood a drink by the publican, that she must have been some kind of spirit-protector on that ill-fated voyage. Sailors were long accustomed to the idea that the wooden figureheads of bare-chested and ferocious women on the prows of great sailing ships were the spirit of their vessel leading them homeward. A woman's bare breasts could calm even the most ferocious waters, or so went the legend, and sailors are a superstitious lot for a reason.

For mariners, Captain Mrs. Patten, a mother, a nurse, and a wife, was a figurehead who had come to life in one of the great sea stories. If there was ever carved in Boston a figurehead of a black-haired, black-eyed young woman who bore a resemblance to a certain Mrs. Patten, that artifact has long since perished, along with her story. Anyone alive in the 1850s or 1860s, had such a figurehead graced the bow, would have required no explanation.

For the women championing the cause of universal suffrage, Mary Ann Patten was also a living symbol. "What a splendid text for the woman's rights people," wrote Philadelphia's *Star of the North* on March 11. After all, if a young girl just nineteen could inspire a crew of unruly seamen to let her take a clipper around Cape Horn in a terrible gale as their master, if women could be captains when permitted, then surely women could be trusted to vote in an election?

**Society was not**, in 1857, ready yet for that bold proposition, but Mary Ann did pave the way for a generation of other women who, in the years that followed, would take the helm and also tell those stories.

Mary Ann's acquaintance, fellow captain's wife Hannah Rebecca

Burgess, who sailed with her husband aboard the clipper ships *Whirlwind* and *Challenger*, would later tell the story of how, like the celebrated Mrs. Patten, she, too, took the helm hundreds of miles from Valparaíso, Chile, when her husband, William, was struck with dysentery in late November and early December 1856.

The two women may, in fact, have encountered each other in January 1857 in Aspinwall. Rebecca landed there on January 19, 1857, after the death of her husband in Chile. On January 19, Mary Ann, feeling fluish with the lingering effects of malaria, was laid up in a hotel, waiting for Joshua to stabilize enough make the last leg of their homeward journey. Their meeting in a small port town: two captain's wives, two women from the Boston area, within a few years of each other in age and direct contemporaries in experience? It would have been quite natural, but these are not the kinds of records—of the lives of two middle-class young women—that make their way into our archives.

All we know for sure is that Rebecca arrived back in New York City at the end of January; Mary Ann and Joshua traveled on the next packet from Aspinwall and arrived two weeks later. Their having met in Panama would make sense, however, of an otherwise curious fact: why Rebecca went to visit Mary Ann in the Battery Hotel on their arrival in Manhattan.

Rebecca's story would not be thrown into the limelight until 1864, when the story of *Neptune's Car* and the captain's wife was an established legend, with the curious New York newspaper article titled "A Possible Relic of Shipwreck," written by the bestselling author of *Two Years Before the Mast,* Richard Henry Dana Jr.

Dana explained that a Bible that had sold in Taiwan as part of the salvage from a shipwreck, with a handwritten dedication *Presented David Graves by Mrs. Rebecca H. Burgess, Boston, February 10, 1857,* had come into his possession. Who was Mrs. Burgess and what, he wondered to a national audience, was the story of this Bible?

Reading the article, with her name written there, Rebecca remembered "I was almost petrified with astonishment." As the papers reported on her correspondence with Dana, the story of the *Challenger*'s voyage was resurrected as another thrilling maritime love story.

Rebecca, too, was catapulted to regional fame and spent her life telling and retelling the story. As the years went on and with each retelling, Rebecca's story cleaved closer and closer to Mary Ann's. By the 1880s, telling the tale to classrooms of local schoolchildren, her biographer records that Rebecca now narrated how the first mate aboard the *Challenger* could not navigate, forcing her to take the helm as captain and save a fortune in cargo. Historians, understandably, have questioned Burgess's later accounts, and remembering, one supposes, always involves a bit of inventing. What is interesting is simply how powerfully resonant Mary Ann's story continued to be decades later. It was a story so good that it was worth adopting.

Nor was Captain Burgess's wife the only one to find inspiration in the tale of Mary Ann Patten. In the late autumn of 1868, about 127 miles off the coast of Calcutta and carrying a cargo of "linseed, jute, and gunny cloth," Thomas McGuire, the master of the *Chieftain*, was struck with dengue fever and passed command of the ship to his wife, Mrs. McGuire, who had sailed with him since the late 1840s.

As *The New York Herald* reported on March 4, 1869, Captain Mrs. McGuire "knew every spar and rope and sail on the vessel. She knew every word of command. She made all the observations herself. She kept the logbook. She was on deck at all hours of the day and night. She watched the barometer." Like Mary Ann Patten, who was in the mind of every reader, she also nursed her ailing husband. Like Mary Ann Patten, who was also on the mind of the New York City Underwriters, she was promptly awarded $1,000 for bringing the ship to port safely. The newspapers were thrilled to report that this wasn't the first time that the intrepid Mrs. McGuire had commanded the vessel in those intervening decades.

By the 1870s, it was no longer unimaginable to anyone that a woman might take the helm in a crisis. Eliza Thorrold continued to run the San Francisco tug, the *Ethel and Marion*, after her husband's death in 1893; when told in 1897 that the law required a qualified captain aboard, she applied for—and received—one of the first tugboat master licenses held by a woman. It would not be until 1939, however, that Myrtle "Molly" Kool, from Saint John, New Brunswick, would become the first licensed female master mariner with a deep-sea command in North America. They were all following in the wake of Mary Ann's story.

**Joshua died intestate.** That meant there would be another delay in resolving the issue of Mary Ann's financial outlook. After his death in July, Mary Ann petitioned the court on August 10, 1857, asking to appoint Dr. Henry Grafton Clark as executor, writing "it being inconvenient for me to administer on the Estate of my late husband Joshua Patten, late of Boston Master Mariner deceased intestate, I do hereby signify the same to your Honor."

The Boston probate records do not contain an inventory to show precisely of what the Patten estate consisted, perhaps because that inventory was delayed until things could be settled with Foster & Nickerson, but the value must have been considerable. Dr. Clark was a prominent figure and lived in a grand double town house on the south side of Beacon Street, near Boston Common, with his wife, Mary, and the fact that Dr. Clark not only agreed to manage probate for Mary Ann but also undertook to "invest and reinvest" moneys for her in August implies there was enough capital there with which to bother—or at least that he thought there would be.

The subscriptions from the newspaper fundraisers amounted to several thousand dollars. In addition to the thousand dollars from

*The Boston Post* and the thousand dollars from the New York Underwriters, the donations from the readers of *The Boston Courier* amounted to $1,399 by autumn. They had owned the house on Main Street in Rockland without a mortgage, as well as the land on the Weskeag River. There had been additional private gifts from prominent merchants in Manhattan.

In addition to these direct supports from admiring fellow citizens, intended to tide Mary Ann over while the finances with the ship's owners were being settled, there was a considerable sum due from Foster & Nickerson. Joshua's $3,000 salary was just one portion of the payment. There was the return on the sale of their private cargo, and Joshua's percentage of the cargo fees coming to her. More importantly, there was the capital saved from their first circumnavigation, which Joshua had left with Foster & Nickerson as an investment.

It's a rough estimate, but if all had gone as expected with Foster & Nickerson, Mary Ann might have reasonably expected to have as much as $25,000 or $30,000 coming to her.

What did that mean in terms of a standard of living? In the 1860s, a ship's caulker—her brothers' trade—earned about $1,000 a year, enough to support a family of six. For just under a hundred dollars a year, you could rent a six-room tenement in Boston like the one in which the Brown family lived on Salutation Street, and, if Dr. Clark were charging the average amount for a physician, the delivery of young Joshua Jr. cost somewhere from $10 to $20, depending on the difficulty of the labor. Much depended on class and one's expectations. A surgeon with a least ten years of experience in the Civil War was paid just over $4,000 a year; a housemaid in the state of Maine made just over $100 per annum.

A sum of $30,000, invested at a 5 percent return or $1,500 per annum, especially if one owned a home without a mortgage, wasn't a competence, exactly, but it wasn't bad for a middle-class young widow either.

Then came September 1857 and the shipwreck of the steamer Mary Ann knew from experience as the *George Law* off the southern coast of America.

**When the steamer** *George Law* sank, with it sank the American economy—and Mary Ann's future.

The ship—refitted and recently renamed the *Central America*—departed from Aspinwall on her scheduled service on September 9, 1857, with 587 people aboard and $2 million of "gold coins, ingots, and bars . . . mined in California." Some of that gold, as usual, belonged to Foster & Nickerson. She ran straight into a hurricane off the coast of the Carolinas.

Desperate passengers and crew passed two harrowing days and nights frantically bailing out a sinking vessel and attempting to load women and children into far too few lifeboats, until the steamer sank on September 12, with the loss of 425 lives and enough gold aboard to set off the Panic of 1857 and bring the American economy to its knees.

The reasons for the financial crisis of 1857 are complex, and gold wasn't the only factor. To put it very simply: Railroad stocks and those same speculative land values that had defined the first part of the nineteenth century were in bubble territory, the bubble burst, and banks started going under. What they were hoping to save them and to arrest the market freefall was the imminent arrival of gold bullion from California. That gold sank into the Atlantic.

Among the businesses to founder in September was Foster & Nickerson, which still held Mary Ann's capital. As *The New York Times* reported, "The whole earnings of Capt. Patten were invested with the owners in New York, who have suspended: hence his widow loses." It meant that, for as long as Mary Ann lived, it would be in greatly reduced circumstances.

To his credit, Dr. Clark did not abandon Mary Ann and did his best to invest what remained of their now modest capital. He proved to be an admirably careful steward. When the estate was finally settled in 1883, twenty-seven years after Joshua's death and after decades of providing financial support for baby Joshua, the residual value was still $2,797, some of which probably included some kind of settlement with Foster & Nickerson, in addition to the $3,491 in expenses that Dr. Clark claimed for managing the investments over several decades. That amount did not include the value of the real estate in Maine, which Mary Ann could never bring herself to sell in her lifetime.

**Mary Ann's lifetime** would not be a long one, and she would not live to see the estate settled. There is no way to manufacture here a different ending.

Mary Ann survived her bout with typhoid fever. As *The Wells Journal*, a Maine newspaper, reported on August 22, 1857, Mrs. Patten was "slowly recovering from the effects of fever [and] is still quite feeble." That the newspapers continued to report on her health is a testament to how deeply engaged the American public remained in the story of her courage well into the autumn.

Mary Ann and baby Joshua lived with her mother Elizabeth and the extended Brown family on Salutation Street for the next several years. The census taken in 1860 shows Mary Ann, age twenty-three, and little Joshua, age three, living in the North End with the Widow Brown and with Mary Ann's younger brothers, Edward (twenty) and William (sixteen), employed as shipyard caulkers. Her brother George and his young family, including Joshua's namesake, were living in nearby Chelsea.

But, while Mary Ann had survived malaria and typhoid fever, she would not survive the tuberculosis that she contracted while devotedly caring for Joshua in 1856 and 1857 during his final illness. The progress of the disease was slow but inexorable. By 1857, there was the telltale cough. By the spring of 1861, Dr. Clark told her mother it was hopeless. Mary Ann, too, was dying.

On March 11, 1861, from her sickbed in North Boston, where she could hear the bells of the Old North Church toll and sometimes the shanties that echoed from the wharves sung by returning seamen, Mary Ann signed her last will and testament. With her as her witnesses were three men: B. C. Clark, perhaps one of Dr. Henry Clark's relations; a shipbuilder named B. F. Delano, and Reverend John Thomas Burrell, the pastor of Old North Church.

The will was short and simple: Mary Ann left everything to baby Joshua. She was already far too sick to contemplate naming a guardian for the boy. That would need to come after. She appointed Dr. Clark as executor and asked that whoever was left to care for her son use the estate for his benefit. She directed that at the age of twenty-one, Joshua Jr. should inherit what remained, and that, if he passed before the age of twenty-one, the estate should go to her mother.

Mary Ann signed the document put in front of her and likely had little idea of what was written on the paper. But the men agreed that her signing something was urgent. If Mary Ann died intestate, it would be months before anyone could make any legal or financial provisions for the orphaned Joshua.

Dying from tuberculosis was a hard business. In the final stages of the disease, those suffering from the infection seemed to waste away, turning to pale, skeletal wraiths in front of those who loved them, giving rise to the common term for the illness: consumption. Racked by bloody coughs that left handkerchiefs scarlet, Mary Ann fought to breathe in a feverish delirium for another week. Then, with one last gasp, her body gave up fighting, as had Joshua's and the racked bodies of the thousands upon thousands of other people before her. In Boston in the 1860s, tuberculosis was responsible for more deaths than any other cause, and it particularly struck down young people in their twenties. In the period from 1853 to 1857, 23,280 people died in Massachusetts from tuberculosis, Joshua among them.

Doctors at the time did not understand yet its root cause—and so did not understand that it was contagious. The leading Boston specialist was Dr. Henry Bowditch, son of the celebrated mathematician Nathaniel Bowditch, who rose from an indentured clerk in a ship's chandlery to sea captain and whose *New American Practical Navigator* remains standard issue for mariners, hypothesized that a residence near a damp or spongy soil, common throughout New England, was the culprit, noting that the disease seemed to pass from generation to generation in certain households. Conventional wisdom also held that—because tuberculosis was known to run in families—some people, whether due to a defect in character or constitution, were more consumptive.

Mary Ann died on March 18, 1861, a week after her will was signed and witnessed. She did not live to see the opening shots fired in the American Civil War on April 12, 1861, though she had long since become a symbol in the years leading up to that national tragedy of what all citizens could agree was the best of what it meant to be an American. That had been part of why her story resonated so deeply in 1857: In a nation divided, everyone could support Mrs. Patten.

Mary Ann's funeral service was at Old North Church, where she had attended since girlhood, and she was buried two days later next to Joshua at the Woodlawn Cemetery. She was twenty-three years old. She left behind a three-year-old orphaned toddler.

**What precisely happened** next to Joshua Jr. and the land in Maine falls through the cracks of recorded history. Like the beginning years of Mary Ann and Joshua's lives, it can only be pieced together from deeds and public records.

The death of the celebrated Mrs. Patten was reported in newspapers across the United States and in Britain as the sad coda to a tragic love story in 1861, and then Mary Ann's story began to fade from public memory. With that fading, the records of their family's domestic life again grow thin and, sometimes, cryptic.

Joshua's father, Abel Patten, too, was dead already. Mary Ann would have learned the news in the spring of 1858, the year after Joshua's passing. He had died on March 12, 1858, in Rockland, Maine, in his seventies and from unrecorded causes.

Deed records show that, following the death of their father, Joshua's sea captain brother, Uriah Patten, sold several properties, including the lands out on the Muscle Ridge Islands, and left the state. He must have done so unexpectedly and without leaving a forwarding address, because the local Masonic lodge record in 1866 notes that he is "supposed dead." He wasn't. His wife, Ann, however, died from one of her seizures in the Augusta Insane Asylum, with years of unpaid medical bills. The town attempted to recover the money, and there were notices in the local papers. Uriah remarried a thirty-year-old widow named Mary Comstock and moved to New York City.

Joshua's stepbrother and cousin, Lemuel, died in 1859, two years after Joshua, only thirty-nine, and he was buried beside Joshua's father, Abel, in the family plot in Rockland.

Sarah Patten lived in Rockland into the 1860s, and the 1860 federal census record shows Sarah Patten owning a home valued at $600 and residing with Joshua's two youngest siblings, John, a seaman, and Charlotte, now married. Sometime in the 1870s, John and his wife, Maria, would move into Mary Ann and Joshua's empty house on South Main Street.

The life of Mary Ann and Joshua's son, Joshua Adams Patten Jr., is poorly documented, but what we know of it cannot be said to be happy.

After his mother's death, the boy continued living with his grandmother, Elizabeth, in the same tenement as his uncles Edward, William, and Thomas, all working as caulkers, and his aunt Isabella, a bookbinder. He is listed in the household in the Massachusetts state census in 1865, when he would have been eight.

Five years later, at thirteen, he was no longer living with his grandmother. By the time of the 1870 federal census, the entire Brown family—his aunt, three of his uncles, his grandmother, spouses, and children—were living together across the river, in Charlestown, but Joshua is conspicuously absent.

He reappears in the 1880 census, now in his early twenties, and is recorded as living with his uncles Edward and William in East Boston. Now, Joshua's profession is listed as "carriage painter," which was a trade that required training.

Presumably, his absence from the family home in the 1870s reflects that period of education. By the 1860s, drawing was a compulsory subject in the Boston public schools, and, while the law required a child to attend school until the age of fourteen, attendance was only required for two six-week periods annually. In the 1870s, fewer than 20 percent of boys attended school after the age of fourteen, and many began working in some capacity by twelve.

Joshua, though, must have demonstrated some artistic talent, because carriage painting was a skilled artistic practice that involved applying and rubbing and smoothing multiple layers of glaze to create luminous finishes and required the ability to paint scrollwork, lettering, and trompe l'oeil effects by hand. The interior of carriages, both steam and horse-drawn, were elaborately and beautifully painted with landscape scenery, mythological scenes, or the portraits of popular actresses. He may have been apprenticed "out" for the customary seven years; more likely he was offered a place in one of the industrial schools opening in the 1870s and 1880s or found employment in a workshop.

It was a career and a training, in other words, with good prospects for employment. During the years of his adolescence, Boston was a city of horses, and the pounding of hooves on pavement and the clatter of bells was the defining sound all around him. There were horse-drawn railways requiring as many as six horses to a carriage at rush hour to haul forty passengers up and down the cobble streets, there were the private carriages of doctors and fine ladies, the merchant wagons loaded with cargo from the docks; all told more than ten thousand horses, from dawn to night, mixed with the ringing of church bells. Decorative painting was fashionable enough that upper-class ladies took classes in the subject as a pastime.

Everything for Joshua should have been promising. There was a little money each year from his parents' estate as income. He had a trade. There was a little house in Maine. He could look forward to a family.

But something happened between 1875 and 1880 that completely derailed his future. Whatever happened would render him unemployed by 1880 and unemployable. It was almost certainly a seizure.

Joshua may have been sickly since childhood. Mary Ann had been seriously ill with malaria late in the second trimester of her pregnancy. She had taken on the steamer passage home quinine, a component of the bark of the cinchona plant and one of the most fortuitous medical discoveries of the 1700s. As a young, first-time mother, though, Mary Ann had been particularly susceptible to a serious infection. The risks for children born to mothers sick with malaria include developmental delays and metabolic disorders, many of which are linked to epilepsy and seizures.

Seizures, especially if they were diagnosed, correctly or incorrectly, as epilepsy were the end of a young man's future in the 1870s. The disease carried a profound stigma. Epilepsy was understood until well into the twentieth century as a mental defect. Those with the disease were unemployable. It also would have been the end of any hope of a family. Until 1956, seventeen American states outlawed marriage for anyone with epilepsy; Britain only repealed that law in 1970. Epilepsy tended to go hand in hand with other neurological disorders, and over time the seizures also created cognitive deficits in sufferers, in a kind of terrible self-fulfilling prophecy. His aunt, Ann Patten, had been confined to the Maine Lunatic Asylum for decades because of seizures brought on by untreated eclampsia, and once the diagnosis was made for Joshua Jr. there was almost no chance that he would also not end his life institutionalized.

His grandmother, Elizabeth Brown, died in 1877, the year that Joshua Jr. turned twenty-one. He lived after her death with his uncles in Charlestown. But, although the 1880 federal census lists his occupation as carriage painter, the census taker tersely records the number of days that he has been employed in the year as zero.

For another few years, while the courts were winding down Mary Ann's estate now that Joshua Jr. had reached the age of majority, he lived with his uncles in the Boston area. In 1883, Dr. Clark settled the estate as executor, and when it was all said and done there was a balance of $2,797 due to the young man, the modern equivalent of about $100,000. There was the land on the Weskeag and the house in Rockland.

The inheritance was not enough to make Joshua rich. But, if he had been able to work, it would have meant a promising and comfortable start for a young man. The problem was, he wasn't able to work. He is also likely to have had ongoing cognitive deficits that affected his judgment. That was the beginning of a downward spiral.

Sometime not later than 1883 Joshua returned to Maine, and he cannot have yet been considered mentally incompetent, because there that autumn he sold the land on the Weskeag River that had been his parents' dream for the paltry sum of $30—less than a thousand dollars in today's values.

The following summer, in 1884, he evicted his uncle John Patten who had been maintaining and residing in the house on South Main Street, and sold that property as well for the shockingly low sum of $50 to a stranger. It's hard to believe that Mary Ann's family would have cast the young man out; more likely he was insistent and impetuous, not unthinkable for any young man in his early twenties confronting a life-altering illness. It is not impossible that the assets were sold in Joshua's name but without his wishing it, to pay back taxes or as part of a commitment order to the city's almshouse and poor farm, because that was where Joshua was headed.

He was probably institutionalized sooner than later and likely by the mid-1880s. By 1900, he had been an "inmate" of the Rockland Poor Farm for more years than anyone could remember. It was one step away from the Maine Lunatic Asylum.

**The poor farm** was a peculiar nineteenth-century institution, not in any way specific to Maine or Rockland, in which a town's "worthy poor"—invalids, "idiots," orphans, the elderly—were housed alongside "paupers," a category of poverty ascribed to the moral failure that might include laziness, homelessness, drunkenness, delinquency, or mental illness. That latter category included epilepsy.

As the social reformer Thomas Hazard put it in 1851, there were four ways of managing the care of wards of the state in the mind of your average nineteenth-century town alderman:

> 1st, by venduing [selling their labor] to the lowest bidder; 2nd, by contracting for their maintenance, with an individual, or individuals [ . . . ]; 3d, by placing all the poor in one Asylum, owned by the town; 4th, by placing all such in an Asylum as are bereft of home and friends, and administering of out-door relief to such as have.

The poor farm was somewhere between the third and fourth options.

The poor farm in Rockland was a rambling, large, old farmhouse, built on the slope of a hill among pasturage in the area known as the Highlands. Down the lane, at the bottom of the hill was an old mill and millpond. Inmates were committed to the farm on the authority of the city overseers for the poor, where they would be expected to work, to the extent their condition and abilities permitted, in exchange for room, board, medical care, and moral instruction. The farm sold its goods at market to offset the costs of running the operation. The elderly and infirm knitted blankets and peeled potatoes. Those strong enough did heavy farm labor. Joshua seems to have been fit enough—apart from the seizures.

In the 1890s, when Joshua was an inmate there, the matron and almshouse keeper were Margaret and Thomas Perry, a local couple in their sixties. They lived at the farm with their son, Albru, and a young housemaid named Harriet Winslow. By the early 1890s, the city physician was Dr. Judkins, who described the permanent residents as "For the most part aged and infirm."

By 1900, Joshua's fellow inmates at the poor farm fell into two clear categories.

Abby Clark was twenty—married and not widowed—and she lived at the poor farm with her three young children, all under the age of three, Herbert, Herman, and Hollis. Little Hollis seems to have been born on the farm that spring. The only other family in residence was George Brewster, his wife, Elizabeth, both in their thirties, and their two small children, George and Edward. Their story, too, is unknown, but generally a family ended up at the poor farm because some misfortune or impairment made the husband unemployable.

The remainder of Joshua Jr.'s fellow inmates were elderly widows and widowers, the youngest being a fifty-eight-year-old widow named Harriet Lord, the eldest an eighty-two-year-old named Aaron Wood. Most of the elderly inmates were men in their sixties and seventies.

Joshua was the outlier. In 1900, he was in his early forties. He was physically able to work. He was not mean or aggressive or unbalanced. He was simply an orphan, with no fortune and with no female relatives to care for him, and prone to seizures and probably by his forties some increasingly significant cognitive delays that left him a kind of social pariah.

On September 10, 1900, he was working down by the millpond where the old wood bridge crosses Meadow Brook. By then, the old gristmill had been turned into a pumping station. As *The Lewiston Sun Journal* newspaper reported later, "Patten was subject to fits," and, while he was doing some farmwork on the bank of the pond, a seizure started.

The young boy working with him looked on, helplessly and in horror, as Joshua's body contorted and thrashed uncontrollably in the water into which he had fallen. The lad—and it can only have been young George Brewster, aged five—ran as fast as he could all the way up the hill and back to the farm to tell his father and Mr. Perry. By the time the men arrived at the millpond, "life was extinct."

Joshua Adams Patten Jr., whose mother and father had traveled the world's oceans and braved Cape Horn in a tempest, drowned alone in a few feet of water on a sunny New England day before the leaves had even started turning.

# Epilogue

## Are There Seas in Heaven, Joshua?

> Write me of hope and love, and hearts that endured.
> —Emily Dickinson, letter, February 1852

This is the end of the Patten family story.

By the time their son died, without any surviving family and destitute, more than forty years had passed since Joshua Jr.'s mother took *Neptune's Car* around Cape Horn in a tempest and fought to save his father and their fortune. By then, the story had long since faded from public recollection, though a new generation of sea captains' wives had felt emboldened to take the helm thanks to the recognition earned that perilous winter by Mary Ann.

When the women of America renewed their fight for suffrage and civil rights in the early twentieth century, Mary Ann's story blazed once again for a brief moment across that horizon. Margaret Fuller had said of women in the nineteenth century, "Let them be sea-captains," believing in it as a dream. Mary Ann brought that dream to life through her intelligence and courage—and through the force of her love for Joshua. When at the beginning of the twentieth century those pressing for votes for women looked for examples, it was stories like Mary Ann's to which they turned. They were stories that helped to pass the Nineteenth Amendment.

And, then, the silence.

But, if this is where the Patten story ends, it is also, I suppose, where my story begins. The lives of Mary Ann and Joshua intersect with my own in ways that have been unexpected. Some of that has been particular, but most of what draws these threads is universal.

Mary Ann and Joshua didn't want to leave when they went to sea. They traveled always with the intention of a homecoming. It was the land and not the sea that drew them. Economics and the forces of globalization in the 1850s pulled them to Cape Horn and to California, and, had Mary Ann and Joshua been able to make just another voyage around the world, perhaps two, *Neptune's Car* would have delivered them back to Joshua's dream on the banks of the Weskeag River.

If they had returned, if they had made the life they imagined in Maine, Joshua and Mary Ann would certainly have met in Rockland my great-great-grandfather, Captain Frank Adolph Peterson, and, perhaps, my great-great-grandmother, the sea captain's wife Adella (Towle). Had they lived long enough on the banks of the Weskeag River in the farm of which they dreamed, maybe they would have met, too, another generation on, my great-grandfather Captain Samuel Lear Keen Peterson and my great-grandmother, Maude (Roche), a shipbuilder's daughter from Prince Edward Island.

Like Joshua's Peabody ancestors, parts of my mother's family arrived on Penobscot Bay in the decades before the American

Revolution, and sea captains and merchant mariners inhabit the branches of that family tree, a particular story. Among those ancestors are the Eames and Waterman families, and over the generations some of those young Eames and Waterman girls married Patten, Peabody, and Bailey boys. Other parts of my family, like so many of our families, arrived hungry and in steerage.

Captain Peterson was twenty-three years younger than Captain Patten, just a single generation apart, and I am sure they would have met, because, like Joshua Patten, Frank soon joined the Masonic lodge in Rockland. By the time the younger Joshua Patten drowned that day in the millpond, Captain Peterson had already retired from the sea as a wealthy man and risen to the lodge grandmaster.

How could they *not* have met if Joshua's story had ended as he had wanted? The population of Rockland today—at just around 7,000 inhabitants—is practically unchanged from what it was the 1860s and 1870s. In these small coastal villages along Penobscot Bay, most people know of each other—and know each other's business. As I imagine that scene, Frank and Joshua would have met one night, as older men, in fellowship and brotherhood, to tell sea stories.

These loose ends of history are nothing more than coincidences, of course. I did not write this story because Joshua hailed from a small fishing village in Maine; the story started, always, with Mary Ann and in Boston.

But if we start to pull and tug at these loose ends of history, something larger does begin to unspool itself, something about the very idea of the stories we choose to forget and those we choose to remember.

This is what stories of average, middle-class and working-class people, of women or mariners or indentured servants look like. Lives, hidden away in church registers, Sunday School attendance books, ship's logs, forgotten churchyards, and probate records.

Those records are invariably incomplete and tantalizing, as much for what they contain and for what they hint at has been lost or left unspoken. There are always lacunae, always places where one must rely, as a historian, on interpretation and learning how to read the silences. In telling Mary Ann's story, I have tried to signal to the reader where the records are rich or lean, to make sense of the gaps, and then have simply got on with telling the story as I believe it happened.

Some people find those silences and that lacuna unbearable. They cannot tolerate any history that works around or narrates the emptiness of our records to recover untold narratives, because it might suggest that history itself is not as black-and-white or as satisfyingly complete as we imagine. But, unless we are willing to sit with ambiguity as writers and as readers, we will only ever read the histories of presidents and princes. They will be the nation builders. We will not have the stories of women who defied convention and persuaded a ship of hard-nosed seamen to trust her to take them safely through the world's most dangerous waters. We will not have the stories of the tens of thousands of people who traveled the oceans in steerage, willingly or unwillingly, from whom so many of us are descended. Nor will we have the story of how a young naval lieutenant, desperate to come home and marry the girl he loved, discovered the secrets of the ocean and how to chart them.

Matthew Maury's charts no longer hold the public in thrall. But perhaps they should. The charts were among the most important technological and scientific advances of the nineteenth century, and, while they represent the first "big data" project in the United States, Maury's charts quickly became, as well, an astonishing example of what crowdsourcing and citizen science could accomplish.

Throughout the 1850s, more than a thousand sea captains every year were sending Maury their logbooks—the logs of tens of thousands of our collective voyages sit in storage. Maury's work—and the unrecorded and unremembered work of generations of mariners who crowdsourced his data and the dozens of assistants in his office who collated and organized it—remains the basis for modern pilot charts still published by the US government and used today by mariners.

In writing and researching this book, I have followed in Mary Ann and Joshua's footsteps, across Drake's Passage and around Cape Horn, as far as Antarctica. But I have also followed other footsteps, along country back lanes and to now-empty housing lots, through dusty archives and reams of microfilm, with the aid of neighbors, wardens, clerks in the town offices, government workers, and local historians, to track the story of Mary Ann and Joshua in their day-to-day lived experience of a nation at a great crossroads, because their story is the story of all those other nameless people whom history has not remembered but who once, out of love and loyalty and hope, did something amazing.

**The quote with** which this book begins is a quote from the poem "Renascence," by the Rockland poet Edna St. Vincent Millay. It describes the view over Penobscot Bay toward the islands from the peak of Mount Battie in Camden. In the opening lines of that poem, Millay writes: "All I could see from where I stood / Was three long mountains and a wood; / I turned and looked another way, / And saw three islands in a bay."

It's a view (and a poem) that, I am sorry to say, I know well. I went to school in Camden, which is just a few miles up the coast from Rockland, and, if you wanted to play hooky there, when I was a young person, without someone calling your mother or your aunt by lunchtime to tattle, one either climbed the mountain or went sailing. I spent many hours staring out toward those islands. I also left school a decent mariner.

Down in the village, Edna St. Vincent Millay's bronze statue stands looking out over Camden harbor and her fleet of what

Mainers simply call "windjammers." These tall-masted, square-rigged great vessels are among the last working remnants of the age of sail, a reminder of the size and scale of *Neptune's Car*, though their only cargo now each summer is wealthy tourists. Maine is no longer at the center of a great international maritime highway, and many of the homes that sea captains built with their riches are gone or have been chopped up into awkward little apartments. Joshua and Mary Ann's house on Main Street in Rockland today is a gas station.

I have sometimes thought that some lines from "Renascence" might have served for the epitaph that I would give Mary Ann and Joshua's love story in this, their final chapter. In that poem, Millay has a verse that reads: "The world stands out on either side / No wider than the heart is wide."

But, if you should visit Woodlawn Cemetery outside of Boston and were to go to see the graves of Mary Ann and Joshua, you would find there has already been left in stone an epitaph that is finer and more fitting, in Mary Ann's voice:

> "Are there seas in heaven, Joshua?
> And is there such a vessel as our Neptune's Car?
> If there is, wait for me, and we shall explore
> the vast and boundless reaches of Eternity."

This is a story about how the small and nearly forgotten lives of two young people are as big and as wide as the American story.

# Acknowledgments

With each new book, the debts mount. I'd like to acknowledge just a few of them here.

I would like to thank the National Endowment for the Humanities (Public Scholar Program) for supporting this book with a yearlong fellowship. In the course of researching this book, I was able to travel to Antarctica and transit Cape Horn, following in Mary Ann Patten's footsteps, though, thankfully, the veracity of that experience did not include an eighteen-day blow in the forecastle of a clipper. A big thanks as well to the Penguins (go Green Team!) for making that excursion to the seventh continent unforgettable.

My thanks in Maine to my mother, Charlene Mazzeo, for tromping through graveyards and scouring old probate records (and for fact-checking); to Donna Perry for driving back roads with us to look for the ruins of the Rockland Poor Farm in a hurricane (mea culpa, officers); to my dad (who still tells a hell of a sea story) and all my dad's shipmates and classmates at Maine Maritime for helping us to track down old Masonic records. Thanks to Ann Morris at the Rockland Historical Society and to Karin Larson at the Warren Historical Society for help finding old title records, to doctoral candidate Andromeda Bainbridge, who kindly assisted with archival research at the Massachusetts Historical Society in the Old North Church collections, and to the curators and archivists at the Sandwich Museum for sharing materials related to Hannah Rebecca Burgess. Plus, a taciturn New England lift of the chin to all my seafaring Maine grandfathers, great-grandfathers, and great-great-grandfathers—John, Samuel, and Frank—for the brine in the veins.

Thanks to the Blue Water Cruising Association of Vancouver Island for the opportunity to learn celestial navigation and to Peter W. Marshall for reviewing this book for historical and nautical accuracy; any errors that persist are entirely my own.

A special thank-you to the people who make writing and books possible: My literary agent, Stacey Glick; my film agent, Lou Pitt; my editors, Hannah Phillips and Brigitte Dale, and the entire team at St. Martin's.

Finally, as always, love and gratitude to Rob and the boys.

# Notes

In an effort to make these notes as economical and as unobtrusive as possible, while also providing a road map for that handful of readers and fellow historians interested in following in these footsteps, I have attempted, where possible, to give the necessary citation information in the running text. Therefore, if I write, for example, that an article appeared in *The New York Times* on January 1, 1857, I do not repeat that same information in a note, trusting that a reader can track that source readily, even if I am quoting directly from the source. Likewise, in cases where I reference a particular historical document, especially manuscript diaries or logs, I give the archival citation only in the first instance and reference the document in the running text, knowing that a reader may, if he or she wishes, find the materials at the first citation. In all other cases, where I cite a text using quotations, that reference is directly attributed; however, it is also that case that, where I am drawing from the arguments of others, if I have cited that same source in the same paragraph, I only make the reference on the first occasion, to avoid having to repeat the same reference in the same immediate area of the text repeatedly. References, in other words, should be understood to refer to a section of text and not as limited to a singular sentence. In order to avoid confusion, variant spellings and misspellings, as sometimes occurred in the press, have been silently standardized. Finally, I do not cite instances of general knowledge, i.e., I assume we all remember from history (and I certainly remember as a professor of the nineteenth century), what, say, the Missouri Compromise was and why it was important for the Civil War. However, all sources to which I have had reference are included in the notes and may be tracked by an astute reader of that marginalia.

## Prologue

2 *He has stood at this helm*: See, among other sources, Paul W. Simpson, *Neptune's Car: An American Legend*, Adelaide: Clippership Press, 2018, 55.

## 1: Penobscot Bay

6 *a full half of all the large sailing vessels*: "Red Jacket," Penobscot Bay History, www.penobscotbayhistory.org/pbho-1/collection/ship-red-jacket.

8 *Those who came home millionaires from the gold rush*: Steven Ujifusa, *Barons of the Sea: And Their Race to Build the World's Fastest Clipper Ship,* New York: Simon & Schuster, 2018, 100, 156.

9 *Nathaniel had fought in the American Revolution*: "Land Grant Application-Nathaniel Patten," Revolutionary War, Maine State Land Office, 706 (2017); Andrew Rothovius, *The Lodge, Including a History of Miles Slip*, ed. F. Stanley Hallett, Milford Historical Society, Milford, NH: The OK Tool Company, 1968.

9 *In the next dozen years, Nathaniel and Hettie Patten*: Bruce Davis, "Re: Nathaniel Patten," Genealogy.com, www.genealogy.com/forum/surnames/topics/patten/631/.

9 *Our Abel styled himself*: Judy G. Russell, "Esquire," The Legal Genealogist, January 9, 2012, www.legalgenealogist.com/2012/01/09/esquire/.

11 *She was the second of at least a dozen children born*: "Lydia Alley," FamilySearch, https://ancestors.familysearch.org/en/LZKS-TZJ/lydia-alley-1778–1830.

11 *It was here that in the winter of 1823 their first son, Enoch*: "Thomaston, Maine, in the 1820 Census," Heirlooms Reunited, January 1, 2020, www.heirloomsreunited.com/2020/01/thomaston-maine-in-1820-census-then-in.html.

## Notes

12 *Just a bit to the south of the Baileys*: "A Brief History of the Hathorn/Olson House," www.maine.gov/doe/sites/maine.gov.doe/files/inline-files/history-olson-house.pdf.

13 *By the 1830s, young Joshua's parents were living*: *Vital Records of Chelsea, Massachusetts, to the Year 1850*, Chelsea, MA: Wright & Potter Printing Company, 1916, 229.

13 *So fearsome and seemingly otherworldly was the epidemic*: Aaron O'Neill, "Child mortality rate (under five years old) in the United States, from 1800 to 2020," Statistica, August 9, 2024, www.statista.com/statistics/1041693/united-states-all-time-child-mortality-rate/; Michael Haines, "Fertility and Mortality in the United States," Economic History Association, March 19, 2008, https://eh.net/encyclopedia/fertility-and-mortality-in-the-united-states/; Crystal Ponti, "When New Englanders Blamed Vampires for Tuberculosis Deaths," History, October 28, 2019, www.history.com/news/vampires-tuberculosis-consumption-new-england.

15 *The Lime Rock Gazette, the Rockland newspaper*: Cyrus Easton, *History of Thomaston, Rockland, and South Thomaston, Maine, from their First Exploration, A. D. 1605; with Family Geneaologies*, Masters, Smith, & Co., 1865, 408, 412.

15 *It would later spawn a lawsuit about claims to adverse possession*: *Peabody v Hewett*, 52 ME 33 (ME 1861), Supreme Judicial Court of Maine.

18 *He must have been home from sea*: "Maine Marriages, 1771–1907," FamilySearch, https://familysearch.org/ark:/61903/1:1:F4DX-WZV; Eaton, *History of Thomaston*, 138.

18 *Like her sister, she'd been born*: "Lemuel C. Bailey," Find a Grave, www.findagrave.com/memorial/160123620/lemuel-c-bailey.

## 2: Boston

21 *All three young men were mariners*: 1850 United States Census, Brunswick, Maine.

22 *She remained for most of a decade an inmate of the asylum*: Maine Insane Hospital, "Maine Insane Hospital Patient Cases, vol. 13, 1858–1864," 2023, *Patient Medical Records (1840–1910)*, 17, https://digitalmaine.com/amhi_medical_patient_cases/17/.

24 *Mary Ann was born in Chelsea*: *Vital Records of Chelsea*, 229; "Mary A. Patten," Find a Grave, www.findagrave.com/memorial/73657321/mary_a-patten.

25 *The confusion seems to stem from a misunderstanding*: "Mary Patten, 19 and Pregnant, Takes Command of a Clipper Ship in 1856," New England Historical Society, updated 2024, https://newenglandhistoricalsociety.com/mary-patten-19-pregnant-commands-clipper-ship-1856/#google_vignette.

27 *"[T]he landlords, runners, and sharks in Ann Street"*: Richard Henry Dana Jr., *Two Years Before the Mast*, Philadelphia: Henry Altemus, 1840, 276.

27 *When their pockets were emptied, "crimpers" hired*: Samuel Eliot Morison, *The Maritime History of Massachusetts, 1783–1860*, New York: Houghton Mifflin, 1921, 354–355.

28 *The best treatment for the "Black Tongue," the doctors said*: Timothy Kent Holliday, "What an 1836 Typhus Outbreak Taught the Medical World About Epidemics," *Smithsonian*, April 21, 2020, www.smithsonianmag.com/history/what-1836-typhus-outbreak-taught-medical-world-about-epidemics-180974707/; Alexander Mercer, "Protection Against Severe Infectious Disease in the Past," *Pathogens and Global Health*, 115, no. 3 (May 2021): 151–167; Stephen Berry and Tracy Barnett, "The Graveyard of Old Diseases," CSI Dixie, May 7, 2019, https://csidixie.org/numbers/mortality-census/graveyard-old-diseases.

28 *"What a dreadful scourge is consumption . . ."*: Mary Fuhrer, "The Disease that Killed the Young and the Beautiful," HistoryNet, February 24, 2021, www.historynet.com/the-young-and-the-beautiful/.

28 *By the beginning of that century, tuberculosis*: United States Centers for Disease Control, "History of World TB Day," October 18, 2023, www.cdc.gov/tb/worldtbday/history.htm; Harvard University Library, "Tuberculosis in Europe and North America, 1800–1922," https://curiosity.lib.harvard.edu/contagion/feature/tuberculosis-in-europe-and-north-america-1800–1922.

29 *If you had stood at the end of Hanover Street*: *The Boston Directory for the Year 1851*, Boston: George Adams, 1851.

30 *Typical of immigrants in the North End in the 1840s*: Joseph Bagley, Alexandra Crowder, and Andrew Webster, "Archaeological Site Exam of the Clough House Backlot," Boston Landmarks Commission report, https://www.boston.gov/sites/default/files/document-file-11-2016/clough_house_site_exam_final_report.pdfclough_house_site_exam_final_report.pdf, 18.

30 *Only 5 percent of seamen in the mid-nineteenth century*: Molly Conway,

"A Study of Boardinghouses for 'Free Colored Seamen' in Antebellum Boston," Primary Research, https://primaryresearch.org/a-study-of-boardinghouses-for-qfree-colored-seamenq-in-antebellum-boston/.

30 *Elizabeth Brown paid between five and ten dollars*: Lauren Middleton, "The Christ church (Old North) Scholars: Meet the Children Who Attended the United States' First Sunday School," Old North, May 23, 2023, www.oldnorth.com/blog/sunday-school-scholars/.

31 *Neither Mary Ann's name nor the names of her older brother George*: Old North Church (Christ Church in the City of Boston), Sunday School Records, 1810–1908, Massachusetts Historical Society.

## 3: Business in Great Waters

35 *"The packet captain, no matter what his age"*: Arthur Clark, *The Clipper Ship Era*, New York: G.P. Putnam's Sons, 1911, 44.

35 *His first command, either that year*: *The Star of the North* (Pennsylvania), March 11, 1857.

37 *Courtship in mid-nineteenth century New England had its own traditions*: Ellen K. Rothman, *Heart and Hand: A History of Courtship in America*, New York: Basic Books, 1984; Captain William L. McClintock, *John Beedle's Sleigh Ride, Courtship and Marriage*, New York: C. Wells, 1841.

39 *Mary Ann and Joshua were married on April 1, 1853*: Lou Rocco, "The People in the Pews: Reverend William Thomas Smithett," Old North, October 16, 2020, www.oldnorth.com/blog/rev-william-thomas-smithett/; Danielle DeVantier, "The Jewells of Old North, Old North, November 28, 2023, www.oldnorth.com/blog/the-jewells-of-old-north/; Theron Metcalf and Horace Mann, *The Revised Statutes of the Commonwealth of Massachusetts, Passed November 4, 1835*, Boston: Dutton & Wentworth, 1836, 477; Old North Church (Christ Church in the City of Boston), Baptism, Marriage, and Burial records (Parish Registers), 1723–1970, Massachusetts Historical Society.

39 *She owned a little house on the south side of Rockland*: Personal correspondence, Ann Morris, Rockland Historical Society; cf. Knox County, Maine, deed register, vol. 18, 286, from Sarah Patten to Joshua Patten.

40 *The Masonic fellowship provided the most reliable form of travel "insurance"*: Roger Burt, "'Wherever Dispersed': The Travelling Mason in the

Nineteenth Century," *Revista de Estudios Históricos de la Masonería Latinoamericana y Caribeña*, 10, no.1 (May–Dec. 2018): 7–40.

40 *As one historian astutely quips*: ibid.

40 *The Sun newspaper of London published, as an item of marine intelligence*: *The Sun* (London), May 30, 1853.

42 *The Cornelia Lawrence was not one of the great "extreme" clippers*: *The Monthly Nautical Magazine*, 1 (Oct. 1854–Mar. 1855), New York: Griffiths and Bates, 1854.

43 *Straight down the road another two or three miles*: "South Thomaston," Maine: An Encyclopedia, https://maineanencyclopedia.com/south-thomaston/.

43 *It had been a strange summer*: Eaton, *History of Thomaston*, 428.

44 *Damariscotta is not twenty-five miles from Rockland . . .* : Lars Bruzelius "Flying Scud," December 1, 1995, www.bruzelius.info/Nautica/Ships/Clippers/Flying_Scud(1853).html.

46 *"Tacking a large square-rigged vessel is considerable of a job . . ."*: Walter McRoberts, *Rounding Cape Horn and Other Sea Stories*, Peoria, IL: H.S. Hill, 1895, 241.

47 *Survival was not assured: A full 75 percent*: "The incidence of Death on Merchant Vessels in 1865," Royal Greenwich Museum, January 22, 2019, www.rmg.co.uk/stories/blog/library-archive/incidence-death-on-merchant-vessels-1865.

48 *Life at sea was never easy*: John D. Whidden, *Ocean Life in the Old Sailing-Ship Days*, Boston: Little, Brown, & Co., 1909.

49 *The 180-foot tea clipper Foochow*: "Proposed Tea Clipper Foo Chow," deck plans, https://doriccolumns.wordpress.com/wp-content/uploads/2023/03/clipperfoochowga.jpg.

49 *The Witch of the Wave, a clipper built in 1851*: qtd. in Laurel Seaborn, "Gamming Chairs and Gimballed Beds: Seafaring Women on Board Nineteenth-Century Ships," *Journal of Maritime Archaeology*, 12 (2017): 71–90.

49 *One sea captain's wife, Rebecca Hannah Burgess*: Manuscript diaries, Sandwich Museum and Historical Association, MA.

## 4: The Road to Liverpool

51 *Mr. Cameron, a burly man with an untamed lamb-chop beard*: Lars Bruzelius, "Maine Clipper Ships," February 7, 1999, www.bruzelius.info/Nautica/Shipbuilding/Shipyards/Clippers(ME).html; Glenn A.

Knoblock, *The American Clipper Ship, 1845–1920: A Comprehensive History*, Jefferson, NC: McFarland, 2014, 266.

52 *The* Flying Scud *and the* Windward *were the newest additions*: Frank J. Mather, "A Clipper Ship and Her Commander," *The Atlantic*, November 1904; Lars Bruzelius, "Pioneer Line of Australian Packets," www.bruzelius.info/Nautica/Ships/Owners/USNM-3(1855)_p144.html.

52 *As one historian has written of Cameron*: "Cameron, Sir Roderick," Glengarry Historical Society, https://glengarryhistoricalsociety.com/dokusoft/!dgb/doku.php?id=cameron_sir_roderick_william.

53 *With a crew of sixty-five men, Elridge*: "The Red Jacket and Her Sapling," The Historical Society of Lancashire and Chesire, https://www.hslc.org.uk/wp-content/uploads/2017/06/67-4-Arkle.pdf, 19; Tim Hatton, "Voyage Durations in the Age of Mass Migration," *Vox EU*, July 31, 2023, https://cepr.org/voxeu/columns/voyage-durations-age-mass-migration.

53 *Hearing of a record in the making, the* Yarmouth Register: William H. Painter, "The Eldrige Brothers: Three Famous Sea Captains of Yarmouth Port" Historical Society of Old Yarmouth, April 14, 2024, www.hsoy.org/blog/2024/4/12/the-eldrige-brothers.

55 *The* Great Republic, *built in 1853 in Boston*: J. Ernest Kerr, *Imprint of the Maritimes*, Boston: The Christopher Publishing House, 1959, 135.

56 *Their mutual destination was Liverpool*: Sir William B. Forwood, *Reminiscences of a Liverpool Shipowner 1850–1920*, Liverpool: Henry Young & Sons, 1920.

56 *To the paying passengers who booked the first-class staterooms*: "Samuel Samuels," Find a Grave, www.findagrave.com/memorial/27676635/samuel-samuels; Samuel Samuels, *From the Forecastle to the Cabin*, New York: Harper & Brothers, 1887, 253, 270.

57 *Longer messages could be sent, of course, in calm weather*: "Signaling at Sea," Shipping Wonders of the World, https://shippingwondersoftheworld.com/signalling.html.

57 *"[W]e clapped on all the sail we could . . ."*: *Proceedings of the Massachusetts Historical Society*, Massachusetts Historical Society, 1932, 9.

58 *"[S]he was giving us a pretty hard rub"*: ibid.

58 *Captain Samuels, now swearing mightily*: ibid.

58 *Or, at least "we presumed it to be the* Flying Scud*"*: "Flying Scud," Pickering Family History, https://pickeringhistory.com/flying-scud/.

59 *The city of Liverpool—from the Old English "liever pol"*: Tim Lambert, "A History of Liverpool," Local Histories, https://localhistories.org/a-history-of-liverpool/.

59 *From the sea, what one saw first on the approach to the harbor*: "History of the Liverpool Docks," *Northern Daily Times*, June 5, 1855.

60 *American packet ships on the emigrant run*: Zoë Alker, "Street Violence in Mid-Victorian Liverpool," (doctoral dissertation, Liverpool John Moores University, February 2014), 127.

60 *Because the warehouses were bonded*: "Construction, heyday and decline," National Museums Liverpool, www.liverpoolmuseums.org.uk/royal-albert-dock-liverpool/construction-heyday-and-decline.

61 *The popular tune in the 1850s was "The Liverpool Judies"*: "The Liverpool Judies," Musicanet, www.musicanet.org/robokopp/shanty/liverpol.htm.

62 *The consul complained that he was short-staffed*: "Nathaniel Hawthorne," Liverpool Footprints, www.liverpoolfootprint.co.uk/hawthorne-n.

62 *American captains passing through Liverpool in the 1850s*: J. A. Picton, *Memorials of Liverpool, Historical and Topographical, Including a History of the Dock Estate*, London: Longman, Green, & Co., 1875, 272; Raymona Hull, *Nathaniel Hawthorne: The English Experience, 1853–1864*, Pittsburgh: University of Pittsburgh Press, 2010, 272.

63 *The consul himself had lived at the boardinghouse on Duke Street*: Julian Hawthorne, *Hawthorne and His Circle*, New York: Harper & Brothers, 1903, 2 vols., ch. 1, 10.

64 *Even more unfortunately, the natives*: Michael Lee Wittig, "John Minor Maury and Nuku Hiva," *The Great Circle*, 43, no. 1 (2021): 1–18.

67 *When he recovered, with a limp and unable to sail again*: Miles P. Duval, "Matthew Fontaine Maury: Benefactor of Mankind," Naval History and Heritage Command, November 13, 2017, www.history.navy.mil/content/history/nhhc/research/library/online-reading-room/title-list-alphabetically/m/matthew-fontaine-maury-benefactor-of-mankind.html.

67 *"With emotions too deep for the organs of speech"*: ibid.

## 5: Pathfinder of the Seas

69 *As the* National Intelligencer *explained the significance*: "Maury's Wind and Current Chart," review, *National Intelligencer* (Washington, DC), January 26, 1848.

70 *"No vessel should go to sea without these charts"*: "W.H. De Courcey Wright," maritime intelligence, *North American* (Philadelphia), May 22, 1848, v. 65, no. 16, 318.

71 *As they left the Mersey River behind them*: Timothy Hatton, "Time on the Crossing: Emigrant Voyages Across the Atlantic, 1853 to 1913," Institute of Labor, no. 16274, June 3, 2023.

71 *By the time the* Flying Scud *arrived back in Manhattan*: "Marine Journal," *The Boston Daily Atlas*, June 29, 1854, v. 22, no. 308; "Maritime Intelligence," *The Weekly Herald* (New York), July 1, 1854, v. 18, n. 20, 208.

73 *The young Mrs. Merriam had been born Mary Parker Bailey*: Charles Henry Pope, *Merriam Genealogy in England and America*, Boston: C. H. Simonds & Co. (privately printed), 1900.

73 *In the summer of 1854, the crews were putting the finishing touches*: "Marine Journal," *The Boston Daily Atlas*, December 13, 1854, v. 23, no. 140.

73 *Captain Nickerson was a member of the Nickerson part*: Longworth's *American Almanack, New York Register, and City Directory for [1842]*, New York: T Longworth & Son, 1842.

75 *A "competence" of $100,000 in capital was the amount*: Knoblock, *American Clipper*, 170; cf. New York Court of Appeals, *Williams v Lawrence*, New York, Douglas Taylor, 1871, 37; *Baron of the Seas*, 25.

76 *Those in his native Connecticut described him*: Obituary, *The Morning Journal-Courier* (New Haven), December 5, 1881.

78 *Sending a ton of tea from Shanghai to London*: Jan Tore Klovland, "A Repeat Sailings Index of Ocean Freight Rates for the 1850s," https://core.ac.uk/download/pdf/30809833.pdf.

78 Neptune's Car *had a cargo capacity of 1,616 tons*: Raymond A. Rydell, "The California Clippers," *Pacific Historical Review*, 18, no. 1 (Feb. 1949): 70–83.

78 *A captain's percentage of the primage could vary*: Lars Bruzelius, "Stag Hound," March 9, 1999, www.bruzelius.info/Nautica/Ships/Clippers/Staghound(1850).html.

79 *A very astute sea captain, with good judgment in tea*: "Information Concerning the History of the Steamer San Francisco," The Mariner's Museum and Park (San Francisco), https://catalogs.marinersmuseum.org/object/CL8611; Clark, *The Clipper Ship Era*, 32.

## 6: The First Circumnavigation of *Neptune's Car*

83 *Captain Samuels's wife, Anne, sailed with him*: Samuels, *From the Forecastle*, 131.

83 *Captain Hussey's fourteen-year-old son*: Gay Montague Moore, *Seaport in Virginia: George Washington's Alexandria*, Charlottesville: University of Virginia Press, 1949.

85 Neptune's Car *cleared Sandy Hook one day and thirty-minutes later*: Carl C. Cutler, *Greyhounds of the Sea: The Story of the American Clipper Ship*, Annapolis, MD: Naval Institute Press, 1984, 312.

85 *At Sandy Hook, Joshua recorded in the ship's log*: ship's log, *Neptune's Car*, National Archives at Boston (NARA), Waltham, MA. Logbooks of U.S. Merchant Vessels (microfilm series), https://www.archives.gov/research/military/logbooks/merchant-vessels.html.

85 *In the middle of this great ocean gyre in the Atlantic*: Ernest Ingersoll, *The Book of the Ocean*, New York: The Century Company, 1898.

86 *As Richard Dana described the splendid power*: Dana, *Two Years Before the Mast*, ch. 3.

87 *Faced with a shortage of crew—because who would risk his life*: Morison, *Maritime History*, 354–355.

87 *Everyone in the North End had known about a brawl*: Conway, "A Study of Boardinghouses for 'Free Colored Seamen.'"

88 *Indeed, they are not entirely understood today*: Julie Beck, "The Mysterious Science of Motion Sickness," *The Atlantic*, February 2015.

88 *As one physician put it in 1846*: F. Willis Fisher, "The Nature and Treatment of Sea Sickness," *Boston Medical Surgery*, 36, no. 26 (1847): 513–518.

92 *The currents in Drake's Passage, at the bottom of the world*: Ryan Smith, Melicie Desflots, Sean White, Arthur J. Mariano, and Edward H. Ryan, "The Antarctic CP Current," Surface Currents in the Southern Ocean, University of Miami, https://oceancurrents.rsmas.miami.edu/southern/antarctic-cp.html.

94 *They told the story of a wave of monstrous proportions*: Paul C. Liu, "A Chronology of Freaque Wave Encounters," *Geofizika*, 24, no. 1 (2007): 57–70.

95 *Off the coast of Vancouver Island, British Columbia*: Carly Cassela, "Gigantic Wave in Pacific Ocean Was The Most Extreme 'Rogue Wave' on Record," Science Alert, September 15, 2024, https://www.sciencealert.com/gigantic-wave-in-pacific-ocean-was-the-most-extreme-rogue-wave-on-record.

95 *Statistical analysis calculates that a ship at sea encounters*: Craig B. Smith, "Extreme Waves and Ship Design," *Tenth International Symposium on Practical Design of Ships and Other Floating Structures*, ABS: Houston, TX, 2007.

95 *One in every 10,000 waves are thought to be "rogue"*: Sherryn Groch, "Scientists Thought These Monster Waves Were Myth. Now They're Racing to Understand Them," *The Sydney Morning Herald*, June 30, 2022.

96 *When hydrographer Captain George Henry Richard arrived*: William Glover, "The Challenge of Navigation to Hydrography on the British Columbia Coast, 1850–1930," *The Northern Mariner*, 6, no. 4 (October 1996): 1–16.

98 *When captain's wife Susannah Weynton found herself*: Susannah Weynton, "Journal of a Voyage to Pacific and American Shores," 1849–1852, University of British Columbia, Special Collections.

100 *Sun blindness and cataracts were occupational hazards*: "The History of the Sextant," https://pgi-shop.de/media/f2/f3/75/1643224352/206.SXT-E.pdf.

## 7: Westward Ho!

102 *Joshua was known for being slow to anger*: Burgess, manuscript diary, Sandwich Museum.

103 *Joshua wrote in relief in his logbook that evening*: ship's log, *Neptune's Car*, NARA.

103 *To understand how rare a passage from an Atlantic port around Cape Horn*: Morison, *Maritime History*, 344.

104 *The islands are often shrouded in fog year-round*: Bonnie Tsui, "The Farallon Islands Are Off Limits to Humans—but Not Wildlife," *The New York Times*, May 19, 2016.

104 *In the watchtower on Loma Alta*: Ujifusa, *Barons of the Sea*, 154.

105 *When Lieutenant Manuel de Ayala became the first non-Indigenous captain*: Carl Nolte, "San Francisco Tides of History," *San Francisco Chronicle*, June 28, 2005.

105 *As Joshua recorded wryly in the captain's log*: Cutler, *Greyhounds of the Seas*, 313.

106 *"Not since the Crusades had such a large assemblage"*: Helene and Jack Lagrange, *Clipper Ships of America and Great Britain, 1833–1869*, New York, G.P. Putnam's Sons, 1936, 224.

106 *Less than 10 percent of the non-native population of San Francisco*:

Timothy G. Lynch, *Beyond the Golden Gate: A Maritime History of California*, Washington, DC: National Parks Service, 2012, 44.

106 *They had lost the $2,000 bonus*: *The Daily Alta California*, vol. 6, no. 107, April 26, 1855; Charles Park, "Development of the Clipper Ship," *Proceedings of the American Antiquarian Society*, vol. 39, pt. 1 (April 1929): 68.

106 *Captain Hussey had brought the* Westward Ho!: *The Daily Alta California*, vol. 6, no. 106, April 25, 1855; "Seaports and Sea Captains, San Francisco 1846–1899," Maritime Heritage Project, www.maritimeheritage.org/news/wharves.html; "Marine Journal," *The Boston Daily Atlas*, vol. 23, no. 278, May 25, 1855; Lagrange, *Clipper Ships of America*, 224.

108 *With the race on and the summer trading season approaching*: "Seaports and Sea Captains, San Francisco 1846–1899."

108 *Joshua's stepbrother and cousin*: Samuel Colville, *Colville's San Francisco Directory, for the Year Commencing October 1856*, San Francisco: Commercial Steam Presses, Monson, Valentine, and Company, 1856, 6; John Lumea, "Joshua Norton at the Rassette House," The Emperor Norton Trust, March 26, 2015, https://emperornortontrust.org/blog/2015/3/26/joshua-norton-at-the-rassette-house.

108 *His young wife, Mary Ann Waterman Bailey*: "Lemuel C. Bailey," Find a Grave, www.findagrave.com/memorial/160123620/lemuel-c-bailey#source.

109 *Goods arriving "ex-Neptune's Car" were advertised for sale*: "Markets," *The Daily Alta California*, June 16, 1855; April 28, 1855.

109 *How much are all these figures in modern dollars?*: "Relative Value Calculator," Measuring Worth, https://www.measuringworth.com/calculators/uscompare/relativevalue.php.

109 *But a gold rush miner could also make $1,000*: Ujifusa, *Barons of the Sea*, 148.

109 *As one historian notes: "No modern bootlegger would dare to hope"*: Park, "Development of the Clipper," 68.

112 *Women could live only on the island of Macao*: "Harriet Low Enters a City Forbidden to Women During the China Trade," New England Historical Society, https://newenglandhistoricalsociety.com/young-puritan-woman-chronicles-china-trade/.

113 *American merchants, capitalizing on the trade, soon followed*: Basil Lubbock, *The Opium Clippers*, Glasgow: Brown, Son and Ferguson, 1946, 320.

113 *When the Chinese emperor attempted to crack down on this illicit trade*: "Commodities, Currencies, and Balancing of the Trade Deficit," Baker

Library, Historical Collections Exhibit, Harvard Business School, https://www.library.hbs.edu/hc/heard/commodities-currencies.html.

113 *By the 1850s, the trade in Hong Kong was divided*: Karl E. Meyer, "The Opium War's Secret History," *The New York Times*, June 28, 1997.

114 *As one British resident remembered it in the 1840s*: Helen Edith Legge, *James Legge: Missionary and Scholar*, London: The Religious Tract Society, 1905, ch. 12.

114 *When Joshua and Mary Ann slipped into Victoria Harbor*: George Lai, "Hong Kong and the Surprising Truth about the British Empire," *The Spectator*, May 18, 2022.

114 *The permanent European population on the eastern side of the island*: C. Chu, "Early Beginnings of British Community (1841–1898)," in *Foreign Communities in Hong Kong, 1840s–1950s*, ed. Gillian Bickley, London: Palgrave, 2016, 17–38, 21; Benjamin Lincoln Ball, *Rambles in Eastern Asia: Including China and Manilla, during Several Years' Residence: With Notes of the Voyage to China, Excursions in Manilla, Hong-Kong, Canton, Shanghai, Ningpoo, Amoy, Fouchow, and Macao*, London: Legare Street Press, 2021, rpt.

114 *There was his fellow Masonic brother, Captain Michael Gregory*: The Daily Alta California, April 13, 1855; Lagrange, *Clipper Ships of America*, 280.

115 *Young hyson tea (the tea of choice at the Boston Tea Party)*: Samuel Lincoln Ball, *An Account of the Cultivation and Manufacture of Tea in China: Derived from Personal Observation during an Official Residence in that Country from 1804 to 1826*, London: Longman, Brown, Green, and Longman, 1848.

## 8: All the Tea in China

118 *The year that* Neptune's Car *arrived in Hong Kong*: Lagrange, *Clipper Ships of America*, 227.

118 *The* Westward Ho! *would sail, alongside Captain Gorham*: Lagrange, *Clipper Ships of America*, 189.

118 *And, because the Chinese had a cultural tradition of satisfying honor*: Lubbock, *Opium Clippers*, 20–21.

120 *Ownership of Chinese Tom was among the wedding gifts*: Krysten Moon, "A Chinese Slave in Alexandria," Southeastern Immigration Project, September 4, 2013, www.southeasternimmigration.org/research/a-chinese-slave-in-alexandria/.

121 *"[M]issionaries in China are made to feel how close they are to eternity"*:

Ellsworth C. Carlson, *The Foochow Missionaries, 1847–1880*, London: Brill, 2002, 11.

121 *While the missionaries were greeted by the local population*: Carlson, *The Foochow Missionaries*, 42.

122 *So, as Eliza continues the story, "Mr. Gibson went to see Capt. Patten"*: Eliza C. Gibson, *California Christian Advocate*, 1916, qtd. in Paul Simpson, *Neptune's Car*, 43.

123 *She had contracted almost immediately on arrival a parasitic dysentery*: Carlson, *The Foochow Missionaries*, 172.

123 *The average life expectancy in the United States*: Aaron O'Neill, "Average Life Expectancy From Birth . . . 1820 and 2020," Statista, August 9, 2024, www.statista.com/statistics/1302736/global-life-expectancy-by-region-country-historical/.

123 *An unexpectedly heartbroken Erastus Wentworth*: Polly Park, ed., *"To Save Their Heathen Souls": Voyage to and Life in Foochow, China, Based on the Wentworth Diaries and Letters, 1854–1858*, Pittsburgh: Wipf and Stock, 1984.

124 *The first of the British tea clippers had set sail for London in early June*: Angus MacKinnon, *Clipper Ships of the Nineteenth Century*, Carlisle, UK: Troon, 1995, 5.

124 Neptune's Car *was commissioned to carry*: National Archives of the United States, General Records of the U.S. State Department, (Record Group 59, microfilm 105), Despatches from U.S. Consular Offices, Despatches from U.S. Consuls, Foochow, China, 1850–1906, vol. 1, July 14, 1849–December 1, 1857.

125 *They may have traveled as far up the Min River*: Stephan Loewentheil, "Why Has It Taken Early Chinese Photography So Long to Emerge from the Shadows?" *Apollo Magazine*, October 31, 2016.

127 *At the bend around St. Katherine's and Wapping*: John Murray, *Murray's Handbook for Modern London*, London: John Murray, 1851, 67.

127 *On Saturday nights, as one resident described the city*: Henry Mayhew, "London Street Markets on a Saturday Night," *London Labour and London Poor*, London: William Clowes and Son, 1851, vol. 1.

129 *By February 26, the final cargo was being put in place*: *Cork Constitution* (newspaper), January 26, 1856.

129 *Several more members of the crew were injured*: "Marine Journal," *The Boston Daily Atlas*, vol. 24, no. 238, April 7, 1856.

131 *The competitors would be* Neptune's Car, *the* Romance of the Seas: "A Heroine of the Sea," *New-York Daily Tribune*, February 18, 1857.

# Notes

131 *The master of the* Snow Squall *that season was Captain Lloyd*: "Maritime Intelligence," *The New York Herald*, July 6, 1856.

133 *As Richard Dana wrote in 1841 in* The Seaman's Friend: Richard Dana Jr., *The Seaman's Friend*, Boston: Thomas Groom, 1841, ch. 2.

## 9: Cape Horn

141 *A young man named Clarence Ray*: "Life On Board: The Watch System," Royal Greenwich Museum, August 12, 2015, www.rmg.co.uk/stories/blog/life-on-board-watch-system.

144 *She flipped through books like* Dr. Ritter's Medical Manual and Medicine Chest: Thomas Ritter, *A Medical Manual and Medicine Chest Companion*, New York: S.W. Benedict, 1847.

## 10: The Tempest

149 *She will need to know the "mean" time far away in Greenwich*: "History of the Nautical Almanac," Astronomical Applications Department, US Navy, https://aa.usno.navy.mil/publications/na_history.

150 *She turns to the section on Cape Horn and reads Lieutenant Maury's guidance*: Matthew Fontaine Maury, *Explanations and Sailing Directions to Accompany the Wind and Current Charts*, Washington, DC: C. Alexander, for U.S. Navy, 1851, 432.

153 *She reads that to treat brain fever*: Audrey C. Peterson, "Brain Fever in Nineteenth-Century Literature: Fact and Fiction," *Victorian Studies*, 19, no. 4, (June 1976): 445–464, 460.

154 *In 1857, when this voyage was over*: William Attfield, "Neptune's Car: A Tale of New York. A Poem," London: Saunders & Otley, 1857.

155 *As* The New York Times *later recounted*: *The New York Times*, February 18, 1857.

156 *They told reporters later, "each man responded by a promise"*: *The New York Times*, February 18, 1857.

## 11: The Land of Mist and Snow

157 *As one maritime historian put it*: Cutler, *Greyhounds of the Sea*, 324.

158 *Sea captain's wife Susannah Weynton was caught in a storm*: Weynton, "Journal of a Voyage to Pacific."

158 *When* Neptune's Car *came through the Strait of Lemaire*: Log of Ship Rapid (Phineas Windsor), logbooks of U.S. Merchant Vessels (microfilm series), National Archives at Boston (NARA), Waltham, MA, https://www.archives.gov/research/military/logbooks/merchant-vessels.html.

158 *Her first masthead was fourteen feet above deck*: *The Boston Daily Atlas*, November 8, 1853.

159 *And that meant that everyone aboard* Neptune's Car *was in mortal danger*: Steve Tredup, "Dangerous Waves and Your Boat," Ocean Navigator, March 31, 2011, https://oceannavigator.com/dangerous-waves-and-your-boat/.

159 *As Hannah Rebecca Burgess, aboard the* Challenger: diary, Sandwich Museum; see also Megan Taylor Shockley, *The Captain's Widow of Sandwich: Self-Invention and the Life of Hannah Rebecca Burgess, 1834–1917*, New York: New York University Press, 2010.

160 *Mary Ann asked the watch boy: Had he made out the ensign*: Robert J. Plowman, "The Voyage of the 'Coolie' Ship Kate Hooper, October 3, 1857–March 26, 1858," *Prologue Magazine*, National Archives of the United States, 33, no. 2 (Summer 2001), https://www.archives.gov/publications/prologue/2001/summer/coolie-ship-kate-hooper-1.

160 *It would not be until 1859 that pyrotechnic signal flares*: Martha J. Coston, *A Signal Success. The Life and Travels of Mrs. Martha J. Coston*, Philadelphia: Lippincott Company, 1886.

160 *The vessel was, indeed, a-hull*: Sam Jefferson, *Clipper Ships and the Golden Age*, London: Adlard Coles, 2014, 6.

161 *"Probably no ship that ever doubled Cape Horn ever had that kind of misfortune"*: "Log of Ship Rapid," NARA.

161 *Half a dozen lay, as one historian puts it, "absolutely helpless in the forecastle"*: ibid.

161 *Hunched over the helm, his arm aching from the strain*: "Log of Ship Rapid," NARA.

162 *"How Mrs. Patten fought that ship" in that last day*: Cutler, *Greyhounds of the Sea*, 325.

165 *The ship's insurer would later write that Mary Ann*: Qtd. in "Women in Transportation, Changing America's History," U.S. Department of Transportation, March 1998, https://www.fhwa.dot.gov/ohim/wmntrans2.pdf, 4.

168 *Mary Ann knew from reading Lieutenant Maury*: Matthew Fontaine

Maury, *The Physical Geography of the Sea*, Washington, DC: T. Nelson and Sons, 1855, 764.

168 *One captain's wife, who recorded the first appearance of an iceberg*: Wood Family Diaries, 1846, W873, item 1.2, Register of the Small 19th Century Ocean Travel Collections, 1834–1861, Online Archives of California, entry of January 22, 1857.

169 *Also in the spring of 1854, the* Medway: "Perils of Cape Horn Passage: Through Sea of Thousand Icebergs," newspaper ephemera, 1924–1985, https://collections.sea.museum/objects/106131/newspaper-clipping-titled-perils-of-cape-horn-passage-thro?ctx=aba8fb15e7c7a0f28d40fe9a484058854a88e4f6&idx=2.

169 *"The dreadful apprehensions that assailed us yesterday"*: Matthew Fontaine Maury, *Explanations and Sailing Directions to Accompany Wind and Current Charts*, Philadelphia: K. C. and J. Biddle, 1854, 184.

169 *The logbook of this journey aboard* Neptune's Car: "Exploring the Antarctica 1840," Naval History and Heritage Command, United States Navy, September 12, 2017, www.history.navy.mil/research/library/online-reading-room/title-list-alphabetically/e/exploring-the-antarctic-1840-the-wilkes-expedition.html.

171 *What complicated matters for Joshua was the fact*: Myra C. Glenn, "The Naval Reform Campaign Against Flogging: A Case Study in Changing Attitudes Toward Corporal Punishment, 1830–1850," *The American Quarterly*, 35, no. 4 (Autumn 1983): 408–425.

172 *American law followed British Common Law*: ibid.

172 *The Supreme Court of the United States found in 1849*: G. J. Rowcliff, "Some Aspects of the Personnel Problem in Our Merchant Marine," *United States Naval Institute*, vol. 64/4/422 (April 1938).

## 12: The Long Way Round

175 *One nineteenth-century Englishman who visited*: Maria Caldecott, *Journal of a Residence in Chile, During the Year 1822*, London: Longman, Hurst, Rees, Orme, Brown, and Green, and John Murray, 1835, 115.

177 *"The men manifested their sympathy by the greatest alacrity"*: *The New York Times*, February 18, 1857.

179 *On the slack tide just after noon on November 15, 1856*: "Marine Correspondence," *New York Herald*, December 15, 1856.

181 *But no law granting a legal right to married women over property*: Zorina Khan, *The Democratization of Invention Patents and Copyrights in American Economic Development, 1790–1920*, Cambridge: Cambridge University Press, 2005, 167–168.

181 *The Rassette House Hotel was a couple of thousand feet*: "Cooper's Eye, Ear and Orthopaidic Infirmary," Pacific Coast Architecture Database, https://v2039.host.s.uw.edu/building/24435/.

182 *This Dr. Harris may have been the well-known pioneer physician*: Colville, *Colville's San Francisco Directory*, 94.

183 *That would not connect San Francisco and New York City until 1861*: *The Daily Alta California*, vol. 13, no. 4231, September 18, 1861.

185 *"Those who saw her enter the harbor"*: *The New York Times*, February 18, 1857.

185 The New-York Daily Tribune *applauded itself*: *New-York Daily Tribune*, February 18, 1857.

185 *One newspaper turned Mary Ann into a "delicate blonde"*: *The Star of the North* (Philadelphia), March 11, 1857.

185 *This same eager reporter was the first to circulate the mistaken story*: ibid.

186 *As one letter writer in early 1857 explained to a correspondent*: *The New York Times*, February 21, 1857.

## 13: The Iron Embrace of the Isthmus

188 *Even walking unaccompanied the handful of blocks*: Paul Freedman, "Women and Restaurants in the Nineteenth-Century United States," *Journal of Social History*, 48, no.1 (Fall 2014): 1–19.

188 *In 1849, the ratio of men to women in San Francisco*: Jacqueline Baker Barnhart, *The Fair but Frail: Prostitution in San Francisco, 1849–1900*, Reno: University of Nevada Press, 1986.

188 *The winter of 1856 was exceptionally cold in California*: *The Daily Alta California*, December 30, 1856.

190 *He was unquestionably back in Maine with his wife and children by 1859*: " Lemuel Bailey," Find a Grave, www.findagrave.com/memorial/160123620/lemuel-c-bailey.

191 *One irate passenger recorded in his diary*: J. S. Holliday, *The World Rushed In: The California Gold Rush Experience*, London: Victor Gollancz Ltd., 1983, 415.

192 *In 1857, the village was an important military fortress*: "Early Images of Acapulco," Early Latin American Photography, https:

//earlylatinamerica.wordpress.com/2014/04/04/early-images-of-acapulco/#_ftnref1.
192 *Young men frequently went ashore for betting, drinking*: Holliday, *The World Rushed In*, 502. Further details in this section at 428–429.
193 *The tourist retorted "kiss my ass"*: Mercedes Chen Daley, "The Watermelon Riot: Cultural Encounters in Panama City, April 15, 1856," *Hispanic American Historical Review*, 70, no. 1 (1990): 85–108.
193 *When the San Francisco newspaper* The Daily Alta California *reported on what came next*: *The Daily Alta California*, vol. 7, no. 137, May 27, 1856.
195 *The locals smoked cigars outside the windows*: Holliday, *The World Rushed In*, 416.
195 *It was celebrated back in New York as a feat of industry*: Robert Tomes, *Panama in 1855, An Account of the Panama Rail-road, of the Cities of Panama and Aspinwall, with Sketches of Life and Character on the Isthmus*, New York: Harper & Brothers, 1855, 52.
195 *Now, they could cross in two and a half hours*: "Journey to a Mission, Chronology Leading to the Arrival of the Sisters of Providence in Washington Territory, 1856," Providence, www.providence.org/about/providence-archives/history-online/historical-timelines/journey-to-a-mission/arrival-aspinwall-panama-city.
196 *"The railroad would soon be found insufficient"*: The Panama Railroad, www.panamarailroad.org/quotes.html.
196 *In the spring of 1856, a year after its opening*: *The Daily Alta California*, 7:133, May 23, 1856; *The Daily Alta California*, vol. 7, no. 137, May 27, 1856.
196 *"Another route is demanded now more than ever"*: *The Daily Alta California*, vol. 7, no. 137, May 27, 1856.
196 *The "Company . . . has power of life and death on the isthmus*: Tomes, *Panama in 1855*, 124.
197 *The entire population—described derisively*: Tomes, *Panama in 1855*, 44.
197 *When Ulysses S. Grant visited Aspinwall*: The Panama Railroad, www.panamarailroad.org/quotes.html.
198 *In the stateroom cabins were "returning Californian bankers . . ."*: Tomes, *Panama in 1855*, 62.
199 *When the* George Law *had departed Aspinwall on December 4, 1856*: *The New York Times*, December 15, 1856.
200 *He had died of tuberculosis*: John F. Trow, *1857 New York City Directory*, New York: Trow, 1857.

200 *The 1860 census records show his widow, Elizabeth Patten*: 1860, United States Census, Massachusetts.

## 14: A Mighty Pretty Woman and a Heroine

202 *As the reporter went on to note*: The New York Times, February 18, 1857.
202 *On Wednesday, it also ran a feature article on Mary Ann*: The New York Times, February 24, 1857.
203 *As* The New York Times *reported to sympathetic readers*: ibid.
204 *In Manhattan, the newspaper readers and the merchant community*: New-York Daily Tribune, February 18, 1857.
205 *The officers on the steamer, keen to show their respect*: The New York Times, February 24, 1857.
206 The New York Times, *still following a story*: The New York Times, February 24, 1857.
206 *When the* Bay State *arrived in Fall River*: The Boston Daily Atlas, vol. 25 no. 198, February 21, 1857.
206 *Readers were delighted to learn that these kind attentions*: The New York Times, February 24, 1857.
206 *The Brown family lived on Salutation Street*: The New York Times, February 24, 1857; "The Salutation / The Green Dragon Tavern," Boston, Historical Marker Database.
207 *When settled into bed in their old room*: The Boston Daily Atlas, vol. 25 no. 198, February 21, 1857.
207 *In New York City, the Board of Underwriters*: The New York Times, February 24, 1857.
207 *Mary Ann's letter of acknowledgment: The New York Times*, March 7, 1857.
209 *And, while the question of the "peculiar institution"*: Erin Allen, "Remember the Ladies," United States Library of Congress, March 31, 2016 https://blogs.loc.gov/loc/2016/03/remember-the-ladies/.
209 *But when suffragettes in the 1840s and 1850s imagined*: Margaret Fuller, Woman in the Nineteenth Century, New York: Greeley & McElrath, 1845.
210 *"If the men of America have seen fit to allow the home"*: The Mount Vernon Ladies' Association, www.mountvernon.org/preservation/mount-vernon-ladies-association.
211 *Florence Nightingale had argued passionately*: Florence Nightingale, "Florence Nightingale's Legacy," Paul S. Russell Museum, Massachusetts General Hospital, www.russellmuseum.org/wp-content/uploads/2020/06/florence-nightingale.pdf.

211 *"Witness," he intoned to the crowd*: Edward Everett, *Orations and Speeches on Various Occasions*, Boston: Little, Brown, and Co., 1856.
212 *Now, playing to the hometown crowd, he went on*: Everett, *Orations and Speeches*.
212 *While the verse is, admittedly, sophomoric*: Attfield, *The Neptune's Car*.
213 *"Why, I 'member goin' a voyage with Cap'n Eaton"*: Harriet Beecher Stowe, *The Pearl of Orr's Island: A Story of the Coast of Maine*, Boston: Houghton, Mifflin, and Company, 1896, ch. 33.
214 *The pressure in the brain, however, also accelerated the deterioration*: Genevieve Timmins, "TB Meningitis Kills and Damages Nerve Cells in Brain Through 'Overstimulation'," Imperial College, London, September 6, 2019, www.imperial.ac.uk/news/192812/tb-meningitis-kills-damages-nerve-cells/.
214 The New York Times, *still following the story*: *The New York Times*, June 15, 1857.
215 The Rockland Gazette, *Joshua's hometown newspaper*: *Rockland Gazette*, June 25, 1857.
216 *Soon The Boston Post joined the action*: *Rockland Gazette*, July 2, 1857.
216 *"A lady on Mount Vernon Street," one newspaper announced*: *The New York Times*, June 25, 1857.
216 The Rockland Gazette, *noting that "Capt. Patten is (or was) a citizen"*: *Rockland Gazette*, June 25, 1857.
217 *From a blind man in London arrived $100*: *The New York Times*, June 27, 1857.
217 *"The merchants of Boston have taken up her case"*: *The New York Times*, June 27, 1857.
217 *"When, in the years to come, the name of Mrs. Patten shall be made the theme"*: ibid.
218 *"Any aid which has been or may be rendered on the part of our citizens to Capt. Patten"*: *Rockland Gazette*, Jun 27, 1857.
218 *On Friday, July 17, 1857, Joshua was transferred to the McLean Asylum*: *The New York Times*, July 25, 1857.
219 *Their physician, Dr. Clark, was a renowned specialist*: Henry Grafton Clark, *Ship Fever, So Called, Its History, Nature, and Best Treatment*, Boston: Ticknor, Reed & Fields, 1850.
219 *The process in general, however, was subject to considerable abuse*: Alison R. Brown, "Reform and Curability in the American Insane Asylums of the 1840s: The Conflict of Motivation Between Humanitarian Efforts

and the Efforts of the Superintendent 'Brethren'," *Constructing the Past*, 11, no. 1 (April 2010), article 4, 23.
219 *The eighty enslaved people whose lives were at stake*: Isabel Sans, "In the 1850s, Maryland Courts Considered Whether Freeing Slaves was Proof of Insanity," Boundary Stones, September 15, 2023, https://boundarystones.weta.org/2023/09/15/1850s-maryland-courts-considered-whether-freeing-slaves-was-proof-insanity.
219 *In 1860, the public was scandalized by the forced incarceration*: Lydia B. Denny, "Statement of Mrs. Lydia B. Denny, Wife of Reuben S. Denny, of Boston, in Regard to Her Alleged Insanity," *Insane Asylum Memoirs, 1842–1890*, Kent State University, https://oaks.kent.edu/insane-asylum-memoirs/statement-mrs-lydia-b-denny-wife-reuben-s-denny-boston-regard-her-alleged.
220 *"Under the control of intelligent and liberal men"*: Frederick Gleason, *Gleason's Pictorial*, Boston: F. Gleason, 1852.
220 *On Monday morning, at 2:00 a.m. on July 20*: *Leicester Chronicle*, August 22, 1857.
220 *"The body," the* New York Times *assured its readers*: *The New York Times*, July 31, 1857.

## 15: The Sea Captain's Widow

222 *What had started as news reports out of San Francisco*: *The New York Times*, February 21, 1857.
222 *She had been romanticized in the poetry of William Attfield*: Walter Scott, *The Monastery: A Romance*, London: Longman, Hurst, Rees, Orme, & Brown, 1820.
225 *Reading the article, with her name written there, Rebecca remembered*: Shockley, *Captain's Widow of Sandwich*, ch. 7.
225 *The newspapers were thrilled to report that this wasn't the first time*: Jeanne Willoz-Engor, "The Remarkable Mrs. Captain McGuire," The Mariner's Museum and Park, July 13, 2022, www.marinersmuseum.org/2022/07/the-remarkable-mrs-captain-mcguire/.
226 *Eliza Thorrold continued to run the San Francisco tug*: "Women in Maritime History," National Park Services, November 16, 2024, www.nps.gov/safr/learn/historyculture/maritimewomenhistory.htm.
226 *After his death in July, Mary Ann petitioned the court*: Index to the Probate Records of the County of Suffolk, Massachusetts: from the Year 1636

*to and Including the Year 1893*, ed. Elijah George, Boston: Rockwell and Churchill, City Printers, 1895.
226 *Dr. Clark was a prominent figure*: Robert Means Lawrence, *Old Park Street and Its Vicinity*, Boston: Houghton Mifflin, 1922; cf. Suffolk Deed, lib. 3, fol. 489.
227 *For just under a hundred dollars a year*: "Prices and Wages by Decade: 1860–1869," University of Missouri Libraries, https://libraryguides.missouri.edu/pricesandwages/1860-1869.
228 *The ship—refitted and recently renamed the* Central America: Chris Bullfinch, "Shipwreck Artifacts to be Featured at August ANA," *Coin World*, June 30, 2022, www.coinworld.com/news/us-coins/shipwreck-artifacts-to-be-featured-at-august-ana-show.
228 *Desperate passengers and crew passed two harrowing days*: Gary Kinder, *Ship of Gold in the Deep Blue Sea*, New York: Atlantic Monthly Press, 1998.
228 *As* The New York Times *reported, "The whole earnings of Capt. Patten"*: *The New York Times*, September 23, 1857.
229 *When the estate was finally settled in 1883*: Probate Records of Sussex County, 1884, v. 559, 309.
230 *With her as her witnesses were three men*: ibid; see also Hall Gleason, *Old Ships and Ship Building Days of Medford, 1630–1873*, West Medford, MA: Medford Co-Operative Bank, 1836.
231 *In the period from 1853 to 1857, 23,280 people died in Massachusetts*: Henry Ingersoll Bowditch, *Consumption in New England: Or, Locality One of Its Chief Causes*, Boston: Ticknor & Fields, 1862.
232 *He must have done so unexpectedly and without leaving a forwarding address*: Genealogy & Family Information, Grand Lodge of Maine, www.mainemason.org/uploads/Patten-Frank-to-Patterson-Moses.pdf.
232 *Sometime in the 1870s, John and his wife, Maria*: "To John E. Hanly of Rockland," July 2, 1884, deed, Knox County, Maine.
233 *By the time of the 1870 federal census, the entire Brown family*: "F. M. Jewell," Find a Grave, https://images.findagrave.com/photos/2023/35/249220330_75daf86c-eecc-4597-aae4-b6f4e18cfefa.jpeg.
233 *He reappears in the 1880 census, now in his early twenties*: 1880, United States Census, Massachusetts, Suffolk County.
233 *In the 1870s, fewer than 20 percent of boys attended school after the age of fourteen*: Chaim M. Rosenberg and Linda Clare Reed, *Child Labor in Greater Boston: 1880–1920*, New York: Arcadia Publishing, 2014, 23;

"An Act Concerning the Attendance of Children at School," General Court of Massachusetts, 1852.

233 *Joshua, though, must have demonstrated some artistic talent*: John Masury, *House-Painting, Carriage-Painting, and Graining: What To Do and How to Do It*, New York: Appleton and Company, 1881; G. W. Clark, *The Carriage Maker and Painter's Guide*, Buffalo, NY: Haas and Kelley, 1870.

233 *The interior of carriages, both steam and horse-drawn*: Mary McIntyre Ferrell, "John Burgum and the Artistry of Carriage Painting," Burgum Foundation, www.burgumfamily.co.uk/pdf_books/John_Burgum_Merri_Ferrell.pdf.

234 *There were horse-drawn railways*: Frances J. Kemp, "Impressions of Boston: 1880–1910," Longyear Museum, https://www.longyear.org/learn/research-archive/impressions-of-boston-1880–1910/.

234 *As a young, first-time mother, though, Mary Ann had been particularly susceptible*: Brooke Dulka, "What Are Metabolic Disorders, and How Can They Cause Epilepsy?," MyEpilepsyTeam, www.myepilepsyteam.com/resources/what-are-metabolic-disorders-and-how-can-they-cause-epilepsy; Meghna Desai, et al., "Epidemiology and Burden of Malaria in Pregnancy," *The Lancet*, 7, no. 2 (February 2007): 93–104.

235 *Until 1956, seventeen American states outlawed marriage for anyone with epilepsy*: International League Against Epilepsy, "The History and Stigma of Epilepsy," *Epilepsy*, 44, no. 6 (September 2003): 12–14.

235 *Epilepsy tended to go hand in hand with other neurological disorders*: Jane McCagh, et al., "Epilepsy, Psychosocial and Cognitive Functioning," *Epilepsy Research*, 86, no. 1 (September 2009): 1–14.

235 *Sometime not later than 1883 Joshua returned to Maine*: "To F. Rice Rowell," October 6, 1883, deed, Knox County, Maine.

236 *By 1900, he had been an "inmate" of the Rockland Poor Farm*: "Joshua Patten," Maine Death Records, 1761–1922.

236 *As the social reformer Thomas Hazard put it in 1851*: Sarah Handley-Cousins, "Little Laborers: Child Indenture in 18th and 19th century America," *Dig: A History Podcast* (November 2022): https://digpodcast.org/2022/11/13/little-laborers/.

237 *They lived at the farm with their son, Albru*: 1900 United States Census, Appleton, Maine.

238 *As The Lewiston Sun Journal newspaper reported later, "Patten was subject to fits*: "Joshua A. Patten Jr.," Find a Grave, www.findagrave.com/memorial/73658263/joshua_a_patten.

## About the Author

**Dr. Tilar J. Mazzeo** is *The New York Times*, *Los Angeles Times*, and *San Francisco Chronicle* bestselling author of numerous award-winning works of narrative nonfiction, including history and biography titles. Formerly the Clara C. Piper Associate Professor of English at Colby College and Professeure Associée in the Department of World Literatures at the University of Montreal, Dr. Mazzeo left the academy in 2019 to focus full-time on writing. A fifth-generation sailor and tenth-generation Mainer (where the Patten story begins), she lives today on Vancouver Island, British Columbia, where, with her husband, she captains a Vancouver 42 offshore sailboat.